TO THE BRINK
AND BACK

Other Books by Jairam Ramesh

Mobilizing Technology for World Development (co-editor)
Kautilya Today: Jairam Ramesh on a Globalizing India
Making Sense of Chindia (also in Chinese)
Green Signals: Ecology, Growth and Democracy in India
Legislating for Justice: The Making of the 2013 Land Acquisition Law (co-author)

TO THE BRINK
AND BACK

INDIA'S 1991 STORY

JAIRAM RAMESH

RUPA

Published by
Rupa Publications India Pvt. Ltd 2015
7/16, Ansari Road, Daryaganj
New Delhi 110 002

Sales Centres:

Allahabad Bengaluru Chennai
Hyderabad Jaipur Kathmandu
Kolkata Mumbai

ISBN: 978-81-291-3780-7

Second impression 2015

10 9 8 7 6 5 4 3 2

The moral right of the author has been asserted.

Printed by Replika Press Pvt. Ltd.

Men make their own history, but they do not make it as they please;
they do not make it under self-selected circumstances,
but under circumstances existing already,
given and transmitted from the past

KARL MARX

Contents

Key Dates and Events between June and August 1991 Covered in This Book

1. 20 June   Narasimha Rao elected leader of the Congress Parliamentary Party (CPP).

2. 21 June
   - Narasimha Rao takes over as prime minister.
   - Ministers sworn in; Dr Manmohan Singh told he is finance minister.
   - The prime minister's broadcast to the nation.

3. 22 June   Portfolios announced; Dr Manmohan Singh officially takes over as finance minister.

4. 23 June
   - A.N. Verma appointed principal secretary to the prime minister.
   - Pranab Mukherjee appointed deputy chairman, Planning Commission.

5. 25 June   The finance minister's prices roll-back controversy.

6. 26 June   The prime minister meets opposition leaders.

7. 27 June
   - Author's fax to Gopi Arora at the International Monetary Fund (IMF).
   - The prime minister and finance minister meet opposition leaders.

8. 1 July
   - First devaluation of the rupee.
   - Congress Working Committee (CWC) meeting.
   - Statement of four economic administrators.

9.	3 July	Second devaluation of the rupee.
10.	4 July	• First trade policy package.
		• Second gold transfer.
		• The West Bengal government's alternatives to the IMF announced.
11.	7 July	• Third gold transfer.
		• The prime minister's press meet in Hyderabad where he was critical of the finance minister.
12.	8 July	Statement of thirty-five economists.
13.	9 July	• CPP meeting (address by the prime minister).
		• The prime minister's address to the nation.
		• The finance minister writes to the chief minister of West Bengal.
14.	11 July	Fourth gold transfer.
15.	12 July	The prime minister seeks a vote of confidence in the Lok Sabha.
16.	15 July	The prime minister wins the vote of confidence in the Lok Sabha.
17.	18 July	Fifth gold transfer.
18.	19 July	Cabinet meeting to discuss the new industrial policy.
19.	20 July	Group of ministers (GoM) discuss the new industrial policy.
20.	23 July	• Cabinet meeting to approve the new industrial policy.
		• Meeting of the union council of ministers to approve the new industrial policy.
		• CWC meeting to approve the new industrial policy.
21.	24 July	• Tabling of the new industrial policy in the Lok Sabha by P.J. Kurien.
		• Presentation of the budget for 1991-92.
22.	1 August	CPP meeting on the budget (with the prime minister presiding).
23.	3 August	CPP meeting on the budget (with the prime minister presiding).

24.	6 August	Small industry package tabled in the Lok Sabha by P.K. Thungon.
25.	10 August	The prime minister's reply to Jyoti Basu.
26.	13 August	Second trade policy package tabled in the Lok Sabha by P. Chidambaram.
27.	14 August	Narasimham Committee on the Financial System announced.
28.	16 August	First stock-taking by the finance minister.
29.	17 August	• Full Planning Commission reconstituted. • The prime minister and finance minister meet trade union leaders.
30.	19 August	The prime minister remarks on Gorbachev.
31.	26 August	The prime minister's reply in the Lok Sabha on industrial policy.
32.	27 August	• CPP meeting on the budget (agriculture). • The finance minister writes to the IMF.
33.	28 August	CPP meeting on the budget (agriculture).
34.	29 August	• CPP meeting on the budget (agriculture). • Chelliah Committee on tax reforms announced.
35.	31 August	• The prime minister meets three national industry associations. • The prime minister meets the Kisan Congress.

I

Narasimha Rao's Entry

For around ninety days, beginning 3 June 1991, I was catapulted into a ringside seat, as Indian economic policy was being transformed. As an aide to P.V. Narasimha Rao—first as he took over as Congress president and thereafter, in the days immediately after he became the prime minister of India—I witnessed profound changes in the trinity of industrial, trade and fiscal policies. I had a Sherpa's role in the design of some of these changes, particularly as they related to industrial policy. This book is based on my own recollections, conversations with some key players in that drama, written records like parliament debates[1] that are not available easily, contemporary newspaper accounts based on official briefings, hitherto unpublished material from Narasimha Rao's archives, minutes of key Congress meetings, along with my own personal notes and papers from that period. The book, therefore, is a personal story, one 'participant-observer's' narrative of the action-packed days of June, July and August 1991, during which time dramatic steps to liberalize and globalize the Indian economy were taken.[2]

---

[1]These verbatim proceedings are presently available online, but only from the year 1999.

[2]The only other person who worked with Narasimha Rao and who has written about his prime ministership is P.V.R.K. Prasad. However, his book *The Wheels behind the Veil* (Hyderabad: EMESCO Books, 2013) deals with the period following April 1992 after Prasad had joined the Prime Minister's Office as media adviser.

To be sure, there had been earlier attempts at reforms. The first two years of Rajiv Gandhi's tenure (1985-87) as prime minister saw a flurry of initiatives to give greater incentives to the private sector to expand. Some economists have written that the growth turnaround of the 1990s and thereafter is anchored in these initiatives. Earlier, Indira Gandhi herself had cautiously begun the process of giving a new direction to regulations when she set up the Economic Administration Reforms Commission under the chairmanship of L.K. Jha; a committee to examine the principles of a possible shift away from physical to financial control under the chairmanship of M. Narasimham; and a committee for restructuring the public sector with Dr Arjun Sengupta as its head. India's first major reform that partially decontrolled the cement industry took place in 1982. Earlier, in May 1979, the Committee on Controls and Subsidies set up by the Morarji Desai government under the chairmanship of Vadilal Dagli submitted its report. Going back even further in time, following the hugely controversial devaluation of June 1966, new measures to attract foreign capital had been announced.

What Rajiv Gandhi began in January 1985 was very important; the process of systematic unshackling undoubtedly started with him. Indeed, in September 1986 he had asked the Planning Commission to prepare a detailed agenda for industrial policy reforms. I was entrusted with this task. A comprehensive action plan titled 'New Industrial Policy Initiatives' had been prepared (Annexure 1). It had advocated, among other things, a more liberal policy towards foreign investment, a loosening of restrictions on the growth of private companies, and the creation of a regulator for capital markets that was to later result in the Securities and Exchanges Board of India (SEBI). But for some strange reason—perhaps having to do with the fact that the politics of the country changed dramatically in April 1987—that note did not go further, even though it was scheduled to be discussed in a meeting of the full Planning Commission.

Then, when V.P. Singh was prime minister for slightly less than a year (1989-90), he asked Montek Ahluwalia[3] to put together a new policy

---

[3]Montek Singh Ahluwalia had been additional secretary to Rajiv Gandhi. V.P. Singh had retained and promoted him as special secretary.

package. In March 1990, V.P. Singh had gone to Kuala Lumpur—after a gap of almost a decade-and-a-half—and impressed with what he saw, directed his key economic aide to do some fresh thinking. This resulted in a truly radical agenda for reforms,[4] but this also never saw the light of day.

June-July 1991 represented a fundamental paradigm shift in economic policy. All that had been done prior to 1991 had aimed to make the system more flexible and responsive. But 1991 marked a whole new beginning. And there could not have been a more unlikely duo playing harbingers of this fundamental change. Both P.V. Narasimha Rao and his finance minister, Dr Manmohan Singh were pillars of the *ancien régime,* stalwarts of the very system they set out to replace. They were, to the Indian economy, somewhat like Richard Nixon was to the American embrace of China in early 1972. The ultimate insiders became the instruments of a profound change—a change that was initially resisted but that came to be embraced subsequently by all political parties. There may have been some mild tweaking here and there, but the fundamentals did not undergo a shift even after Narasimha Rao and Manmohan Singh left office in May 1996.

How did I get to being where I was in this epochal period of June-July 1991? I had quit the Planning Commission in January 1991 and was working with Sam Pitroda[5] and R.D. Pradhan[6] as part of the

---

[4]This document titled 'Towards a Restructuring of Industrial, Trade and Fiscal Policies' was comprehensive in scope and was an agenda for radical reform, most of which was to be accomplished after June 1991. It was prepared in May 1990 and got leaked thereafter, which led to a furore within the V.P. Singh cabinet since neither the Commerce nor Finance Ministries were particularly enthusiastic about the agenda. The Planning Commission was also hostile to it. It has become part of economic folklore as the 'M' document, a name given to it by the economist Ashok Desai who was chief consultant in the Ministry of Finance between December 1991 and September 1993. If there is one single document that contains the economic reforms programme of the Rao government and of subsequent ones as well it is this 'M' paper.

[5]Sam Pitroda was a close adviser of Rajiv Gandhi on technology but was entrusted with numerous other assignments as well.

[6]R.D. Pradhan was union home secretary and governor of Arunachal Pradesh during

'back office' election campaign team of Rajiv Gandhi. My primary role was to prepare position papers on economic issues and give ideas for the election manifesto. As Rajiv Gandhi started his campaign in early May 1991, I started preparing talking points for his rallies and passing them on to his close friend Suman Dubey[7] who travelled with him. I had no formal position in the Congress but was generally seen as part of Rajiv Gandhi's circle of assistants.

◆

A colossal tragedy struck on 21 May 1991 when Rajiv Gandhi was assassinated. Like everybody else, I was completely shattered. On 22 May, the Congress Working Committee (CWC) had an emergency meeting at 5 p.m. This meeting, presided over by P.V. Narasimha Rao, decided to elect Sonia Gandhi as Congress president. But the very next day, she declined, and a few days later, on 29 May, the CWC met again with H.K.L. Bhagat presiding; Narasimha Rao was elected as Congress president.[8]

◆

I had never met Narasimha Rao, although I had been in the government for a decade in various capacities. I knew of him by reputation, of course, as someone who had been chief minister of Andhra Pradesh between 1971 and 1973, where he took land reforms promised by Indira Gandhi seriously, but ended up paying a heavy political price by being ousted. I knew that Indira Gandhi and Rajiv Gandhi trusted his

---

Rajiv Gandhi's prime ministership and had started working with the ex-prime minister in 1990 without a formal position as such, when he was also a member of the Maharashtra Legislative Council.

[7]Suman Dubey, a well-known journalist, was a school and university friend of Rajiv Gandhi and had worked as an adviser in the Ministry of Information and Broadcasting between 1986 and 1989.

[8]How Narasimha Rao came to be (s)elected as Congress president has been described by K. Natwar Singh in *One Life is Not Enough: An Autobiography* (New Delhi: Rupa Publications, 2014).

sage advice and drafting skills. I knew that Rao had been chairman of the committee to prepare the Congress' manifesto for the 1991 Lok Sabha elections. But I did carry one negative impression of the man. In February 1987, Rajiv Gandhi—then holding the post of finance minister after the sudden transfer of V.P. Singh from the Finance to the Defence Ministry—had promised a 'white paper' on the public sector in his budget speech as a first step to reforming state-owned enterprises. A group of six CMDs (chairmen and managing directors)— headed by V. Krishnamurthy, then the chairman-cum-managing director of the Steel Authority of India Limited (SAIL)—was set up, and I had prepared the first working draft for the group to consider. Thereafter, the group submitted a final version to the prime minister, after which it went to a Committee of Secretaries. This committee then proceeded to mangle it—entirely unsurprising, since no bureaucracy would really like to give true autonomy to public sector companies. The revised draft went to the cabinet. Thereafter a Cabinet Committee was set up under the chairmanship of Narasimha Rao to finalize the white paper. The white paper was never published, and in my mind, Narasimha Rao came to be a symbol of procrastination, delay and the status-quo. I felt that a golden opportunity to redefine the relationship between public sector companies and the government—to delink management from ownership, to transform the managerial and technological capabilities of these companies that occupied 'the commanding heights' of the economy—was lost.

R.D. Pradhan took me to meet Narasimha Rao, if memory serves me, on 30 May 1991, so that he could be informed about how the 'non politicos' around Rajiv Gandhi were contributing to the election campaign. Rao said he knew of me and asked me to continue with whatever I was doing. He told me that he was not an expert on economic issues and that I should coordinate meetings with Pranab Mukherjee[9] and keep briefing him on these subjects. He said that on 2 June he would be having his first interaction with the media and that I should quickly prepare a statement that he could use. I promptly

---

[9]Pranab Mukherjee was a former finance minister and a leading ideologue of the Congress.

did so, but was disappointed that what I had drafted was not used. This would not be the last time such an event would occur.

On 3 June 1991, Narasimha Rao asked me to accompany him on his first election tour to Farrukhabad, Hardoi and Lucknow in Uttar Pradesh. He was most agitated about the fast-unto-death that the Telugu Desam Party (TDP) supremo N.T. Rama Rao had been observing in Hyderabad, demanding justice for the victims of the violence that had erupted after Rajiv Gandhi's assassination. I kept giving periodic updates on the situation there—and this was an era when there were no mobile phones! Apart from this, there was hardly any conversation between us. Besides, we were mostly in a helicopter. However, Rao did say that Dr Zakir Husain had been one of the most urbane and cultured Indians and that he was happy to launch his election campaign as Congress president from the constituency of his grandson, Salman Khurshid.

Subsequently, Pranab Mukherjee and I met Narasimha Rao at 12, Willingdon Crescent (now Mother Teresa Crescent)—then the office of the Sanjay Gandhi Memorial Trust—on three separate occasions, between 5 and 18 June 1991, to discuss the state of the economy, the tasks ahead for a new government and the immediate priorities if the Congress came back to power. While Mukherjee would do most of the talking in these sessions—his phenomenal memory for detail and his vast knowledge of economic management on full display—I would be asked for my views every now and then. One session was taken up to look at the interim budget that the Chandra Shekhar government had presented on 4 March 1991. In another session, N.D. Tiwari[10] and Margaret Alva[11] were also present and we discussed a check-list I had prepared on the immediate tasks for the incoming prime minister. It read like this:

---

[10]N.D. Tiwari was minister of finance and commerce between 1987 and 1988, after which he became the chief minister of Uttar Pradesh for the third time.
[11]Margaret Alva was union minister of state, personnel, public grievances and pensions in the Narasimha Rao government.

IMMEDIATE ECONOMIC TASKS

1. Review of monsoon prospects and contingency plans
2. Review of the price situation with a specific focus on foodgrains and edible oils
3. Review of availability and distribution of essential commodities
4. Review of balance of payments position with main focus on export performance
5. Review of the RBI [Reserve Bank of India] credit policy
6. Announcement of kharif procurement prices
7. Formulation of budget in the context of promises made in the manifesto
8. IMF [International Monetary Fund]/World Bank/ADB [Asian Development Bank] loan. Talks with USA, Japan, UK, Germany on bilateral assistance
9. Finalization of Eighth Plan with focus on employment
10. White paper on economy during NF [National Front] and JD(S) [Janata Dal: Samajwadi] rule
11. Key appointments
    - Finance Ministry
    - Financial institutions
    - Planning Commission
    - Commerce, Industry Ministries

Narasimha Rao was elected as the leader of the Congress Parliamentary Party (CPP) on 20 June 1991.[12] He asked me to prepare a speech and, once more, in my enthusiasm, I offered a draft assuming that it would be used. Again, it was totally ignored. Rather, at the meeting, after being felicitated by many of his colleagues, Narasimha Rao spoke in both English and Hindi without relying on notes. As he communicated with his audience, Rao seemed especially nostalgic about Rajiv Gandhi and

---

[12]The various maneuverings leading up to Narasimha Rao's election as leader of the CPP have been described in P.C. Alexander, *Through the Corridors of Power* (New Delhi: HarperCollins, 2004); R.D. Pradhan, *My Years with Rajiv and Sonia* (New Delhi: Hay House, 2014); and B.G. Deshmukh, *A Cabinet Secretary Looks Back* (New Delhi: HarperCollins, 2004).

sought the support of MPs (members of Parliament) in the name of his departed leader. Then, focussing heavily on the manifesto, he said that perhaps, Rajiv Gandhi had a premonition that this would be his lasting legacy because he had ensured that the 1991 manifesto would be the most competent and meticulous programme of action. Finally, Rao likened the Congress' performance in the recently-concluded elections to that of a great cricketer missing his century by a solitary run.[13] More than this, what I vividly recall is the beginning of Rao's address; he claimed that he preferred dialogue to speech and promised more such sessions in the future. Little did he realize that he would be forced to fulfil this assurance much sooner than he had planned, on account of the budget of 24 July 1991—a budget that would change the country.

After the CPP speech, Narasimha Rao asked me to meet Mani Shankar Aiyar[14] and M.J. Akbar[15] and work out a 'broadcast to the nation' for him to deliver the next day. The three of us met at Akbar's residence and exchanged ideas. As in the past, I put together a draft and promptly gave it to Narasimha Rao. A few hours after becoming prime minister, Rao did give his broadcast to the nation. But once again, Rao relayed what he himself had prepared with the assistance of the cabinet secretary, Naresh Chandra, and the principal information officer, I. Ramamohan Rao.

◆

On the evening of 20 June, Naresh Chandra met Narasimha Rao and handed over a top-secret eight-page note highlighting the urgent tasks awaiting the new prime minister. While the note had been prepared by different ministries, especially the Finance Ministry, it was the

---

[13]Of the 521 seats for which elections had been held in the general elections, the Congress had won 232 seats and along with its allies had a strength of 246 in the 10th Lok Sabha, short by 15 of a majority needed. (Source: Election Commission.)
[14]Mani Shankar Aiyar was Rajiv Gandhi's close aide and then a newly-elected Congress MP.
[15]M.J. Akbar, now a Bharatiya Janata Party (BJP) MP, was a Congress MP between 1989 and 1991.

cabinet secretary who finally put it all together. When he saw the note, Narasimha Rao's first response was: 'Is the economic situation that bad?' To this, Naresh Chandra's reply was, 'No, sir, it is actually much worse.' He quickly briefed the incoming prime minister about what needed to be done and added that a default had to be avoided at all costs. He also informed Narasimha Rao about the efforts of the Chandra Shekhar government in seeking assistance from the IMF, adding that it would be better to do whatever had to be done immediately—rather than wait for IMF assistance, then respond, and give the impression of acting under international pressure.

On the evening of 21 June 1991, the new prime minister—before informing me that he would be getting Ramu Damodaran, who had worked with him earlier, as his private secretary—said that I should join his office soon and basically focus on what had to be done immediately.[16] He asked me not to wait for formal orders and instead, start working closely with his newly-appointed finance minister, Manmohan Singh— someone I knew well since he had recruited me into the Planning Commission in August 1986. Indeed, when Manmohan Singh saw me at the prime minister's residence on the evening of 21 June, where he had come to give a detailed briefing, he smiled at me and said, 'Jairam, now is the time to do all the things you wanted us to do while in the Planning Commission.' My appointment as officer-on-special-duty in the Prime Minister's Office (PMO) was notified a day or two after the prime minister had, at the suggestion of Dr P.C. Alexander,[17] appointed as his principal secretary, A.N. Verma[18]—another man I knew and enjoyed a warm personal relationship with. I could

---

[16]R.D. Pradhan in *My Years with Rajiv and Sonia* (New Delhi: Hay House, 2014) recounts how he persuaded Narasimha Rao, after he became prime minister, to induct me into his office, invoking a conversation with Sam Pitroda—a conversation that Pitroda denies ever having taken place!

[17]P.C. Alexander had been principal secretary to two prime ministers, Indira Gandhi and Rajiv Gandhi. He had served as the governor of Tamil Nadu from 1988 to 1990.

[18]A.N. Verma had been secretary in the Ministries of Commerce and Industry and was then appointed secretary of the Planning Commission during the Chandra Shekhar regime, when Naresh Chandra, his 'junior' from the 1956 batch of the Indian Administrative Service (IAS), was appointed cabinet secretary.

even share a joke in his company—on one occasion, suggesting that with him, Naresh Chandra and Suresh Mathur (then industry secretary), the 'Kayasth mafia' would rule. Verma only laughed and said, '*Badmaash ho tum!* (You are a trouble-maker!)'

This, then, is how I came to be where I was in that momentous period. The years of revival lay ahead and have been written about extensively. But June–July–August 1991 were early days of survival. The later impressive growth record of the Indian economy lent a certain amount of retrospective coherence to what got done in the initial weeks.

My stint with the prime minister was exceedingly short. But it was not uneventful and not without opportunities to play a small role in a truly landmark undertaking. I must, though, emphasize that this book is not *my* story at all. It is a story of how I saw Narasimha Rao and Manmohan Singh shake up India, and how, incidentally, some Sherpas helped them along the way.

2

The Economic Crisis of Early 1991

What was the crisis that the country faced when Narasimha Rao took over as prime minister and Manmohan Singh became finance minister?

It was simply this: India's foreign exchange reserves had dropped precipitously, so as to be sufficient for just two weeks of imports. Normally, a safe level at that time was reckoned to be three months of import cover. Foreign exchange reserves were US$3.11 billion at the end of August 1990. By mid-January 1991 they had fallen sharply to just US$896 million.

The first pressure on the reserves had come from the trebling of oil prices following the Gulf War of August 1990. To make matters worse, India had to repatriate thousands of workers from Kuwait back home. Obviously, their remittances, which helped the economy manage its balance of payments, stopped. Exports to Iraq and Kuwait also came to a halt and we lost US$500 million or thereabouts on this account alone.

The second pressure came from political instability within the country. The nation—particularly the capital—was rocked by violent agitations against the implementation of the Mandal Commission recommendations on reservations for other backward classes (OBCs). By October 1990, the V.P. Singh government was tottering. At this time, non-resident Indians (NRIs)—whose deposits were a valuable source of dollar support to the economy—started withdrawing their money from Indian banks. The flight started in October 1990 and about US$200 million went out in just three months. The flight was to accelerate in the April–June 1991 period to almost US$950 million. It started declining slowly thereafter and the flight became an inflow only after the February 1992 budget.

The third source of pressure came from India's short-term borrowings in the late 1980s (between 1986 and 1989), that took place because interest rates were low—it made sense then. But with a growing loss of international confidence in the Indian economy— particularly because of the political situation beginning August 1990— interest rates began to go up and the cost of international credit increased considerably. Simply put, we could no longer borrow to 'roll over' the short-term debt.

Inflation was as much of a serious problem. The average annual rate of inflation during the five-year period 1985/86–89/90 was 6.7 per cent. But in 1990–91 (that is, for the financial year ending 31 March 1991), it had shot up to 10.3 per cent. It kept rising, reaching a peak of 16.7 per cent by the end of August 1991. High inflation in India in relation to the inflation rates in countries that were our major trading partners meant that the real effective exchange rate (that is, the nominal exchange rate adjusted for relative prices) had appreciated after October 1990. This made our exports expensive and non-competitive.

GDP (gross domestic product) growth had averaged 5.6 per cent per year during the tenure of Rajiv Gandhi and it remained at around that level in 1990–91 as well. It is this that led critics of the IMF route, taken by Narasimha Rao and Manmohan Singh, to argue that India was facing not a problem of solvency but really one of liquidity. In reality, however, the two are not distinguishable in a sharp way, and it was certain that the short-term liquidity crisis carried the seeds of medium- and long-term insolvency. The crisis would definitely have impacted growth performance, sooner rather than later.

India's short-term external debt had ballooned to alarming levels. By end-March 1991, short-term debt, whose original maturity was twelve months or less, had reached over US$8.5 billion, which was about 10 per cent of the country's total external debt. Worse, short-term debt whose residual maturity was twelve months or less—that is, all principal replacements due under all loans and credits in twelve months or less—was much higher at around US$13.6 billion. These were staggering amounts, especially given that our foreign exchange reserves (including gold) at the end of March 1991 amounted to no more than US$5.8 billion.

◆

Chandra Shekhar replaced V.P. Singh as prime minister on 10 November 1990, and Yashwant Sinha became finance minister. It was a curious arrangement. The Congress, with 195 MPs and as the single largest party in Parliament, was giving outside support to a new party, then with 54 MPs, which formed the government. Nobody expected this peculiar situation to last very long and differences cropped up soon, first over the issue of permitting refuelling by US military aircraft and then over economic policy. In December 1990, the finance minister had announced a slew of measures to cut imports—which soon began to impact, indeed substantially reduce, both industrial production and exports.

By February 1991, when preparations for the budget were in full swing, Pranab Mukherjee sensed that new taxes would be imposed to raise resources. Along with the Congress president, Rajiv Gandhi, Mukherjee called on President R. Venkataraman. Venkataraman writes thus in his memoirs:

> On February 13, Rajiv Gandhi again called on me with Pranab Mukherjee, my successor as Finance Minister in 1982. Pranab Mukherjee told me that he had a discussion with Yashwant Sinha and that he felt a harsh budget would be inappropriate at that time. He was also worried that inflation would be sparked off and bring unpopularity to the Congress if it supported these measures. Since Yashwant Sinha had earlier discussed the economic situation with me, I told Pranab Mukherjee of some of the compulsions of the Finance Minister. As an old colleague of mine, I explained to him that the current inflation was not due to cost-push or demand-pull but largely due to excessive liquidity

and that budgetary action was unavoidable to control inflation. The whole discussion was in the nature of an academic exercise rather than consultation on programmes to be adopted.

On February 19, the Prime Minister met me again at 8pm. He said [...] that he was presenting a vote on account to Parliament and not a regular budget. He added that matters had been discussed and settled between his party and the Congress (I). He hoped to conclude the Parliament session by the end of March.[19]

Earlier, the all-powerful CWC had met at 10 a.m. on 19 February and the record of that meeting reads thus:

Political Situation

While discussing the political situation, some members pointed out to newspaper reports that Congress (I) wanted to withdraw its support to the Chandra Shekhar government. Some others said that our party was supporting a minority government which was unable to tackle the economic crisis and other vital issues. In their opinion this government should be changed today itself instead of a few months. However it was general opinion in the meeting that the party stands by its commitment and it was its responsibility to see that the government did not fall during voting in Parliament but it was up to Janata Dal (S) to be very careful about floor management.

Economic Situation

A study paper as prepared by Shri Pranab Mukherjee on the economic situation was circulated to the members before discussion started.

The Congress president describing the present economic situation as very grave, informed the meeting that India did not have money to repay the loans, neither could it buy fertilizers, etc. The members also expressed concern on the grim economic situation of the country and called upon the Govt. to take the nation into confidence before asking the people to sacrifice particularly

---

[19]R. Venkataraman, *My Presidential Years* (New Delhi: HarperCollins, 1994).

because in this financial year Rs 5890 crore were sought to be raised by taxation and increase in administered prices. The members were of firm view that a "Vote on Account" will be supported if it is presented in accordance with the Congress Economic Policy.

A note prepared by Pranab Mukherjee, which was discussed by the CWC, influenced the thinking of the party and its top leadership in the first two-three months of 1991 (Annexure 2). As part of the note, Mukherjee had said:

> The immediate task before the government is to remove the sense of panic and frustration and to restore confidence in the system. [...] In order to generate resources for development, Government must join radical economic reform in line with international trends of de-regulation, competition and decentralization. To achieve national objectives and to tone up the functioning of the Public Sector, the following steps have now become necessary:
>
> 1. The objectives of the public sector should be redefined to include
>   a. Self-reliance
>   b. Return on capital employed
>   c. Essential and infrastructural services.
> 2. Financially unviable units with low social responsibility should be privatized through formulated 'exit policy'.
> 3. Greatest importance should be attached to performance, improvement and recruitment of top executives, reward and punishment systems, and performance evaluation systems should be redesigned to achieve these objectives.

It was clear that by mid-February 1991 the Congress had decided that, instead of a regular budget, an interim budget would be presented which would keep the system going till end-July, by which time a regular budget would be placed before Parliament. The expectation, clearly, was that by then there would be some improvement in the economic scenario.

Accordingly, Yashwant Sinha presented an interim budget or technically a vote-on-account on 4 March 1991. Two days later, in response to the furore caused by two Haryana police constables spying on Rajiv Gandhi's residence, Chandra Shekhar submitted his resignation and subsequently elections were announced for May 1991.

◆

The crisis of early 1991 has been written about extensively by economists. It was by no means the first macroeconomic crisis that India faced but it was the most serious. There had been crises during 1965-67, 1973-75 and 1979-81 as well. The most comprehensive analysis of these crises is by Vijay Joshi and I.M.D. Little. Little, incidentally, was Manmohan Singh's doctoral thesis adviser at Oxford University. Joshi and Little write:

> The crisis of 1990 had its roots in the policy stance taken in the aftermath of the second oil shock (1979-80). At that stage, exports stagnated due to real exchange rate appreciation. There was little current account adjustment. The fiscal position deteriorated. Both domestic and foreign debt increased rapidly. As a result, the underlying macroeconomic situation in 1985/86 was unsatisfactory.
>
> There were some good policy decisions in the second half of the decade. The exchange rate was managed more flexibly and exports grew rapidly in response. There were moves toward industrial deregulation and trade liberalisation which contributed to rapid industrial growth. The policy environment was also benign. The terms of trade improved and world trade was buoyant.
>
> The major mistake in macroeconomic policy lay in neglecting the danger signs evident in 1985/86 on the fiscal front. Fiscal deterioration was allowed to proceed apace. As a consequence, the current account deficit continued to worsen and domestic and foreign debt continued to increase at a dangerous rate. By the end of the decade, the macroeconomic fundamentals were out of joint. Even strictly a temporary shock like the Gulf War was enough to trigger a full-scale crisis. [20]

---

[20] Vijay Joshi and I.M.D. Little, *India: Macroeconomics and Political Economy: 1964-91* (New Delhi: Oxford University Press, 1994).

And what about the man who was to be finance minister very soon? What was his thinking at this time? Manmohan Singh had been economic adviser to Chandra Shekhar for a very brief while and had become chairman of the University Grants Commission (UGC) in mid–March 1991. This must have given him time to reflect—and reflect he did, publicly, at least on three occasions before being inducted into the cabinet.

In an interview he gave to Sanjaya Baru of *The Economic Times* on 5 March 1991, when he was still economic adviser to Chandra Shekhar, Manmohan Singh spoke of the dark clouds that had already gathered:

Q: But the foreign exchange bottleneck is still there. We went to the IMF in 1981 and once again now.

Dr. Singh: This was a way of dealing with structural change and responding to the two oil shocks in 1979 and now. In 1981 we needed the support because we had begun to liberalise the trade regime. There was no problem in handling that situation. I think the problems came later. Since the mid–eighties we have borrowed excessively and the fiscal deficit has gone out of control. We could have avoided this situation if we had attended to the balance-of-payments problem much earlier. Then there is the fact that the terms of assistance have hardened [...] International interest rates have gone up, our debt profile has worsened and the terms of commercial borrowing have hardened.

Q: Would you then advocate approaching the IMF for even more than what we have already secured?

Dr. Singh: In the short run there is no alternative. We are very vulnerable at the moment. But an IMF loan is no solution either. Ultimately India has to raise its own resources. We have to step up our exports.

On 6 April 1991, by which time he had become chairman of UGC, Manmohan Singh delivered the convocation address at the Institute of Rural Management, Anand and said:

India is now faced with a severe budgetary crisis and an unsustainable deficit in our balance of payments. A steady decline in public savings rate from about 3.2 per cent of GDP in 1985–86 to 1.4 percent in 1989–90 has been a major contributory factor. We have made an excessive use of borrowing both at home and from abroad to finance public spending. The productivity of public spending has also been far from optimal.

Finally, on 15 April 1991, he delivered the convocation address at the Indian Institute of Management (IIM), Bangalore (now Bengaluru) and had this to say about the economic situation:

India's twin deficits—fiscal deficit and balance of payments deficit—have reached unsustainable limits. We have over-borrowed both at home and abroad to finance the growth of public spending. Thus, hard decisions are needed to overcome this crisis.

Manmohan Singh had offered a pointed diagnosis. Little did he realize that he would soon be called upon to administer the bitter medicine as well.

Interestingly, back in the early 1970s, Manmohan Singh had articulated equally intrepid views. The first intellectually solid and empirical assault on the economic policies of the 1950s and 1960s (more of the latter actually) came from Jagdish Bhagwati and Padma Desai in their classic *India: Planning for Industrialization* (London: Oxford University Press, 1970). Manmohan Singh reviewed this book in 1972 in *The Indian Economic and Social History Review* when he was chief economic adviser in the Ministry of Finance, and concluded by writing:

In view of the growing complexity of the Indian economic structure, the planning instruments have to be continually kept under review. It would be tragic if we were to become prisoners of instruments which, howsoever suitable at one stage of development, turn out later to be fetters on further development. Professor Bhagwati and Mrs Desai's book is a welcome contribution to the debate on the efficiency of Indian planning techniques and should help stimulate some fresh thinking on instruments of controls. There is certainly a need to recognise that the knowledge available to civil servants is not necessarily superior to that of entrepreneurs and that the fact that some direct controls are good does not mean that more controls are better than less controls. At the same time, it would be much too presumptuous to claim that modern neo-classical economics has answers to all the economic problems in all parts of the world and that an efficient framework is always one based on the principles of economic liberalism.

Clearly, the man who would become finance minister in June 1991 was no prisoner of dogma and certainly no idealogue!

3

The Inevitability of Dr Manmohan Singh as Finance Minister

21 June 1991 dawned, and I was up earlier than usual. Knowing that the prime minister-designate, Narasimha Rao, was an early riser, I called him up at around 6.30 a.m. and asked him whether he had any instructions for me, since in a couple of hours he would be sworn in as prime minister. He asked me to reach 12, Willingdon Crescent by 8.30 a.m. Upon reaching, in the adjoining waiting room, I found S.K. Mishra, the then principal secretary to the prime minister; Naresh Chandra; and M.K. Narayanan, the director of the Intelligence Bureau. We were told that Rao was closeted with P.C. Alexander and that it would take some time. I guessed that the two were discussing the names of those to be invited for the swearing-in in about four hours.

The four of us were engaged in some general chit-chat when the buzzer of Khandekar's telephone was pressed from inside. R.K. Khandekar was Narasimha Rao's Man Friday, and when he put the receiver down, I asked whether I should go inside. His reply was: '*Nahin thoda aur wait kijiye. Abhi Manmohan Singh se milane ko kaha hai*. (No, wait for a bit. For now, he has asked to be connected to Manmohan Singh.)' I immediately understood that Manmohan Singh was to be invited as minister in the new cabinet, and that in all probability he would be given the finance portfolio.

P.C. Alexander has written with authoritative and, at times, hilarious detail in his memoirs on how Manmohan Singh came to be appointed:

I met Rao on 20 June immediately after his election as CPP leader and showed him my draft proposals. He spent quite some time with me dissecting them and specified to me the additions and deletions he wished to make. The next step was to match the man to the ministry.

Narasimha Rao had earlier hinted [to me] that he was thinking of choosing a professional economist as the finance minister. During his discussions with me on 20 June he had mentioned the name of Dr. Manmohan Singh and that of Dr. I.G. Patel, another well-known and experienced economic administrator who had been recommended to him by a few influential individuals. I told him, without any hesitation, that my personal choice would be Dr. Manmohan Singh and I briefly explained why. I could see that Rao was very happy at my wholehearted endorsement of Manmohan Singh. He then said that since the Finance Minister's post was a political one, he hoped that Manmohan Singh would not hesitate to join politics. I asserted that I was confident that Manmohan Singh would accept the offer. Being a good friend, I would be able to persuade him even if he expressed reservations about acceptance and I would tie up the loose ends, if any, quickly.

On 20 June when I telephoned Manmohan Singh's house his butler informed me that he was on a trip to Europe and was expected to reach Delhi only much later that night. I left word that I would call again early in the morning the next day. When I telephoned his house at 5 a.m. on 21 June his butler told me that he was fast asleep and could not be disturbed. However, I insisted that I had to meet him without any delay and told him my name again hoping that my identity would make a difference. But it made no impression upon the man. Upon insisting that I had to talk to Dr. Manmohan Singh very urgently, he came on the line. I just told him that I had to meet him immediately, without giving any reason and that I would be reaching his house within a few minutes. When I arrived there, he had gone back to sleep as he was obviously jet-lagged. He could not have possibly guessed that I was on a very important mission—not only to him but also to the nation as a whole. He was hurriedly woken up again and I straight away conveyed to him my message. His immediate question was: What is your reaction? My response was that, if I had any other view, except to support his appointment as finance minister, I would not have met him at that unusual hour. He was happy upon hearing this view but asked me whether I thought Rao would stand by him even if some of his own cabinet or party colleagues were to oppose his proposals and plans as finance minister at a later stage. I assured him on behalf of Rao that he would have the latter's full trust and support. Manmohan was delighted at this assurance and gladly accepted the offer and requested me to convey his thanks to Rao. He reminded me with great warmth how he felt especially happy that I was again becoming an instrument in a major change in his official career. I told him that he was Narasimha Rao's choice and my role in his appointment was mainly because I happened to be his friend as well as Rao's.

I went to Rao's house directly after taking Manmohan Singh's leave and informed him about the latter's positive response and that I had conveyed the assurance that Rao would fully back Manmohan Singh in the discharge of his duties as finance minister. Rao felt very happy that he had succeeded in selecting the right man for this vital post when the country's financial position was at its nadir.[21]

Some years later, as I got to know P.C. Alexander better, I asked him what had prompted him to choose Singh so forcefully. He told me that he knew how much confidence Indira Gandhi had in Singh and that, at heart, Singh was a Congressman in the Nehruvian mould. I never summoned the courage to ask Rao himself about his choice, although one of his closest aides recalls that Rao had suggested Singh's name to replace him as deputy chairman of the Planning Commission. (Rao had been minister of planning and deputy chairman of the Planning

---

[21]P.C. Alexander, *Through the Corridors of Power* (New Delhi: HarperCollins, 2004).

Commission between November 1984 and mid-January 1985, and had been entrusted with the defence portfolio as well in January 1985.) It is clear that the prime minister had seen his finance minister-designate at the closest of quarters for almost a decade-and-a-half.

R. Venkataraman—or RV, as he was popularly known—who was president of India through the crucial months of 1991, further confirms this:

> Narasimha Rao called on me at 7.30 p.m. [on 20 June] and I offered him my warmest congratulations [...] Narasimha Rao wanted my suggestion for the post of Finance Minister in view of the acute foreign exchange crisis facing the country. He said that he would prefer one with some knowledge of the international financial institutions and experience in dealing with them. I told him that in that case he would have to go outside the ranks of his party and suggested two eminent names. The Prime Minister later chose Dr. Manmohan Singh with whose excellent work in the South Commission he was familiar. [22]

◆

Would Rajiv Gandhi have appointed Manmohan Singh as his finance minister had he come back as prime minister? Of course, this question cannot be answered definitively but can only be speculated upon. However, R.D. Pradhan has stated this possibility in his remembrances:

> By mid-May 1991 [...] RG [Rajiv Gandhi] had sensed that he would be back in power. He had asked me to start making the necessary preparations in case he had to assume responsibility. I came up with a seven-page document which Sam Pitroda had transferred onto his laptop.
>
> Given the grave financial situation faced by India then, we knew that the first priority would be the appointment as finance

---

[22] R. Venkataraman, *My Presidential Years* (New Delhi: HarperCollins, 1994). Manmohan Singh had been secretary general of the South Commission in Geneva between 1987 and late 1990.

minister of a highly qualified economist with a sound knowledge of financial management and one who commanded the trust of the [IMF] and the World Bank. RG had tentatively cleared three names: Dr. I.G. Patel, Dr. Manmohan Singh (both former governors of the Reserve Bank of India) and S. Venkitaramanan (then the RBI governor). Sam Pitroda and I knew Dr. Patel very well as a result of previous interactions with him. IG, who was earlier director of the London School of Economics, turned down the offer. Dr. Manmohan Singh was at that time out of India in connection with the work of the South-South Commission presided over by the former chancellor of the Federal Republic of Germany, Willy Brandt [sic].

RG had asked me to visit Bombay and to contact Dr. Manmohan Singh through S. Venkitaramanan [...]

On 20 June 1991, as soon as it became clear that PV [Narasimha Rao] would become the next Prime Minister I briefed him on a range of important matters that we were dealing with prior to RG's death. I particularly pointed out that RG had cleared the name of Dr. Manmohan Singh as the next Union Finance Minister in case Dr. I.G. Patel was not available. [23]

Rajiv Gandhi's esteem for Singh also comes through in Mani Shankar Aiyar's comments. Aiyar was amongst the closest of Rajiv Gandhi's aides even in the years after the latter had ceased to be prime minister. He had quit the Indian Foreign Service (IFS) in 1989 and became officer-on-special-duty to the Congress president in early 1990. When I asked him to recall the 1991 period, this is what he wrote to me very colourfully on 3 June 2015:

In February 1991, I called on the Chief Economic Adviser, Dr. Deepak Nayyar to collect some reference material for my Sunday columns. He gave me the material readily enough but pressed me to stay so that he could inform me of the condition of the economy. For the next thirty minutes, Dr. Nayyar sent the

---

[23]R.D. Pradhan, *My Years with Rajiv and Sonia* (New Delhi: Hay House, 2014). Actually the name of the commission that Pradhan refers to was the South Commission which was chaired by Dr Julius Nyerere, former president of Tanzania.

shivers down my spine [as he explained] how India was on the verge of bankruptcy. I rushed from North Block to 10 Janpath and, on learning that Rajiv Gandhi was about to commence a CWC meeting, got George's [Rajiv Gandhi's private secretary] permission to barge through the door. I requested Rajivji to come to one side as I had important information to impart to him. He seemed amused rather than bemused and, after hearing me out for a few minutes, asked why I did not address the whole of the CWC rather than just himself. Accordingly I did so. Rajivji asked me not to go away but wait with George till the CWC meeting is over. When I returned to the room, he beamed as usual and informed me that none of the CWC members had understood a word of what I had said! He then instructed me to call on Dr. Manmohan Singh and ask him to meet Rajivji as soon as possible.

I went to Dr. Manmohan Singh's Pandara Road residence where Mrs. Gursharan Kaur met me at the verandah to say that her husband was not at all well and could I come back later? I said I did not really need to converse with him but only convey a message of a couple of sentences which was a matter of urgent importance. She kindly let me into Dr. Singh's bedroom where I succinctly gave my message and leant my ear towards Dr. Singh's mouth to hear him whisper that I should tell Rajivji that he would meet him as soon as possible.

◆

Clearly, Manmohan Singh as finance minister was 'an idea whose time had come', to adopt a famous phrase by Victor Hugo—a phrase to be used by Singh himself in his maiden budget speech on 24 July 1991.

Singh's sobriety and quiet dignity were his hallmarks, just as his experience as an economic administrator was unmatched. There had been noted 'professionals' as finance ministers before, like Shanmukham Chetty, John Mathai and C.D. Deshmukh. But none matched the combination of academic brilliance and wide administrative experience of Manmohan Singh.

However inevitable and inspired his appointment may appear in retrospect, the fact remains that it was a surprise to almost everybody. Pranab Mukherjee, who had been finance minister between 1982 and 1984 in the Indira Gandhi government, was widely considered to be the favourite for this coveted post. After he had re-joined the Congress (after founding another party in 1986, the Rashtriya Samajwadi Congress in West Bengal), for all of 1990 and early 1991, he had been advising Rajiv Gandhi and had been his interlocutor with Yashwant Sinha (who was finance minister in Chandra Shekhar's government). On 20 June 1991, just a day before Rao's swearing-in as prime minister, Pranabda—as he was popularly called—gave a detailed interview to the journalist R.K. Roy (to be carried the next day in *The Times of India*) in which he had pretty much laid out the broad economic agenda of the Rao government (Annexure 3).

Q: The Congress wants to roll back prices. What is the targeted rate of price rise the party has in mind?

A: Inflation cannot be zeroed but it can certainly be brought down from the current double-digit rate to 8 per cent or even lower, that was the average in the eighties. I would start with this kind of a modest target. As regards rolling back prices, the government has some fiscal manoeuvrability in this regard, as also administrative measures available to it. I would not like to amplify upon this now. [...]

Q: You are talking about resuming the plan but the IMF wants economic liberalisation.

A: We want planning and liberalisation. We must give room for play to the private sector. The public sector must vacate the areas in which the private sector has the capability to come in. The public sector must move into the difficult areas of advanced technology.

Q: You are not averse to conditional assistance from the IMF?

A: No. Actually, the government [of V.P. Singh] ought to have taken advance action in 1990. The conditionality would have been less harsh.

Q: But surely the Congress government could have gone to the IMF in early 1989?

A: You see, in 1989 the mix between short-term borrowing and the lines of long-term credits available to this country was fair. The proportion of short-term credit rose in 1990, before the Gulf War. If the Congress had been returned to power, we would have gone to the IMF in 1990.

However, Pranabda's appointment as finance minister was not to be. Instead, on the evening of 22 June 1991, the prime minister told me that he was soon going to appoint Pranab Mukherjee as deputy chairman of the Planning Commission and that I should keep in close touch with him. This appointment was made the very next day and when I called on him, the new deputy chairman told me that I should keep meeting him regularly to discuss both economic and political matters. He also told me that I should continue to work as an aide to the prime minister, and he had earlier conveyed this to 'PV'—as he used to refer to Narasimha Rao at all times.

This repeated reference to 'PV' always reminded me of high-school chemistry where students are taught Boyle's law, which is mathematically represented as PV=constant, where P is the pressure of a given quantity of gas and V is its volume. The political 'PV', similarly, was unflappable.

4

The Flap on the Roll-back of Prices

Manmohan Singh was officially given the finance portfolio on 22 June 1991. Three days later he held his first formal press conference. It was a virtuoso performance where he laid out the government's priorities in economic policy in the clearest manner possible. On one issue though, what he said created a storm.

◆

The Congress' manifesto for the 1991 Lok Sabha elections had made a departure from the usual staid practice and ended up with a programme of action for the first hundred days (as also for the first 365, 730 and 1,000 days). P. V. Narasimha Rao was chairman of the manifesto drafting committee which included Pranab Mukherjee and Mani Shankar Aiyar. But it was P. Chidambaram—who would become the commerce minister in Rao's government—who was the principal author of the idea of a separate programme of action as well as its contents. I could see that Pranab Mukherjee was not entirely convinced that we had done a wise thing, but Chidambaram was very persuasive and had his way.

In the 'First 100 Days' section of the 1991 manifesto, the Congress pledged to, among other things:

★ Arrest price rise in essential commodities and, in particular, roll back prices to levels obtaining in July 1990 in the case of

1. Diesel;
2. Kerosene;
3. Salt;
4. Edible Oils;
5. Cycles and two-wheelers;
6. Electric bulbs;
7. Cotton sarees and dhotis of 40s count or below;
8. Stoves including smokeless chulhas;
9. Newsprint;
10. Postcards, inland letters and envelopes.

Actually, somebody should have questioned the practicality of this pledge but there was no time for a discussion. The manifesto had to come out quickly since it had already been delayed and, in any case, the general opinion was that manifesto promises are meant to be just that—promises to make the party appear good.

◆

At the 25 June press conference, the finance minister was asked about inflation. What he said first was unexceptionable:

> It would be wrong to say that I have a magic wand to bring down prices. What I can promise is that in three years time prices could be made stable if a strategy of macroeconomic management is pursued now.

But he went on to say that he had no readymade mechanism by which he could fulfil the Congress (I) poll promise of rolling back prices of a select group of commodities to their July 1990 levels.

This admission was naturally played up the next day in all newspapers and it appeared that the new government had started with a self-goal. The prime minister was perturbed and so was his political secretary, Jitendra Prasada. Prasada first sent for me and said that the finance minister's statement was a huge embarrassment and was politically most unwise. Next, the prime minister asked me to see him. I could sense that he was clearly irritated. He had received letters of protest from MPs like Rajni Ranjan Sahu and Gurudas Kamat. He expressed some frustration with economists not being sensitive to politics. He was worried that this could create a backlash against the government within the party.

He was right. At a meeting of the CWC on 1 July 1991, the finance minister's admission on prices came under sharp attack—mostly by a senior leader from Uttar Pradesh, Ram Chandra Vikal. On 7 July, at a press conference in Hyderabad, in a bid to douse the flames, the prime minister said that the finance minister's statement was not a reflection of the government's decisions and that the government was bound by the 1991 manifesto—earning for Manmohan Singh the only public rebuke of sorts from his boss in their five-year partnership.

A number of my friends in the Congress called me and asked me to tell the finance minister to issue a statement saying that 'he was misquoted'. Knowing Manmohan Singh, I did nothing of that sort, but for months had to bear the wrath of senior Congressmen for canvassing the idea of a hundred-day agenda. I took this in my stride knowing full well that I was not its real author. Pranab Mukherjee, too, told me that 'people should realize that we seek a mandate for five years and not for a hundred days'. Since both he and Singh were key figures in the drafting of all subsequent manifestos, this fracas over the roll-back ensured that the Congress never included a specific and separate hundred-day agenda as part of its election promises in 1996, 1999, 2004, 2009 and 2014.

5

The One-pager to Our Man in the IMF

On 26 June 1991, I met Gopi Arora, then India's executive director at the IMF, and for many years a close adviser of both Indira and Rajiv Gandhi. He was visiting New Delhi. It was he who had first got me into the Ministry of Industry in August 1985. We had become close even though I was not part of the 'left brigade' of which he had been a leading light.

Arora told me that our credibility was rock bottom but that Manmohan Singh's appointment as finance minister had aroused considerable hopes and expectations. He went on to add that his experience with the prime minister over the past decade told him that he was very cautious and indecisive. Arora also said that he had conveyed to the prime minister that I would be very useful to him and that I should be given wide space to function.

Arora's concern was that devaluation was essential, but given the Congress' views on it, clouded by the June 1966 experience,[24] he was not very hopeful. Devaluation apart, his main concern was with the broader reforms agenda. He needed something urgently to convince the IMF board that the Narasimha Rao government meant business, could be taken seriously, and was also committed to new thinking. He told me that he had spoken to the prime minister and finance minister

---

[24]In June 1966, Indira Gandhi had devalued the rupee substantially. This is discussed later in the book.

at length and he wanted me to put together some ideas quickly that he could use in his discussions at the IMF.

That very night, I jotted down a few thoughts and showed them to the prime minister late at his residence. He liked what he saw but wanted to make no commitments. He believed that the note I had prepared could be sent to Gopi Arora 'informally'—not as a statement of official policy but as a summary of the directional shifts we were contemplating. Clearly, Rao wanted to maintain an element of deniability in case anything went wrong or the note leaked.

Thus, it was that on 27 June 1991, I used the fax machine in Jawahar Bhavan—in the custody of R.D. Pradhan who was managing the election campaign management office of the Congress—to send the note to Gopi Arora.[25]

		SECRET
		27.6.91

Phase I(7–10 days)

1.	Industrial Delicensing
2.	Amendments to MRTP
3.	Changes in FERA
4.	Export Initiatives
5.	Sale of Public Sector equity
6.	Cut in Non-plan Loans to Public Sector
7.	Cut in Export Subsidy.
8.	Package for involvement of foreign companies in oil exploration.
9.	Package for Private Sector participation in power sector.
10.	NRI Deposits.
11.	Increased utilisation of Foreign Aid.

Phase II(Budget)

1.	Increase in Fertiliser Prices.
2.	Increase in Sugar prices.
3.	Increase in issue price of Foodgrains.
4.	Freeze on Govt. D.A.
5.	Cut in other subsidies

---

[25]R.D. Pradhan in *My Years with Rajiv and Sonia* describes this event but sadly, gets the dates wrong. He says it happened on 22 June. It could not have since the note itself is dated 27 June in the original.

Arora thanked me for my initiative and said that my comments would be very useful in his meetings with the managing director of the IMF and other senior officials. As we had agreed, no mention was made of devaluation in the faxed note.

◆

26 June 1991 was also the day the prime minister met some key opposition leaders separately. These included Chandra Shekhar, V.P. Singh, L.K. Advani,[26] Harkishan Singh Surjeet[27] and some others.

The next day, he called an all-party meeting. Those who attended included L.K. Advani, George Fernandes,[28] Somnath Chatterjee,[29] Indrajit Gupta,[30] Madhu Dandavate,[31] P. Upendra,[32] Harkishan Singh Surjeet and Yashwant Sinha. Senior officials were also present. There was some bonhomie given that the prime minister had been in office for under a week, and also because he knew each of those attending very well. The finance minister, too, was no stranger to the audience. The meeting served as a good political gesture so very early in the game and the meeting lasted about an hour-and-a-half.

The finance minister gave an extensive briefing on the state of the economy, a comprehensive picture of the financial crisis facing the country, and a clear signal that a default on international payment obligations had to be averted at all costs. He also indicated that talks had already started with institutions like the IMF and the World Bank,

---

[26]L.K. Advani is a leader of the BJP, and during Rao's tenure, was the leader of the opposition.

[27]Harkishan Singh Surjeet was a CPM (Communist Party of India [Marxist]) leader.

[28]George Fernandes had been railways minister in the V.P. Singh government and was a key member of the Janata Dal.

[29]Then a member of the CPM, Somnath Chatterjee was an MP from Bolpur, West Bengal.

[30]From the CPI (Communist Party of India), Indrajit Gupta was an MP from Midnapore, West Bengal.

[31]Madhu Dandavate was finance minister in the V.P. Singh government and a Janata Dal MP.

[32]P. Upendra of the TDP had been the leader of the opposition in the Lok Sabha during the prime ministership of Rajiv Gandhi.

who had been friends of India.[33] There was no endorsement for the course of action the finance minister was recommending and seeking support for. But the leaders of the political parties appeared reconciled to the idea that some drastic steps would have to be taken to preserve and protect India's global prestige. However, there was also an all-round view that under no circumstances could subsidies be sacrificed at the altar of IMF support.

I had been in Jamaica in the late 1970s when that country had taken IMF assistance and had seen 'It's Manley's Fault (IMF)' scribbled on walls—in reference to the role that the country's prime minister, Michael Manley had played in that episode.[34] I was beginning to wonder when there would be graffiti, especially in Calcutta (now Kolkata), saying, 'It's Manmohan's Fault!'[35]

---

[33]In a rare joint statement issued on 21 May 1991, reflective of the special relationship that India had enjoyed with the IMF and the World Bank for almost four decades, Barber Conable, president of the World Bank, and Michel Camdessus, managing director of the IMF said: 'Mr. Rajiv Gandhi's death is a tragic loss for India and the international community at large. The Bank and the Fund have long been associated with India's economic development. This will continue. During the recent Interim and Development Committee meetings in Washington in April, an informal meeting of the major donors of the Aid-India Consortium was held to discuss India's economic and financial situation. The Indian authorities said then that they were preparing, in consultation with the Fund and the Bank, a programme of corrective policies aimed at strengthening their economy. We will continue to work to that end and thus to provide the basis for support by the Fund, the Bank, and all other members of the India Consortium, which remains strongly committed to India's economic development.'

[34]Jamaica's prime minister, Michael Manley, saddled with an ailing economy, approached the IMF for balance-of-payments support. The terms of the May 1978 agreement— which made the government devalue its currency, impose new taxes on consumer goods, and reduce expenditure—aggravated political and social tension within Jamaica, and led to unrest, violence, and opposition protests.

[35]Many of Manmohan Singh's critics would write and say that he had worked in the IMF and/or the World Bank. The truth, however, is that he never had.

6

The Devaluation Trauma

Right from the beginning, the prospect of devaluation horrified the prime minister. It was not surprising. He belonged to a generation that believed that the 6 June 1966 devaluation forced upon Indira Gandhi was a political and economic disaster. Little did he realize that almost exactly a quarter of a century later, he would be in the hot seat. Of course, numerologically, 6.6.66 couldn't be matched!

While the truth of the devaluation episode under Indira Gandhi[36] is considerably more complex than is popularly held, it is also a fact that the US and other Western donors did not keep their side of the bargain and the international support promised to India as a quid pro quo for devaluation did not materialize. This could well have been for the political stances India took on issues of concern to the Americans, especially Vietnam.

Even before he became prime minister, Narasimha Rao had quizzed Pranab Mukherjee and me on the pros and cons of devaluation.

---

[36]Two insider accounts of that episode are B.K. Nehru, *Nice Guys Finish Second* (New Delhi: Viking, 1997) and I.G. Patel, *Glimpses of Indian Economic Policy* (New Delhi: Oxford University Press, 2002). B.G. Verghese, then the prime minister's information adviser, writes in his memoirs, *First Draft: Witness to the Making of Modern India* (New Delhi: Tranquebar, 2010) that the night before the devaluation, Indira Gandhi tried to relax by watching *Doctor Zhivago* and *Those Magnificent Men in Their Flying Machines*, but she admitted, 'I am scared stiff'.

Two or three days after he assumed office, Rao informed me that Nikhil Chakravartty, the respected editor of *Mainstream*, had met him and told him that devaluation should be avoided at all costs. He further informed the prime minister that Dr Arjun Sengupta, the noted economist who had worked with Indira Gandhi during 1981–84 and had subsequently been India's executive director at the IMF, was firmly of the view that devaluation was unnecessary and that if given an opportunity he could help negotiate an IMF package without its dreaded conditionalities. The prime minister respected Nikhil Chakravartty and wanted me to speak directly to Arjun Sengupta, who was in Delhi then.

I met Sengupta, who I knew well, and he reiterated what he had told Chakravartty. He was keen to come back to India from Brussels, where he was our ambassador, and in keeping with his seniority, wanted to be designated principal finance secretary; this, he felt, would grant him clout with the IMF. Sengupta asked me to convey to the prime minister that he had also served as an adviser to Michel Camdessus, the managing director of the IMF, which gave him a unique position vis-a-vis the organization. I transmitted whatever Sengupta told me faithfully to Narasimha Rao. Nothing happened further on that front.

But then, on 30 June 1991, the prime minister asked me to meet him late in the evening at Hyderabad House, the official meeting place maintained by the Ministry of External Affairs, where he was hosting an Iftar dinner. When I met him after the banquet, he appeared very perturbed and said that he did not fully accept the business of 'two-step devaluation' which was being forcefully advocated by the finance minister. Later, I was to learn that Manmohan Singh had sent the prime minister a top-secret handwritten note suggesting devaluation—but in two phases. One devaluation was bad enough, but two in quick succession seemed to have shaken Rao. President R. Venkataraman, who had been finance minister under Indira Gandhi, had cautioned the prime minister and finance minister about a radical step like devaluation. While Venkataraman was against the very idea, that it was proposed to be carried out by a 'minority government' made it even more unacceptable!

I did not know what the finance minister had written to the prime minister. But I took the prime minister through the arguments for a two-step devaluation—that the first step was needed to test the waters and establish our credibility, and the second would be the real change. I told him that the markets were expecting a two-step devaluation. I also recall having told the prime minister that it was high time that we acknowledged that the exchange rate was a matter of, not pride, but a price. I reminded him that there was scholarly evidence to suggest that the 1966 devaluation was not such an economic disaster as it was made out to be. But I could see that Narasimha Rao was completely unconvinced. He let me go after about ninety minutes. That was the first time I got to know that devaluation was on the cards.

♦

As it turned out, the first devaluation of the rupee—against major currencies (the dollar, pound, yen, mark and franc)—of between 7 per cent and 9 per cent took place on 1 July 1991. Within forty-eight hours, on the morning of 3 July, the second devaluation of about 11 per cent against the major global currencies was carried out. Thus the rupee had depreciated by something like 18 per cent in just two days.

The prime minister was certainly not amused. In fact, a little after the first devaluation, in the early hours of 3 July, he called up Manmohan Singh asking for the second devaluation to be halted. The finance minister argued with him but to no avail. Thereafter, Manmohan Singh called Dr C. Rangarajan, the deputy governor of the RBI, at around 9.30 a.m., to ask him to hold back the second stage devaluation—only to be told that it had already been carried out that very morning at 9 a.m. The finance minister was, of course, delighted that this had been done, but conveyed the news to the prime minister less enthusiastically.

The two-step devaluation decision was taken purely between the prime minister and the finance minister, and was conveyed to the governor and deputy governor of the RBI. The finance minister had wanted it that way because he felt that given the 1966 experience, the cabinet would never give its consent.[37] Of course, financial markets had expected the devaluation, although there were varying expectations regarding the exact quantum of change.

Once the second devaluation was announced, markets reacted positively and industry circles also welcomed the move. But predictably, the news caused a furore in Parliament and great sullenness within the Congress itself. The finance minister and the RBI governor, on their part, took great care never to use the word 'devaluation', always referring to it as 'an adjustment of the exchange rate of the rupee'.

The finance minister called an unscheduled press conference on 3 July after his conversation with the prime minister, and defended the two-step devaluation, enumerating in detail the benefits that would accrue to the economy. But more importantly, he emphatically ruled out further downward revisions and gave a firm assurance that no further devaluations would take place.

In an interview with the journalist Paranjoy Guha Thakurta (Annexure 4), when asked why he had opted for devaluation, and a two-step one at that, he said:

> We, in this country, live under certain illusions—economists have been responsible for it—that devaluation is something immoral, anti-national. You look around the world. Over the past year, both the Soviet Union and China have gone in for massive devaluation of their currencies. Our people—the economists, the journalists, the politicians—somehow believe that devaluation is sinful and dishonourable. It is nothing of that sort.
>
> The exchange rate is just a price. If you are in the business of selling, *your* price has to be competitive. And who are our competitors? They include South Korea, the countries of south and

---

[37]The 6 June 1966 decision was taken by the prime minister on the advice of four key officials—L.K. Jha (the prime minister's secretary), S. Bhoothalingam (the finance secretary), I.G. Patel (the chief economic adviser) and P.C. Bhattacharya (the governor of the RBI)—and ratified by the cabinet the previous day, on a Sunday. 'The prime minister had agreed more by faith than understanding'; based on the interviews of the author with S. Bhoothalingam, 14 April 1983, and L.K. Jha, 27 April 1983.

south-east Asia, and Pakistan. Look at what they have done. I think their exchange rate policies have been aggressive and designed to enhance their competitiveness. Now, if in this situation, we do nothing, our balance of payments, which is already precarious, would worsen further.

[...Regarding why devaluation was in two stages] to be honest, I had to test the reaction of the market, test the political reaction and prepare the country for a bigger devaluation. That was why we launched a trial balloon. The initial reaction was favourable, the market took it calmly. [...]

Q: Did you go in for a sudden devaluation instead of a gradual one—say, spread out over a month—because time was running out?

A: A gradual kind of devaluation could not have been done in the present situation. Normally, you have creeping devaluation which is not noticed. If I allowed a gradual slide, the rupee could have suddenly slumped. In this country and abroad, people were saying that the rupee was so weak that no government would be able to sustain its value. The ideal thing to do would have been to devalue at one go, but I had to prepare domestic public opinion. I'm grateful that the Prime Minister has understood the gravity of the problems.

The prime minister, on his part, was clearly a reluctant protagonist in the two-step devaluation drama. But once it happened, he defended it aggressively, both in Parliament and outside. On 7 July, he spoke to K.K. Katyal of *The Hindu* and answered questions on devaluation thus:[38]

Q: The thrust now will be on economic reforms, structural adjustments as the Finance Minister has been saying. Somehow the assurance that, in this process, the independence of judgement would be preserved is missing. Would you like to say something?

PM: It is not missing. We have been emphasising it time and again. In fact he has been saying that the main request for all these reforms would be to see that we do not lose our economic

---

[38]The interview appeared in *The Hindu* on 10 July 1991.

independence. If we go on drifting we would certainly have lost it, if not now, after six months. In the next one week or two, we would have been defaulters. And once you become a defaulter, a country of India's size, what will happen is something that you can easily imagine. Then what happens? Can you keep your economic independence after that? Therefore what the Finance Minister said is absolutely correct and what I say is this is the only way of keeping our economic independence in the long run. We had to take hard decisions so that we don't go into a situation where it becomes irretrievable. Then you lose economic independence. So it is in order to prevent that horrendous situation that these decisions were taken.

Q: What haunts both experts and non-experts is the experience of 1966. The rupee was devalued but exports did not pick up. Could there be assurance that 1966 would not be repeated?

PM: We will have to carefully weigh the steps which need to be taken hereafter and we are at it. We have not really left anything for test and I am sure that whatever might have happened at that time, I am not quite sure what to say about that because I was at least personally not fully aware of the details—so without making any comment about what happened in 1966 this time I may say that we will not leave anything to drift. We will take all the consequential actions that are needed and we are already taking those steps.

On 8 July 1991, the prime minister's interview with Prabhu Chawla of *The Indian Express* appeared, and here, too, the prime minister was unapologetic and anything but defensive.

Q: Given the minority character of your government, do you feel confident as Prime Minister?

A: Yes, I do feel more confident now. Although the responsibility is very heavy, the Congress party can discharge this very effectively. And the kind of response which the Government has got from the people during the last three weeks has provided us greater confidence.

Q: Is it due to this that you have resorted to strong economic measures like steep depreciation of the rupee?

A: We mean business now. The country could not wait any longer. These decisions should have been taken long ago.

Q: But is it not improper to push through such strong measures without proving your majority on the floor of the House?

A: These steps were so urgent that I could not have waited. Both from the point of view of time and substance I had to do what I did.

Q. Was it done under IMF pressure?

A: No, it was done because it was more or less in the pipeline. It was done because much time was lost in not taking these decisions earlier. I am glad we have done it. If we had not done it, the alternatives would have been disastrous.

The Katyal and Chawla interviews were quintessential Narasimha Rao. He philosophized like nobody else could, but got his point through—that there was no alternative to devaluation. He remained emphatic, although I very well knew, as did the finance minister, how deeply uncomfortable he was with the move, and had, in fact, tried hard to stop the 3 July devaluation.

The devaluation decision proved very contentious and criticism did not stop. In Parliament, the finance minister had to face much flak from across the political spectrum. But he took the fight to his critics much to the delight of the prime minister and all of us.

On 16 July 1991, for instance, the Rajya Sabha witnessed this exchange during question hour. It was in response to a question asked jointly by Gurudas Dasgupta of the CPI and Ajit Jogi of the Congress. Dasgupta actually asked the question.

Shri Gurudas Dasgupta (West Bengal; CPI): My question to the hon. Minister is that the balance of payments position cannot be corrected if there is no increase in the export India does. Over the last ten years there have been a number of so-called adjustments in the exchange rate and even then there has been no appreciable improvement in the export of the country. In 1966, devaluation was resorted to. Even then for the first few years export increased by only 4.5%. In this background, I would like to know how the hon. Finance Minister is optimistic that there can be increase in export so that the balance of payments position can be corrected.

[…] Part (b) of my question is this. There is a danger that the increase in export may be over-counter-balanced by the increase in the price of import […]

Part (c) of my question is whether the devaluation was resorted to because the Government of India was under duress from the non-resident Indians and also that it was under duress because of the World Bank conditionalities for getting the loan.

Dr. Manmohan Singh: I would like to answer the last part of the question first. We were not under any duress from anybody then and we are not [under] duress now. This was a sensible decision to do in the circumstances in which our country was placed and is now. Therefore, I don't have to bow to the IMF or to anybody else to do what is in the best interest of the country.

Shri Gurudas Dasgupta: The Prime Minister said yesterday that the banks would have been underrun if devaluation was not done. What have you to comment on that?

Dr. Manmohan Singh: The Prime Minister was mentioning the objective conditions prevailing then and what we did was a response mechanism which stopped those types of destabilising activities becoming a flood. This is not a question of functioning under duress at all. The first part of the question is: will devaluation lead to an increase in export? The hon. Member has referred to several previous instances. Let me say that in this country there seems to be a strange conspiracy between the extreme left and extreme right that there is something immoral or dishonourable about changing the exchange rate. But that is not the tradition. If you look at the whole history of India's independence struggle before 1947 all our national leaders were fighting against the British against keeping the exchange rate of the Rupee unduly high. Why did the British keep the exchange rate of the Rupee unduly high? It was because they wanted this country to remain backward and they did not want this country to industrialise. They wanted the country to be an exporter of primary products against which all Indian economists protested. If you look at Indian history right from 1900 onwards to 1947, this was a recurring plea of all Indian economists—not to have an exchange rate which is so high that India cannot export, that India cannot industrialise. But I am really surprised that something which is meant to encourage the country's exports, encourage its industrialisation is now considered as something anti-national.

This was Professor Manmohan Singh at his scholarly best. He was also unusually combative. After all, his doctoral dissertation was on India's exports and he had challenged the 'export pessimism' syndrome of the 1950s. I mentioned this to a couple of colleagues and said that sitting in the Officials Gallery and listening to the finance minister answer questions and make his interventions was a wonderful lesson in real-world macroeconomics.

7

The Continuing Gold Sales Controversy

Nothing exemplified the magnitude of India's financial crisis in the early part of 1991 better than the need to use our gold reserves to raise money to pay for the country's imports. This showed that we had become totally bankrupt. Of course, under Section 33(5) of the Reserve Bank of India (RBI) Act, 1934, the RBI had the power to keep 15 per cent of its gold outside India[39] and it could exercise that power on its own. But that power had never been exercised till the early months of 1991.

It was Prime Minister Chandra Shekhar and Finance Minister Yashwant Sinha—on the advice of the RBI Governor S. Venkitaramanan—who first decided to use our gold reserves to raise foreign loans to keep the wheels of the economy moving. On 16 May 1991, 20 metric tonnes of confiscated gold held by the Government of India was leased to the State Bank of India (SBI). Two days later, SBI entered into a sale transaction with a repurchase option with the United Bank of Switzerland. This was before the Rao government came to power. This helped raise about US$200 million.

Once the new government came to power, gold transfers continued. This time it was the RBI that transported a total of 46.91 tonnes of gold to the Bank of England over four days—4, 7, 11 and 18 July

---

[39]The law specifically states: 'Of the gold coin and gold bullion held as assets, not less than seventeen-twentieths shall be held in [India].'

TO THE BRINK AND BACK ■ 45

1991 (the last of which took Parliament by surprise). This enabled the country to borrow 'for a period of one month at a time a total sum of about $400 million to help us tide over the serious liquidity problems we were facing.'[40]

The SBI transaction involved the sale of confiscated gold at the prevailing market price with the option to repurchase it within six months. The four RBI transactions, on the other hand, did not mean outright sales but were meant only for 'parking' that gold in the vaults of the Bank of England, permissible by law, against which the Bank of England advanced the RBI some temporary financial assistance.

Right from the start, Parliament was agitated about the gold transfer issue. Members cutting across party lines protested loudly. Congress MPs did not spare their own government. On 12 July, the matter rocked question hour and there were heated exchanges between the finance minister, and K.P. Unnikrishnan and Chandrajeet Yadav, both of whom had been leading lights of the Congress in the past.

> K.P. Unnikrishnan (Kerala; JD [Janata Dal]): Sir, the distinguished Finance Minister for whom I have high respect, regard and affection [...] I would also request him not to quibble around and acquire the habit of politicians and to be straightforward in this House and tell the truth [...] There has been another transaction. It is said that it had been taken for safe custody of Bank of England walls, as though our walls are not protected. A former Reserve Bank Governor, his former colleague has called it a national humiliation. I would like to know why the second transaction was necessary.
>
> Dr. Manmohan Singh: [...] He has made a reference to the statement of my distinguished predecessor as the Governor of the Reserve Bank, Dr. I.G. Patel. I had spoken to him this morning [...and] he has been grossly misquoted. He had not said that what we have done is dishonourable or a humiliation. What he has said is that all of us should feel very sad that we brought our country to this pass that these transactions have to be done. I share that perception and all of us in this House and our people outside

---

[40]Statement of Finance Minister Dr Manmohan Singh on gold transactions, Lok Sabha, 18:00 hours, 18 July 1991.

must reflect as to what has gone wrong with this country that we have to do such painful things.

But there were some fine moments of statesmanship, too, when the finance minister defended his predecessor, Yashwant Sinha, who was being attacked by Congress MPs during question hour in the Rajya Sabha on 16 July:

Dr. Manmohan Singh: Mr. Chairman Sir, there is no relation between the stock of gold held by the Reserve Bank or the Government and the price level of the country. So this decision in regard to gold which was taken by the previous Government— some gold went when they were in power, some gold went when we were in power—if you are asking what impact it will have on prices, my answer is a plain "no"—that there is no relation between what was done and the domestic price level.

The second question that was asked was, was this transaction absolutely necessary and at what level was the decision taken? I am convinced that in both these cases these transactions were very necessary. The former Finance Minister and the former Prime Minister took these decisions. It was not a happy decision. I know that the then Prime Minister was greatly pained by that decision and I share the sense of pain. It is not something of which I am very proud—that I have to sell the country's gold—but the House must appreciate the situation in which this country stands [...] We are not very proud of what we have done but you have my assurance that we considered all options, the pros and the cons, the costs and the benefits. In the circumstances, this was the best possible decision that could be taken.

Shri Yashwant Sinha (Bihar; SJP [Samajwadi Janata Party]): Sir, I am very grateful to the Finance Minister for the way he has spoken. I must say that it has been a totally non-partisan approach that the Finance Minister has brought to bear upon a question to which unnecessary sentiment is sought to be attached [...] I must point it out because the Finance Minister has justified what our Government had done and I must express my gratitude. At the same time, I must also say that I am very glad that he has put the record straight because a junior spokesman of that party called it a national betrayal. He does not agree with that and I am glad about that.

Sadly, that was the first and last time Yashwant Sinha was so magnanimous. After that, he never lost any opportunity to taunt, bait or criticize Manmohan Singh, first as finance minister, and later as prime minister, in the bitterest language possible. I have always believed that this was because he was sore that the credit for ushering in economic reforms was not given to him, but was instead rightly bestowed on Manmohan Singh.

We had thought that all gold transactions had been completed by 16 July 1991. But reports of a fourth transaction hit the headlines on 18 July. Parliament was agog once again. It was then that it was decided that the finance minister would make an authoritative statement on the gold transfers from the RBI to the Bank of England. Accordingly, he made this statement in the Lok Sabha late at 6 p.m. on 18 July itself. He recounted the history of all transfers and why they had become essential. But the two important new points he made were:

1. The movement of gold had to be done without prior public announcements for security reasons.
2. No further gold transfers would take place.

The prime minister mused about gold once or twice. This was particularly so after Atal Bihari Vajpayee, a leading member of the BJP, who would become India's eleventh prime minister, had spoken on the budget in the Lok Sabha on 5 August 1991. Vajpayee had said:

[…] There is about 10,000 tonnes of gold in our country, out of which 5,000 tonnes is hoarded and 5,000 tonnes have been brought into the country through smuggling. If we succeed to […] get 2,000 tonnes of gold from the public—I am not talking of 5,000 tonnes of gold but only 2,000 tonnes of gold […] it would be worth 36 billion American dollars […]

If we sell gold worth 25 billion dollars to clear our debts and invest the rest of gold in such a way that it would fetch us 10 percent profit, then it would help us in overcoming the financial crisis.

My view, which I shared with the prime minister, was that what the BJP leader was suggesting was unrealistic given the role gold plays in our lives; in any case, it was a suggestion for the medium-term. It was no solution for the days and months ahead. For that, the IMF route was the only way out, something that the V.P. Singh and Chandra Shekhar governments had recognized.[41]

◆

What might Rajiv Gandhi have done vis-à-vis gold? The Congress was vocally critical, no doubt, but what is to be made of this oral recollection by S. Venkitaramanan, while taking part in a symposium organized by the Rajiv Gandhi Foundation in November 1994, two years after he had retired as the governor of the RBI? He recalled thus:

> I was Governor of the Reserve Bank and we had this severe crisis. I had the permission of Chandra Shekhar to interact with him [Rajiv Gandhi]. I had gone to him and said: 'Sir, it worries me that we should have this country going through tremendous crisis of foreign exchange and we have three billion dollars' worth of gold in our reserves. I want to use it. I know that your party colleagues are against it and publicly you have expressed, your party has expressed this view.' He [Rajiv Gandhi] said: 'It is nonsense. How can you allow this country to go through with this situation without using the gold you have? If you want, I will come out and say [it].'[42]

Alas, that never came to pass.

---

[41]Under various borrowing windows of the IMF, India took US$660 million during July–September 1990 and US$1.8 billion in January 1991. India was to later borrow US$221 million in July 1991, US$639 million in September 1991, US$117 million in November 1991, US$265 million in January 1992 and US$650 million in February–March 1992. This demonstrates vividly how precarious the economic situation was and how dependent we had become on the IMF for balance-of-payments financing well after the reforms blitz of July 1991.

[42]See *Rajiv Gandhi's India*, Volume 2, volume editor V. Ramachandran (New Delhi: UBS Publishers, 1994).

8

The Default Option Remembered

In June–July 1991, one issue kept nagging the prime minister—that of debt rescheduling. It was obvious that some political leaders and their economist-friends had got to him. Thus, one of his early queries to me was: 'Why can't we renegotiate our loans like we had done in the 1960s?' It is not that he was suggesting a default or anything close—but certainly, the matter bothered him.

My response was that the two situations were not comparable. In the 1960s all our debt was to multilateral institutions like the World Bank and to bilateral aid agencies. It was certainly true that the Aid-India Consortium,[43] as it was then called, had renegotiated India's debt obligations. But the situation in 1991 was totally different. This was short-term debt and debt owed to commercial institutions. This was more like the Latin American situation and I told the prime minister as much. I allowed myself a rare moment of levity in one of these meetings when I repeated the well-known line to him: 'Sir, it is true that when you owe somebody 500 dollars, you should be worried; but when you owe somebody 5 billion dollars, *he* should be worried.' The prime minister was not amused. Therefore, on a more serious note, I reminded him that his finance minister had been crying

---

[43]The Aid-India Consortium, led by the World Bank, was organized in 1958 as an international network to support the economic development of India.

himself hoarse that India would not default and there should be no ambiguity on this matter.

I had never known the finance minister to be aggressive. His style was measured and calibrated. But on this subject, I found him unusually strident—and rightly so. There were far too many voices raising the issue of debt rescheduling. On 23 June, just a day after assuming office in the North Block, the finance minister, while speaking to the United News of India, had categorically stated that there would be no default on repayment. He had said that India had a reputation for 'financially sound behaviour' and went on to add that 'we will build on that and do whatever is necessary to maintain the country's credit-worthiness and honour all our commitments'.

The matter got raised in the Rajya Sabha again during question hour on 16 July 1991, as the following exchange will reveal:

Shri Sukomal Sen (West Bengal; CPM): [...] Sir, the question is, India is heavily indebted, true. Not only India but many other third world countries are also heavily indebted to the IMF or other commercial banks and they have the same problem. Now, if the Government of India wants to review the situation in a broader perspective, I would like to know from the hon. Minister whether instead of sending out gold immediately and going to the IMF, the Government unitedly with other third world countries would demand a moratorium on all foreign debts for the next few years so that India and other third world countries can tide over this crisis.

Dr. Manmohan Singh: Mr Chairman, Sir, that is a different question. I have stated categorically.

Mr. Chairman: He wants to know whether India will try for a moratorium in cooperation with other countries in a similar situation.

Dr. Manmohan Singh: The Prime Minister has stated it categorically and I have stated it categorically that we are honour-bound and duty-bound to honour all our commitments. About what happens in collective forums of the third world, I think, we will consult all other countries. We have been doing so before and we will continue to do so hereafter. But let nobody get any impression that this country is out to renege on its international obligations. That will be a sad day for India and we will avoid it under all conditions.

◆

I thought the idea of debt rescheduling had died in the prime minister's mind because of the tough stand taken by the finance minister. But I was to discover later that it may have still lingered there. On 20 September 1992, I attended a lecture by Dr I.G. Patel in memory of Govind Ballabh Pant in New Delhi titled 'Freedom from Foreign Debt'. The prime minister must have received a garbled version from some of those present, for the next morning I received a call from him. He asked, 'Jairam, has IG [as Patel was often referred to] called for debt rescheduling?' Fortunately, I had the circulated text of the lecture handy and read out the paragraph that had set the prime minister thinking. Patel had said:

> On a more general plane, there is no reason why we should seek a reduction in our official debt by negotiation. If debts to much richer countries like Poland and Egypt could be written off, there is no reason why we should be singled out for martyrdom simply because we have honoured all our obligations so far.

I encouraged the prime minister to read the full lecture, and sent it across to him. That was the last I heard of it.

9

Statements: Right and Left

On 1 July 1991, four of the country's most distinguished economists-cum-economic administrators issued a joint statement supporting what Manmohan Singh had set out to do. The finance minister himself gently nudged P.N. Dhar (or PND, as he was often called) to take the lead, assemble the influential quartet, and, as a united force, support bold liberalization. Manmohan Singh had worked with PND in the 1970s when the latter was secretary to Indira Gandhi and Singh was chief economic adviser in the Ministry of Finance.[44]

Apart from PND, the other three names suggested themselves. I.G. Patel had held senior positions in the Government of India and had, as we know, been governor of the RBI between 1977 and 1982 and later served as the director of the London School of Economics. M. Narasimham, a grandson of S. Radhakrishnan, had a distinguished

---

[44]This was incidentally the period when Manmohan Singh first came to the notice of Indira Gandhi and earned a name for himself. The rate of inflation was 20.2 per cent in 1973-74 and 25.2 per cent in 1974-75 on account of the first oil shock and drought. The rate of inflation fell to -1.09 per cent in 1975-76; 2.1 per cent in 1976-77; 5.2 per cent in 1977-78; and actually 0 per cent in 1978-79. There is wide consensus amongst scholars that the package of extraordinarily tough fiscal, monetary and incomes-policy measures announced in July 1974 helped destroy the demon of inflation in the late 1970s. Manmohan Singh was the principal author of the package, which P.N. Dhar and B.D. Pande (then the cabinet secretary) helped sell to a beleaguered prime minister. The three were entrusted with the responsibility of getting the package implemented.

career in the RBI, the World Bank, the IMF, the ADB and the Ministry of Finance. R.N. Malhotra was an IAS officer who had specialized in economic management and had been at the helm of affairs in the RBI between 1985 and 1990. The four were very close professionally and personally, not only amongst themselves but also with the finance minister. The prime minister knew of M. Narasimham and had great respect for IG, having considered him briefly for the post of finance minister.

I had some idea that a joint statement from these four gentlemen was in the works. The noted journalist and former MP, R.K. Mishra, then chairman of the Observer Research Foundation (ORF), had told me about it and I had then alerted the prime minister. ORF had, in fact, organized the release of the joint statement on 1 July at the Parliament House Annexe with both the finance and commerce ministers present, along with P.N. Dhar. Another such function took place on 5 July. When the statement finally came out, it received wide media coverage because of the impeccable credentials and reputation of the signatories. I called up the two I knew well—PND and Narasimham—and conveyed to them the prime minister's deep appreciation for their statement. Besides, I knew that PND was close to senior Congress leaders and felt that the statement would be read by these leaders with great interest and seriousness (Annexure 5).

After a couple of days the statement was forgotten, but suddenly it hit the headlines again. In our enthusiasm to give the statement the widest possible circulation, I think I suggested to the finance minister that perhaps we could send it to all MPs. The finance minister liked the idea and so did the prime minister. But instead of sending the statement to the MPs under a separate cover, we allowed ourselves to have it sent to the MPs along with the usual papers that get distributed to them by the Lok Sabha and Rajya Sabha Secretariat.

On 11 July 1991, as soon as its session commenced, all hell broke loose in the Rajya Sabha as the following extract from the proceedings will reveal:

Shri Dipen Ghosh (West Bengal; CPM): Sir, I have addressed a letter to you. Two days ago among the parliamentary papers package there was one statement purported to have been signed by Mr. I.G. Patel, Mr. Narasimham, Mr. Malhotra and [one] other economist. *(Interruptions)*

Mr. Chairman: I have received your letter. *(Interruptions)*

Shri Dipen Ghosh: Why [is] this statement being circulated among other papers? They are neither ministers nor Members of Parliament. How can this paper be circulated? *(Interruptions)*

Shri A.G. Kulkarni (Maharashtra; INC [Indian National Congress]): This is not proper. Comrade Bhupesh Gupta used to say, "Why don't you go to Russia and China and see what is happening?" *(Interruptions)*

Mr. Chairman: He says something else. Please sit down.

Shri A.G. Kulkarni: No. How do you allow him?

Mr. Chairman: I allowed him. Now you please sit down. *(Interruptions)* I will explain to you. *(Interruptions)*

Shri Dipen Ghosh: How could it find its way into the parliamentary papers? This is unauthorised use of the Parliamentary Secretariat surreptitiously for sending the papers to the Members of Parliament. *(Interruptions)* I [take] exception to this unauthorised use of Parliamentary Secretariat Office for circulating a particular point of view about the Indian economic situation for finding solutions. If it is for enlightening the Members, there are 35 other economists who have also issued statements, who have also issued a call and whose views should also have been circulated. *(Interruptions)*

Mr. Chairman: It is all right. Now, please listen. *(Interruptions)*

Smt. Renuka Chowdhury (Andhra Pradesh; TDP): This is total erosion of the Indian Parliamentary system. *(Interruptions)*

Mr. Chairman: Everybody has understood. I have already told you here and I am repeating it: it was a mistake on the part of the Secretariat to do it. It was not correct. That is all. *(Interruptions)*

Shri Dipen Ghosh: You should make an enquiry as to who is responsible. *(Interruptions)*

Mr. Chairman: No paper like this should be circulated and I hope that the Secretariat will keep it in view that no unauthorised paper is circulated to Members in any way at any time. *(Interruptions)* […]

Shri Yashwant Sinha (Bihar; SJP): May I make one point […] We are completely reassured by what [was] said, that extraneous papers should not have found a place in the parliamentary papers which were circulated. But I think the point which has been raised is a very important one. *(Interruptions)*

Mr. Chairman: I agree. *(Interruptions)*

Shri Yashwant Sinha: We must decide and we must know under whose influence, under what inspiration those papers were circulated and what circumstances. The House must be taken into confidence. *(Interruptions)*

Shri Dipen Ghosh: We want to know. *(Interruptions)* The Finance Minister must explain. *(Interruptions)*

Shri Yashwant Sinha: It was done in a casual manner. This is a very serious thing. We want to know who was behind this. *(Interruptions)*

Mr. Chairman: The Secretariat has informed me just now there was a letter from the Parliament Assistant of the Finance Minister in which it is stated: '250 copies of English and 100 copies of Hindi version of Joint Statement: Agenda for Economic Reform are sent herewith. Finance Minister desires that the same are circulated among the Members of the Rajya Sabha today positively.' […]

Shri Yashwant Sinha: Shall we leave it at that?

Mr. Chairman: Of course.

Shri Yashwant Sinha: The Finance Minister must appear in this House. He must explain [why] he wanted that that particular paper be circulated.

Shri Dipen Ghosh: The Leader of the House [should] be asked to explain. He owes an explanation to this House.

The Leader of the House (Shri S.B. Chavan): I will inquire into the matter. I will find out from the Honourable Minister of Finance as to why it is that he thought it necessary that this should have been circulated.

Shri Jagdish Prasad Mathur (Uttar Pradesh; BJP): This shows the ignorance of the Finance Minister about the procedures. That is all.

Hectic back-channel negotiations then commenced with the minister of Parliamentary affairs, Ghulam Nabi Azad, playing a key role in settling the controversy. Finally, on 15 July, at the stroke of the noon hour, the chairman of the Rajya Sabha made the following announcement:

On 11th July, 1991, several Members raised in the House a matter regarding circulation of a statement purporting to have been signed by Prof. P.N. Dhar, Shri I.G. Patel, Shri Narasimham, Shri R. N. Malhotra along with parliamentary papers. They also observed that the circulation of such an unauthorised paper was not correct. The Home Minister who is also Leader of the House, assured in the House that he would enquire into the matter. I have now received a letter from the Finance Minister, Shri Manmohan Singh, which reads as follows:

> Respected Chairman, may I request you to recall the proceedings of the Rajya Sabha on 11th July 1991 regarding the circulation of joint statement issued by Prof P.N. Dhar, Dr. I.G. Patel, Shri M. Narasimham and Shri R. N. Malhotra on Agenda for Economic Reform. I wish to express my sincere apologies for the unintended lapse in strict adherence to the procedure for circulation of such papers. I have taken note of the points raised by the Hon. Members as well as the ruling given by you on the subject, and I would like to assure you that the prescribed procedure will be strictly followed in the future.

In view of the above, I treat the matter as closed.

I called on the finance minister that very evening, and his relief that the joint statement controversy had been resolved was all-too-evident. But neither of us had bargained for yet another eruption, this time in the Lok Sabha the very next day.

Sometime after noon on 16 July, the speaker of the Lok Sabha made this statement: 'I have received a letter from the Hon. Finance Minister regretting circulation of the views of economists. I think the matter can be closed with that.' But it was not to be so easily disposed of as the following exchange will reveal:

Shri Somnath Chatterjee (West Bengal; CPM): What is the letter? (*Interruptions*)

Mr. Speaker: He has regretted. (*Interruptions*)

Mr. Speaker: He has now expressed his regret. (*Interruptions*)

Shri Somnath Chatterjee: Why should they utilise the Lok Sabha Secretariat for this purpose? They should not pressurise the Lok Sabha Secretariat. The Secretariat people are very experienced. The Lok Sabha Secretariat must have been pressurised.

Mr. Speaker: There are two aspects. One aspect relates to the Finance Ministry. The other aspect relates to the legislature Secretariat. As far as the Finance Ministry is concerned, I have received a letter and the matter should rest over there. As far as this Secretariat is concerned, I am personally looking into it for appropriate action. (*Interruptions*)

Shri Somnath Chatterjee: I am not blaming them. I am not blaming the Secretariat. The Secretariat people know their job. That is why I say they must have been pressurised.

Shri Ram Naik (Maharashtra; BJP): This is being informed to [the] Lok Sabha today. We have seen that [the] Rajya Sabha has been informed yesterday. Sir, both the Houses should be treated on par.

Mr. Speaker: About what?

Shri Ram Naik: About this incident of expressing the regret by the Finance Minister, the Rajya Sabha was informed yesterday. But this is being announced here today. At least in such matters, both the Houses—Lok Sabha and Rajya Sabha—should be treated on par.

Mr. Speaker: Do not prolong it. I received the letter only in the evening. Maybe that letter [had] been written yesterday only. It came to my notice only in the evening. I am informing you now. It is not necessary that you should prolong it.

This finally set the controversy to rest. But there had been tension for six days. The intentions were right. But yes, the procedure was certainly unconventional and hackles were justifiably raised. It was a valuable early lesson in how to deal with Parliament.

◆

In retrospect, the mistake we made was not in circulating the other statement mentioned by CPM leader, Dipen Ghosh, when he fired his salvo on 11 July. This was a statement issued by thirty-five of the leading 'leftist' economists of the country in the nation's capital on 8 July (Annexure 6). They included former members of the Planning Commission like C.H. Hanumantha Rao, Arun Ghosh, Rajni Kothari and G.S. Bhalla; former West Bengal finance minister, Ashok Mitra; and noted academics like I.S. Gulati and Bhabatosh Datta. This statement was significantly at variance with the one issued by PND and company in that it rejected the inevitability of approaching the IMF for short- and medium-term assistance. While its analysis of what had gone wrong in 1990 and 1991 was not radically different from that of the quartet, the thrust of its recommendations was not faster and deeper regulation or an expanded role for the private sector. Rather, it was critical of the devaluation measures and wanted no cut in subsidies.

The significance of this statement was that three top officials serving the government in key positions—the finance secretary, foreign secretary and the chief economic adviser in the Ministry of Finance—

were in full sympathy with it and did not hide their support, much to the irritation of the principal secretary to the prime minister and, I suspect, even the finance minister.

10

Jyoti Basu Writes to the Prime Minister

On 4 July 1991, the West Bengal government released a document titled 'Alternative Policy Approach to Resolve BoP[45] Crisis' (Annexure 7). In it, it called for an increase in income tax rates, cuts in non-development expenditure, the collection of tax arrears and the unearthing of black money. Soon after, the West Bengal chief minister, Jyoti Basu, wrote to the prime minister and finance minister, sending them this document.

After taking over, both the finance minister and the prime minister had called for a national debate. Now they had one. The finance minister promptly responded on 9 July,[46] and wrote:

My effort [...] is that somehow we should avoid a situation where we are declared a defaulter. If that eventuality comes about despite my efforts, it would be the saddest day in the history of Independent India. Moreover, judging by the experience of Latin American and African countries in the last decade, a default situation will certainly mean that the decade of the 90s will also be a decade of reckless inflation and rising unemployment. It will,

---

[45] Balance of payments.

[46] My best efforts to locate this letter failed. Consequently, I have used excerpts of the letter that appeared in *The Hindu*, 10 July 1991, p. 4. I can confidently assert that this was an authoritative leak!

in other words, become a lost decade as has been the case in Latin American and most countries of Africa during the 1980s.

Referring directly to the recommendations in the note, Manmohan Singh went on to write:

It is my honest assessment that the alternative policy approach does not provide a way out of the balance of payments difficulties at the present juncture. The non-resident Indians will not send any money to India so long as our reserves remain at the dangerously low level that they are now. As regards import compression, you very well may be right that in the previous years there was some fat in the import bill. However, in the last five months a savage import cut has been imposed and today there is no scope for any further import compression. Even the import compression that is now in place will have serious consequences. It will hurt industrial production, lead to large-scale unemployment and will give rise to serious unrest and disruption.

That Jyoti Basu enjoyed a close friendship with and the esteem of the finance minister was evident by the latter's almost instantaneous response to the former's letter. What later became clear was that the prime minister also had enormous respect for the West Bengal chief minister. He was not satisfied that his finance minister had responded; he told his principal secretary and me that he, too, would like to reply. Hence, on 10 August, he wrote to Jyoti Basu. The prime minister's letter was more political than that of Manmohan Singh. He lauded West Bengal's record in land reforms and democratic decentralization as worthy of emulation by other states. To placate the Left parties, he promised that the letter of intent to be signed with the IMF would be tabled in Parliament.[47] The prime minister saw no contradiction in

---

[47]The finance minister's letter to the managing director of the IMF dated 27 August 1991 was tabled in the Rajya Sabha on 16 December 1991, by which time much of the sting of having gone to the IMF had been lost. There were some hilarious moments while finalizing the letter of intent. An early draft shared by IMF officials spelt 'labour' as 'labor' and 'programme' as 'program' and I had to point to the principal secretary that such obvious slips-ups would demonstrate the real authorship of the letter of intent!

what Jyoti Basu and the thirty-five economists (in the previous chapter) were advocating and wrote that, in fact, the 24 July 1991 budget had implemented many of the suggestions being made. Dr Asim Dasgupta, the West Bengal finance minister, released the prime minister's reply in Kolkata on 20 August. I was happy that he had done so—not the least because now, I would not be accused of orchestrating the leak!

II

Chidambaram in Quick Action

With the urgent need to arrest declining exports immediately and boost them in the medium-term, it was obvious that trade policy changes were a matter of priority. The PMO did not take any direct interest in designing these changes, despite the fact that A.N. Verma, the prime minister's principal secretary, had been commerce secretary. This was because in Montek Ahluwalia, the secretary of commerce, we had a man who knew exactly what needed to be done; and in P. Chidambaram we had a super-efficient, 'hands on' commerce minister.

My only side-role in this area was on the night of 3 July 1991[48] when I was summoned by the prime minister at about 9 p.m. On entering his drawing room, I found the finance and commerce ministers in his company. After a brief discussion, a decision was taken to abolish the export subsidy in the form of cash compensatory system—or CCS, as it was popularly known—that was given to exporters. Indeed, after the two-step devaluation, it made little sense to continue with this subsidy.

The finance minister wanted an immediate announcement of this decision, but I told the trio that it was rather late to give out the news for it to have any impact in the papers the next day. Nonetheless, I

---

[48]The events of 3 July 1991 have been discussed in greater detail by Montek Ahluwalia in a festschrift, published in honour of P. Chidambaram, titled *An Agenda for India's Growth*, edited by Sameer Kochhar (New Delhi: Academic Foundation, 2013).

did some quick thinking and decided on my own that I would inform *The Economic Times* since the CCS issue was of interest to the exporters who read that daily. Accordingly, *The Economic Times* the next day had a front page box news-item that read thus:

CCS SYSTEM MAY BE REPLACED BY REP LICENSES
New Delhi Bureau
New Delhi, 3 July

The government is likely to abolish export subsidies in the form of cash compensatory support.

They are likely to be replaced by a modified replenishment (rep) license system.

The decision to abolish CCS is believed to have been taken late on Wednesday night in view of the currency realignment in the last 48 hours.

According to government sources an official announcement on the abolishing of CCS is expected on Thursday.

As soon as I reached office on 4 July, A.N. Verma conveyed to me the prime minister's unhappiness that only one paper had carried the news. Obviously, some of his friends in the media who felt left out had complained to him. I told the principal secretary that it was around 11 p.m. or so that I was told to communicate this decision and that given the late hour I had tried to get it out in the best way possible. But my explanation did not wash and I was told to be more careful in future.

As far as the substantive trade policy reforms themselves were concerned, P. Chidambaram announced them officially on the morning of 4 July. After the devaluations of 1 and 3 July, this was the third major move of the Rao government. The commerce minister was in his element and handled the press meet with his characteristic aplomb and dexterity. But as soon as the package was announced—and the fact that the office of the Chief Controller of Imports and Exports (CCI&E) would be abolished—there were howls of protest within Udyog Bhavan which housed the Ministry of Commerce. The protests continued even as the minister, in his defence, took recourse to the Congress' 1991 manifesto and its commitment to abolish five regulatory agencies in the first 730 days in office. A compromise was struck a little later and the CCI&E took on a new avatar, Indian-style, as the DGFT (Directorate General of Foreign Trade).

It took less than ten hours, as Ahluwalia writes, to get the 4 July trade policy reforms approved by the prime minister and the finance minister. The reforms themselves—anchored in removal of discretionary controls in the form of licensing, and in the linkage of all non-essential imports to exports (other than in the case of petroleum, fertilisers, steel and other essential purchases)—were widely welcomed by industry. They vastly simplified the procedures for imports while giving a huge boost to exports. Besides, they granted a large degree of automaticity in the issue of replenishment licenses which were being renamed exim (for export-import) scrips.

The commerce minister, for the first time ever, unambiguously declared that the rupee would be made fully convertible on the trade account in three to five years. This meant that Indian currency could be freely exchanged for dollars to import goods. This was actually accomplished in less than two years.

But the former prime minister, Chandra Shekhar, was most unhappy and very biting in his criticism in Parliament. He accused the government of becoming a slave of the World Bank and said that the 4 July package had been prepared by that organization. The commerce minister issued a pointed rejoinder on 19 July giving the long lineage of the 4 July package. In his defence, the commerce minister pointed out that the basic blueprint for trade policy reforms was prepared by the Abid Hussain Committee,[49] which had submitted its report way back in December 1984, and this blueprint was further expanded in June 1990 when V.P. Singh (a former commerce minister himself) was prime minister. But the most telling riposte was the revelation of the

---

[49]The Abid Hussain Committee on Trade Policies (1984) contained recommendations regarding import policies and export-promotion strategies—including the exemption of CCS.

commerce minister that Chandra Shekhar's Cabinet Committee on Trade and Investment (CCTI) itself had on 11 March 1991 approved a new export strategy which contained the main elements of the 4 July package; the commerce minister at that time was Dr Subramanian Swamy.

The 4 July package was only the first step. Much remained to be done. This was but natural since a highly complex system built over a period of more than four decades was being dismantled. The system was so convoluted and opaque that I used to joke that the most eagerly awaited import–export document every year was not the one on trade policy, but rather, Takht Ram's commentary on it.[50] Besides, the name of the organization itself—the Office of the Chief Controller of Imports & Exports—betrayed a particular mindset, where a case could be made for controlling imports, but controls on exports were to be pioneered at one's peril.

Finally, on 13 August 1991, the commerce minister made a detailed statement on trade policy in the Lok Sabha, going beyond the 4 July initiatives. A new package for 100 per cent export-oriented units and for units in the export-processing zone was announced. Public sector monopoly on the import and export of items was considerably curtailed. Details of how the new exim scrip instrument would operate were made explicit, as were those for the system of advance licenses to provide exporters with duty-free access to imports. The statement demonstrated that the Rao government was determined to push through both policy and institutional reform in support of accelerating exports. The commerce minister conveyed this in so many words.

---

[50]Takht Ram was a retired officer of the CCI&E who had spent years in that organization.

12

The Curious Case of the Prime Minister's
9 July Speech

The prime minister addressed the nation again on Doordarshan and over All India Radio on 9 July.[51] He may have felt that with Parliament about to begin the next day he needed to send political signals regarding his overall approach. Like in the past, he asked me for a draft. Having learnt my lessons well, I gave it to him in the full expectation that it would not be used one bit at all.

I was pleasantly surprised. The speech the prime minister delivered was entirely in keeping with the draft I had given him. He said:

> When I spoke to you last, I promised quick and bold measures to restore our sick economy to health. We have taken the first step to fulfil that promise. This is the beginning. A further set of far-reaching changes and reforms is on the way.
>
> For the last eighteen months, there has been paralysis on the economic front. The last two governments postponed taking vital decisions. The fiscal position was allowed to deteriorate. The balance-of-payments crisis became unmanageable. Non-resident Indians and foreign leaders became more and more reluctant to

---

[51]I tried to get hold of the officially printed copy of this speech from the Ministry of Information and Broadcasting but was unsuccessful. Finally, an official copy was made available to me in June 2015 by P.V. Prabhakar Rao, Narasimha Rao's youngest son (Annexure 8).

lend money to India.

Consequently, India's external reserves declined steeply and we had no foreign exchange to import even such essential commodities as diesel, kerosene, edible oil and fertilizer. The net result was that when we came to power, we found the financial position of the country in a terrible mess.

Desperate maladies call for drastic remedies. And that is what we have done. And that is what we will continue to do.

Exchange Rate Adjustment

The Reserve Bank changed the exchange rate of the rupee. This was done so that we can export more. More garments, more leather products, more gems and jewellery, more agricultural products made in India will be sold abroad. This will not only earn us foreign exchange but also create new employment at home.

And why do we need to earn foreign exchange so badly? Not to import luxury items but to buy commodities like kerosene and diesel, fertilizers, edible oil and steel. We produce these commodities, but what we produce is not enough. We are stepping up our production, but for some time, we have to import.

The adjustment in the exchange rate will discourage the import of non-essential goods. And will therefore save foreign exchange for the import of essential goods of mass consumption. It will also end uncertainty about the future of our currency and will encourage non-resident Indians to send more money to be deposited in their accounts in India.

After changing the value of the rupee we undertook a major overhaul of the trade policy. Our message was simple—you cannot import if you do not export. We cut down on export licenses so that our exporters do not face hurdles. We eliminated subsidies so that the money saved could be better deployed in welfare and employment programmes.

My objective is to make India truly self-reliant. Self-reliance is not a mere slogan for me. It means the ability to pay for our imports through exports. My motto is—trade, not aid. Aid is a crutch. Trade builds pride. And India has been trading for thousands of years.

Friends, Rajiv Gandhi came to power in 1984. He first understood the need for India to change her traditional way of thinking and doing things. He realized that if India is to survive and prosper, fundamental economic reforms must be carried out. He did that. What we have done is a continuation of the policies initiated by him.

Social and Economic Philosophy

In my first address to you I had outlined the agenda of my government. We stand committed to that agenda. The Budget which will be presented on July 24 will clearly articulate the social and economic philosophy of my government, the broad outlines of which are evident in our actions.

What is this outline?

We believe that a bulk of government regulations and controls on our economic activity have outlived their utility. They are stifling the creativity and innovativeness of our people. Excessive controls have also bred corruption. Indeed, they have come in the way of achieving our objectives of expanding employment opportunities, reducing rural–urban disparities and ensuring greater social justice.

We believe that the Nation, as well as the Government, must learn to live within its means. Normally, a family borrows money to buy an asset and not to meet daily expenditure. So it is with the Government. There is much fat in Government expenditure. This can and will be cut.

We believe that Government concessions must be for the poor and the really needy. Over the past few years, expenditure on this has increased substantially and in many instances the concessions are being enjoyed by people who are not in dire need of them. This must change

India Cannot Lag Behind

We believe that India has much to learn from what is happening elsewhere in the world. Many countries are bringing in far-reaching changes. We find major economic transformation sweeping large countries like the Soviet Union and China, as well as small countries in Eastern Europe. There is a change in outlook, a change in mindset everywhere. India too cannot lag behind if she has to survive, as she must, in the new environment.

Our commitment to work for the uplift of the poor, the underprivileged and the disadvantaged is firm and irrevocable. We believe that this is best achieved if Government concentrates on providing drinking water, on expanding education, on fighting social discrimination, on creating jobs, on establishing infrastructure. Our measures must reflect this ideology.

I wish to assure you that while we are restructuring the economy to make it more productive and efficient, prices will be kept under the strictest control. We will ensure adequate availability and supply of essential commodities.

Friends, it will be dishonest for me to pretend that the job of repairing our economy will be easy, quick or smooth. Each one of us will be called upon to make sacrifices. This is no time for partisan politics. I need the cooperation of each and every one of you. I need your support, your understanding. Together, we will succeed.

I could not believe that the prime minister had conveyed my speech to the nation *in toto*. There was now a spring in my step, and I shared my excitement with the principal secretary the very next day. He was phlegmatic as ever and said that perhaps the prime minister had been too preoccupied to find the time to draft his own speech. Nonetheless, I felt mighty pleased that the master draftsman had actually used my draft. Indeed, this time, as a result, the style of his speech was more direct and pointed; it stood out in contrast to the normal Narasimha Rao offering, given its pithiness. There wasn't much philosophy. I would not know it then, but this was my first and last success with him as far as speeches went.

But the story of this speech does not stop here. In January 1993, the Ministry of Information and Broadcasting brought out the first volume of selected speeches of the prime minister, from his assumption of office in June 1991 up to June 1992. Strangely—and it could have been done only with his approval—the 9 July 1991 broadcast to the nation does not figure in the collection. The volume starts with his very first speech of 22 June 1991 and then jumps to his speech in the Lok Sabha on 15 July 1991. The omission is bizarre, to say the least, and it would appear that the prime minister did not wish to leave behind this speech for posterity in his published collected works, although copies of the speech had been officially printed and circulated after it had been delivered.

If it were any other speech, it would not have merited much attention. But this was an address to the nation after all. And it was his very first address devoted exclusively to economic issues, in which he explained the country's predicament in simple, easy-to-understand language and laid out his government's agenda clearly. I have no idea why this happened! I can only recall the unforgettable conversation in 'Silver Blaze' in *The Memoirs of Sherlock Holmes*:[52]

[Inspector Gregory:] 'Is there any point to which you would wish to draw my attention?'

[Holmes:] 'To the curious incident of the dog in the night-time.'

[Inspector Gregory:] 'The dog did nothing in the night-time.'

'That was the curious incident,' remarked Sherlock Holmes.

[52]Arthur Conan Doyle, *The Memoirs of Sherlock Holmes* (London: Doubleday, 1894).

13

The Sanskritist Prime Minister

On 15 July 1991, the motion of confidence—moved three days earlier—came up for voting in the Lok Sabha. But before the actual vote, the House was treated to a vintage Narasimha Rao performance. It was his first major speech in the Lok Sabha as prime minister. Rao had been given briefs on different subjects. But he decided, as always, to speak not from text but spontaneously.

That day, the prime minister was at his philosophical best. At times, what he said appeared convoluted, but that was par for the course. He defended what the government had done since it had taken over. He was not partisan but made the point effectively that the situation he had inherited had left his finance minister and him with no other option but to embark upon a series of tough measures—gold sales, devaluation, talks with the IMF, and trade reforms, with industrial liberalization also imminent.

The highpoint of Rao's forty-five minute intervention came when he lapsed into Sanskrit:

> What have I done? What had the government done? We know that there are no alternatives to what we have done. We have only salvaged the prestige of this country. *Samutpanne ardham tyajati panditah*. This is precisely what we have done. I do not say that the economy has been booming or is going to boom immediately. What I am saying is s*arvanshe samputpanne*.

I could see that most people did not understand what the prime minister was saying. I recall A.N. Verma looking at me with a puzzled expression, then whispering, '*Kaho, Pandit, kuch samjhe?* (Tell me, wise one, do you comprehend this?)' Later, I told Verma that the Sanskrit saying in the prime minister's speech means that the wise man, in the event of total ruin, wriggles out by giving up half his possessions; this is done in the hope that he will save himself from total destruction by using what is left properly.

Even if Rao's expressions made little sense to those present, he definitely appeared Upanishadic. Moreover, he had unknowingly served notice to the BJP—Sanskrit was not its monopoly!

The prime minister was not yet done with Sanskrit in the Lok Sabha. He went on:

> Naturally, there is a long distance to go. This is not all. This is
> not the final solution, this is only the beginning. If you do not
> have a beginning, you cannot have an end. Therefore, the journey,
> the *mahaprashthana*, starts today after taking these decisions.

I think *mahaprashthana*[53] may have been more easily understood by those present, but I am not entirely sure. Regardless, it was a nice Indian way of describing the economic reforms programme and giving it a spiritual dimension, as it were. Besides, as the prime minister spoke, I recalled that in his speech to the CPP on 20 June, he had—drawing from the Congress' own legacy—underlined that the relationship between the leader and the people is spiritual and not related to posts!

That Narasimha Rao could draw from ancient wisdom to throw light on current issues is further revealed by his unpublished manuscript, 'Liberalisation and the Public Sector' (Annexure 9). In this, while reflecting on the perils of India falling into a debt trap, Narasimha Rao recalled Cārvāka philosophy, which proclaimed, '*Rinam krithva ghritam pibet*. (Make debts and enjoy yourself.)' He went on to explain

---

[53]*Mahaprasthanika Parva* or 'Book of the Great Journey' is also the seventeenth of eighteen books that make up the Mahabharata and deals with the ascent of the Pandavas to Mount Sumeru.

why this ancient school of Indian materialism said so: '*Bhasmeebhutasya dehasya punaraagamanam kuthah*. (Once your body is consigned to the funeral pyre, where is it going to come back from?)' Rao concluded by saying that when it comes to a state or the nation, this reckless outlook is still more disastrous since the state and the nation will last forever, unlike the individual. I only wish I could have discussed this further with Narasimha Rao since I believe the materialist traditions in Indian philosophy have been unfairly downplayed and distorted in favour of mysticism and spirituality.[54] These materialist traditions, incidentally, are all-too-evident now.

As far as the 15 July vote itself was concerned, it was a foregone conclusion once the Left parties and those that made up the National Front (like the Janata Dal) decided to walk out. The BJP voted 'no', but was hopelessly outnumbered. While the non-BJP opposition was very critical of the Rao-Singh economic policies, clearly it did not want the government to fall.

And so, we lived another day.

---

[54]One of the most fascinating books I have ever read is Debiprasad Chattopadhyaya, *Lokayata: A Study in Ancient Indian Materialism* (New Delhi: People's Publishing House, 1959).

14

The K.N. Raj Interview

The prime minister was quite sensitive to what eminent economists were saying about his government's policies even though he did not show it. I witnessed this first-hand when, perhaps on 25 or 26 July 1991, I sent him an interview that Dr K.N. Raj had just then given *Frontline* (Annexure 10). As part of the interview, when he was asked what his views were on the finance minister's assessment that there was no alternative to a large IMF loan if India were to tide over the economic crisis, Raj said:

> There are two propositions here. One, that there are certain conditions attached by the IMF to the extension of the loan. Second, that we have no alternative. I do not myself know what are all the conditions that have been imposed. But I have sufficient confidence in Manmohan Singh because he has very wide experience. He is not another economist; he is a person who has worked in a very wide range of organisations so that he is familiar with the entire background. [...] So I have no reason to question his assessment.

Further, when asked if India would stand to lose her economic independence if she were to accept an IMF loan, Raj said:

> I am not terribly bothered about the leftist position because they have a high-minded, doctrinaire approach when they are out of

power. If the leftists were in power today I know exactly what
they would have done. They would have accepted these [loan
conditions]. So that does not affect my judgment.

Now, K.N. Raj had an awesome reputation both as an economist
and an institution-builder, and—on his return from the London
School of Economics, when he was only in his late twenties—he
had singlehandedly written sections of the First Five-year Plan. In
the early 1960s, he had headed a committee that had recommended
major changes in policies regarding the planning and distribution of
steel. K.N. Raj was generally regarded as 'left-of-centre' and therefore,
when I read the interview, that too in a magazine that was decidedly
pro-Left, I thought it was hugely significant to bring it to the prime
minister's notice right away.

The prime minister asked for a couple of copies of the Raj
interview, which I sent. I asked him what he had thought of it. He
replied that if 'Raj has given us a certificate it means a lot'.

Ten years later, I recounted this episode when Manmohan Singh
and I dined with K.N. Raj and his family in Thiruvananthapuram. K.N.
Raj recalled that once, in the late 1970s or early 1980s, Narasimha
Rao had showed up at the Centre for Development Studies—that
Raj had established in Kerala's capital—just to have a conversation.
He also recalled that word had been sent to him after the interview
had appeared that the prime minister had appreciated it.

My own impression is that while Narasimha Rao was being buffeted
by criticism from all sides, he took solace in the Raj interview and
the encomiums paid to the man he had selected as finance minister.

I also know how much the finance minister appreciated the public
display of support by a legendary figure, at a time when he was under
sustained attack in Parliament and outside by his friends—including
S.K. Goyal, Chandra Shekhar's longstanding economic alter ego, who
had once enthusiastically backed Manmohan Singh's appointment as
economic adviser to the prime minister in November 1990.

15

The Industrial Policy Reforms Drama

As soon as I joined the PMO, A.N. Verma called Suresh Mathur,[55] Rakesh Mohan[56] and me for a discussion. He told us that this was a golden opportunity to get something done in the space of industrial policy reforms since the prime minister had deliberately kept the industry portfolio to himself. I knew that both Mohan and Verma had laboured hard to bring about changes in industrial policy when V.P. Singh had been prime minister and Ajit Singh had been in the Ministry of Industry. But those attempts had been thwarted because of opposition from within the cabinet.

Thereafter, Mathur, Mohan and I met a couple of times. The first draft was prepared by Mohan. By about 7 July 1991 we had finalized what we wanted to sell to the prime minister. I had kept the finance minister in the loop at every stage. In fact, at one point of time, when we were discussing reforms to the anti-monopoly legislation (popularly known as the Monopolies and Restrictive Trade Practices [MRTP] Act), I told him that the minister of state for law, justice and company affairs, Rangarajan Kumaramangalam, or Ranga as we

---

[55]Suresh Mathur was then the secretary in the Ministry of Industry. He had a 'let's get it done' approach, and like Verma, had sharp political antennae.

[56]Rakesh Mohan was then economic adviser in the Ministry of Industry. He had studied the textile and small-scale industries closely and had been advocating changes in industrial policy for three years.

called him, was not terribly happy with what we were suggesting—namely, the plain and simple abolition of clearances for industry under an Act that had been made in 1969 when there was concern that licensing had, somewhat paradoxically, led to the concentration of economic power. I had been trying to convince Ranga of the need to be radical regarding MRTP and not just remain incremental. I knew that if he would not get convinced, there was little chance of his senior minister, the old warhorse, Vijaya Bhaskara Reddy, coming on board for this crucial reform measure.

The finance minister then did something that stumped me momentarily. He called Ranga and me to his room and became very emotional. He told his young colleague how he had worked with his father—the redoubtable Communist leader Mohan Kumaramangalam, who later joined Indira Gandhi's cabinet—and how pragmatic and open to new ideas his 'good friend Mohan was'. For about ten minutes, Singh reminisced about Ranga's father and told him to consider what he would have done at this crucial juncture of India's history. Ranga came out of the finance minister's chamber telling me, '*Yaar, Sardar ne kamaal kar diya.* (Singh has taken me by surprise!)' Ranga added, 'Let me work on my old man [Vijaya Bhaskara Reddy] now.'

After Suresh Mathur, Rakesh Mohan and I had finalized the package, Verma asked me to prepare a note, which could be shown to the prime minister to get his broad, informal approval before it went to the cabinet. Accordingly, I prepared a five-page note summarizing what we were contemplating by way of industrial policy reforms. I added a couple of points on my own based on my earlier efforts of September 1986:

MRTP

Objective: To Shift the Focus of MRTP from a priori control on growth and expansion of industry to effective check on monopolistic and unfair trade practices.

1. MRTP not to be applicable for expansion of present undertaking and establishment of new undertaking.

2. Provision relating to mergers, takeovers and amalgamations to be repealed.

3. Additional powers to MRTP Commission for undertaking preliminary investigations into complaints received from individual consumers or states or central government and also undertaking investigation into complaints relating to monopolistic trade practices.

4. Enlarge powers of MRTP Commission by giving it the powers of a civil court.

5. Empower Director General of Investigation and Registration to make applications to the Commission relating to monopolistic trade practices.

6. Streamline the definition of "unfair trade practice" so as to eliminate the burden on the Director General or the MRTP Commission to prove actual loss or injury having been caused to the consumer before any action can be initiated.

7. Expand the present definition of service to bring the activities of chit fund companies within the ambit of the restructured MRTP.

8. Increase the limit of penal provision by prescribing higher penalty for contravention of any order of MRTP and offences mentioned in the MRTP Act.

9. Provide enabling power to MRTP Commission to compound offences.

FOREIGN INVESTMENT

OBJECTIVE: Give a clear and unamibiguous signal
          that foreign investment is welcome

1. Increase in present foreign equity limit of 40% to
    60%.

2. Automatic permission for investment upto 60% in
    all Appendix I industries.

3. In non-Appendix I industries automatic permission
    for investment upto 60% subject to balancing of
    profits and dividends whenever they are made with
    net foreign exchange earnings.

4. No necessary linkage with technology agreements.

5. Automatic permission for foreign technology
    agreements upto lumpsum payments of Rs 1 crore,5%
    royalty for domestic sales and 8% for exports,
    subject to total maximum of 8% over 10 year period.

6. Government to create a window for negotiating and
    working with 20-30 large companies in select
    areas. Investment programmes of these companies to
    be cleared on a composite basis.

INDUSTRIAL LICENSING

OBJECTIVE: Confine licensing to essentials.

1. All industrial licenses to be abolished except for
    short negative list and projects beyond certain
    size.Criteria for inclusion of industries in
    negative list-security, environment,

2. Industrial licensing to be done only for projects
    of over Rs 200 crores in non-backward areas and Rs
    500 crores in backward areas.or projects with
    capital goods requirements of greater than
    $ 25 million.This should also not be necessary
    if no free foreign exchange is required for
    capital goods.

3. No location restrictions from Central government
    except for four largest metropolitan areas where
    restrictions may apply to locations within 30 kms
    of periphery.

PUBLIC SECTOR

OBJECTIVE: To strengthen public sector in key and core areas and give their operations a commercial orientation.

1. All non-commercial obligations imposed on public enterprises to be made transparent.

2. Modernisation programmes for public sector in core areas of steel, energy and engineering to be finalised in the next three months.

3. Boards of public enterprises to be made more professional and given greater role.

4. Delays in appointments at Board level to be eliminated and procedures for timely succession planning instituted.

5. Public sector to vacate non-strategic areas and areas where private sector has demonstrated capability.

    * Hotel Corporation of India
    * ITDC
    * Modern Food Industries
    * Hindustan Latex
    * Mandya National Paper Mills
    * Hindustan Newsprint
    * Computer Maintenance Corporation
    * Bharat Leather Corporation
    * Hindustan Paper Corporation
    * Nagaland Pulp and Paper Company
    * TAFFCO
    * Tyre Corporation of India
    * Hindustan Photofilms
    * Central Electronics
    * Hindustan Prefab Ltd
    * Electronics Trade and Technology Development Corporation
    * Scooters India
    * National Bicycle Corporation of India
    * Cycle Corporation of India
    * Orissa Drugs and Chemicals
    * Rajasthan Drugs and Chemicals
    * UP Drugs and Pharmaceuticals
    * Bengal Chemicals and Pharmaceuticals

6.   Partial disinvestment in select public enterprises
     to be carried out in favour of public,financial
     institutions and mutual funds.

               * Air India
               * Indian Airlines
               * Mahanagar Telephone Nigam
               * Indian Oil
               * Maruti
               * BHEL
               * Bharat Petroleum
               * Hindustan Petroleum
               * HMT
               * Hindustan Organic Chemicals
               * IPCL

7.   Problem of chronic loss making enterprises to be
     tackled.Reference to be made to BIFR for
     revival/rehabilitation/closure packages.

EXIT POLICY

     OBJECTIVE: Facilitate closure of unviable units
               while protecting interests of labour.

1.   Adjustment Assistance Fund to be created to
     assist workers affected by industrial
     restructuring.

2.   Amendments to be made to Sick Industrial
     Companies Act to capture incipient sickness.

3.   Strengthen BIFR so that it becomes an effective
     instrument for enforcing an exit policy.Give
     BIFR authority to override provisions of Urban
     Land Ceilings Act.

4.   Create special mechanisms to deal with backlog
     of sickness in cities like Kanpur,Ahmedabad,
     Bombay and Calcutta.Permit closures of terminally
     sick units and sale of assets.Provisions of
     Urban Land Ceilings Act to be suspended in such
     cases.

5.   Change current norms concerning promoters' equity
     so as to increase promoters' stake in projects
     floated by them;minimum equity stake of promoter
     to be 25%.

6.   Industrial Disputes Act to be reviewed to make
     exit easier without adversely affecting the
     interests of workers.

SMALL INDUSTRY

OBJECTIVE: Reshape existing policy to promote
faster growth of small industry

1. Create new segment of tiny industry with
   investment in plant and machinery less than
   Rs 10 lakhs.

2. Divide support to small industry into one-time
   support and sustained support.Only tiny sector
   eligible for sustained support-excise benefits,
   concessional rates of interest,reservation/
   price preference,priority in raw material
   allocation,testing facilities.One time
   support available to both small and tiny sector-
   capital investment subsidy,loans,contribution to
   cover promoters' equity etc.

3. Make small-scale sector eligible
   for foreign equity participation

This note went to the prime minister, probably around 8 July
1991. As it turned out, the section that I had inserted, namely on
exit policy, got eliminated in the version approved by the prime
minister because it was considered too politically volatile. Verma
told me that I should not be too exuberant and the inclusion of
exit policy would only jeopardize the other initiatives. On 9 July,
the prime minister addressed the CPP on the eve of the Parliament
session and said that the economic revival of the country was the
first item on his agenda. He added that his government would, in the
next four days, announce a comprehensive and coordinated package
of industrial reforms.

When I opened the *Hindustan Times* on 12 July, I was shocked,
to put it mildly. My entire note had been carried with the banner
headline 'Industrial Licensing to Go'.

INDUSTRIAL LICENSING TO GO

By Kalyani Shankar
New Delhi, July 11

SALIENT POINTS

- *Foreign equity to go up from 40 per cent to 51 per cent and permission to be automatic.*
- *A new package for tiny sector.*
- *MRTP asset limit to go up from Rs 100 crore to Rs 1,000 crore.*
- *A special Empowered Board to negotiate with 40 to 50 giant international firms to approve direct foreign investment.*
- *Phased manufacturing programme to go.*
- *Locational limit only 30 km around metropolitan cities of Bombay, Delhi, Calcutta and Madras.*
- *Liberal policy towards small sector and a promotional package for tiny sectors.*

Abolition of all industrial licences except for a short negative list, automatic permission for foreign direct investment upto 51 per cent and increase in foreign equity limit upto 51 per cent, a new package for the tiny sector with increase in investment limit to Rs 5 lakh are some of the bold and innovative measures contemplated in the new industrial policy.

The draft policy is being finalised under the direct supervision of Prime Minister P.V. Narasimha Rao, who is also holding the Industry portfolio, Union Finance Minister Dr Manmohan Singh, Ministers of State for Industry P.K. Thungan [sic] and Mr. P.J. Kurien and other concerned Ministers are also involved in the policy making.

The policy, which is being given final touches, will be placed before Parliament next week.

Additional powers to the MRTP Commission, increase in asset limit to Rs 1,000 crore for the MRTP companies from the present Rs 100 crore, automatic permission for foreign technology

Rajiv Gandhi flanked by P.V. Narasimha Rao and Madhavsinh Solanki at the release of the 1991 Lok Sabha election manifesto of the Congress on 16 April 1991. This document was extensively used by Narasimha Rao and Dr Manmohan Singh to defend economic reforms in June, July and August 1991.

A meeting of the Congress Working Committee (CWC), under the chairmanship of P.V. Narasimha Rao on 22 May 1991, that unanimously decided to elect Sonia Gandhi as Congress president—an offer she declined a day later.

Prime Minister P.V. Narasimha Rao with two immediate ex-prime ministers, Chandra Shekhar and V.P. Singh, on 21 June 1991.

*P.V. Narasimha Rao's first press conference
as Congress president on 2 June 1991.*

*Dr Manmohan Singh's press conference of 25 June 1991
that led to the flap on the roll-back of prices.*

The prime minister's meeting with opposition leaders and the finance minister's briefing on the economy on 27 June 1991.

P.N. Dhar and three other economists issued 'An Agenda for Economic Reform' on 1 July 1991 that led to an uproar in Parliament subsequently. Here is P.N. Dhar with Dr Manmohan Singh and P. Chidambaram at a seminar on the statement.

The prime minister with Julius Nyerere, former president of Tanzania and chairman of the South Commission, of which Dr Manmohan Singh was secretary general between 1987 and 1990.

Dr Manmohan Singh on his way to presenting his first and most historic budget on 24 July 1991.

Protests outside Dr Manmohan Singh's North Block office on 9 August 1991. Such a protest is unimaginable these days. It will never be permitted!

Prime Minister Narasimha Rao and Finance Minister Manmohan Singh meet trade union leaders at the prime minister's residence on 17 August 1991. G. Ramanujam, co-founder of INTUC (Indian National Trade Union Congress), is to Narasimha Rao's right.

The first meeting of the reconstituted Planning Commission on 19 September 1991 with Sharad Pawar, Pranab Mukherjee P.V. Narasimha Rao, Manmohan Singh, Balram Jakhar and the author in the background.

agreements for Appendix-1 industries upto a lump sum of Rs one crore are some of the other bold measures contemplated.

According to the draft policy, permission will be automatic for foreign direct investment upto 51 per cent equity in Appendix-1 industries. Capital goods imports will be automatically approved if they are financed by foreign equity or buy back arrangements. A special empowered board is also proposed to be constituted to negotiate with 40 to 50 large international firms and approve direct foreign investment in select areas. This is aimed at attracting substantial foreign investment which may also provide access to high technology and foreign markets and these projects will be considered in totality and cleared fast.

Also majority foreign equity holdings may be allowed for trading companies which are primarily engaged in export activities.

In Non-Appendix industries, automatic permission upto 51 per cent will be allowed subject to balancing of profits and dividends with net foreign exchange earnings.

As far as the industrial licensing is concerned, the objective of the Government is to confine licensing to essentials. Industrial licenses are proposed to be abolished except for a short list of industries related to security and strategic concerns, social reasons, hazardous chemicals and overriding environmental reasons.

The negative list includes the core sector, sugar, all types of automobiles, specified luxury goods, drugs and pharmaceuticals, tobacco products and petroleum products.

Industries reserved for the small sector, however, continue to be reserved.

Industrial licensing will be required only for projects of over Rs 200 crore in non-backward areas and Rs 500 crore in backward areas or projects with capital goods requirements of more than $25 million. In projects which require imported capital goods, automatic clearance will be permitted if the foreign exchange availability is ensured through foreign equity, foreign lines of credit or foreign borrowing.

In other cases, the capital goods imports will be cleared by the special industrial approvals committee.

Yet another significant policy measure contemplated is that there will be no location restrictions from Central Government except for the four metropolitan cities of Bombay, Delhi, Calcutta and Madras. In these metropolitan cities restrictions may apply to locations within 30 km of periphery.

Phased Manufacturing Programme (PMP) is also likely to be abolished in view of the exchange rate adjustment and new trade policy.

All existing registration schemes for industries like Directorate General of Technical Development, DLR and EIR may be abolished.

As far as the MRTP and FERA relaxations, the Government proposed to shift the focus of MRTP from a PRIORI control on growth and expansion of industry to effective check on monopolistic and unfair trade practices.

It also proposed to repeal provisions relating to mergers, takeovers and amalgamations of MRTP companies in the Act. Additional powers to the MRTP Commission like giving it the powers of a civil court, provision of enabling power to compound offences, and additional powers for undertaking preliminary investigations into complaints from individual consumers. The Director General of Investigation is also proposed to be empowered to make applications to the MRTP Commission relating to monopolistic trade practices.

The Government is also contemplating to raise the asset limit of the MRTP companies to Rs 1,000 crore from the present Rs 100 crore. In fact, the apex trade bodies like FICCI [The Federation of Indian Chambers of Commerce and Industry], ASSOCHAM [The Associated Chambers of Commerce of India] and others have been demanding the increase of asset limit for a long time. The last time the asset limit enhanced was in 1985 when the Rajiv Gandhi Government increased it from Rs 25 crore to Rs 100 crore.

For the tiny sector, priority would be given in credit supply. The district industries centre would be strengthened and restructured. For the small and tiny sector, Government also proposes to dismantle inspector raj, simplify procedures, remove bureaucratic controls and cut down paper work.

A new scheme of integrated infrastructural development for small-scale industries to facilitate location of industries in rural and backward areas and to promote stronger linkages between agriculture and industry is also proposed in the draft policy.

Another significant step is to provide access to the capital market. The Government may allow equity participation—both foreign and domestic—in the small-scale sector upto 24 per cent of the total shareholding.

In the small sector, regulatory provisions relating to management of private limited companies will also be liberalised. A new package for promotion of tiny units is the main thrust of the government's new policy.

Regarding public sector, the Government is yet to finalise its view. It is not yet known if the public sector will form part of the new industry policy paper. However, the thinking appears to be that there should be disinvestment in selective public sector undertakings. Whether the profit making PSUs alone should be disinvested in a selective manner or it should be a mix of profit and loss making public sector undertakings is also yet to be decided.

I knew my goose was cooked and I would definitely be held responsible for the leak. I immediately ran upstairs, carrying the newspaper with me, and barged into Verma's room as soon as he arrived (which was around 9.15 a.m.). I displayed the paper and told him that I was not responsible and there had never been any contact between me and the journalist whose byline had appeared. I went to the extent of telling the principal secretary that he should immediately order an IB (Intelligence Bureau) probe which would vindicate me completely. Verma heard me out for a couple of minutes, smiled as he always did, and simply said: '*Relax, yaar. Khamakhan pareshaan ho rahe ho. Ja ke apna kaam karo.* (Relax. You're fretting for no reason! Get back to work.)' I was flummoxed by the nonchalance with which my remonstrance had been dismissed, but decided to let the matter go. Perhaps, there is some truth in the adage that 'often the ship of state leaks from the very top'!

◆

Initially, we had planned to release the industrial policy reforms separately. Indeed, all public statements made by the prime minister first on 9 July and then again on 15 July in the Lok Sabha suggested this. Then, there was a view that the reforms should form part of the budget that was to be presented on 24 July. That was certainly the finance minister's view. I found myself encountering, perhaps, my only disagreement with him in that period when we worked together. I argued that the industrial policy reforms were truly revolutionary and to have maximum impact they had to be announced separately. The prime minister seemed to agree with my contention and asked me to prepare a speech for his use, if and when he presented the industrial reforms package in Parliament. I prepared a speech and sent it to him. But, as it turned out, the speech was never used since the prime minister decided not to speak. Alok Prasad, then the prime minister's private secretary, returned the draft to me pencilling along the margin 'pity this was never used'.

Sir:

I rise to place a statement on some new industrial policy initiatives that my Government will take.

The statement is detailed and lists out the measures we will adopt to accelerate the pace of industrialisation in the country.

I will make only some brief remarks to place these initiatives in their proper perspective.

For some years now there has been growing consensus that we need to do something different in the next phase of industrial development.

The first phase served us well.

We built up infrastructure.

We established basic industries.

We attained self-sufficiency across a broad spectrum.

And we opened up new areas to industrial growth.

But somewhere along the line weaknesses also developed.

We lost our share of world markets even in traditional areas of strength like textiles.

We could not keep abreast of changes in science and technology and introduce these changes in our industry. Obsolete technology has meant increased energy consumption, greater use of raw materials and higher costs and prices.

Forgetting the old maxim-protect the infant,nurture the child and strengthen the adolescent-we protected the producers for too long thereby making them complacent about quality and productivity.

We allowed controls on growth and expansion to proliferate.These controls have stifled innovativeness and have bred corruption.Indeed,they have come in the way of achieving our objectives of expanding employmkent opportunities,reducing rural-urban disparities and ensuring greater social justice.

Rajiv Gandhi understood clearly the need for a bold new approach in the context of the challenges India will face in the years ahead.

He realised that blind dogma has no place in the modern world.

He understood that India has to be an integral part of the international trading and financial system.

In the years that he was Prime Minister,a number of initiatives were taken ,in his own words,to reduce controls without losing control.

What further changes he would have brought about in his second innings is reflected in the manifesto of the Congress Party.The manifesto reflects his approach-pragmatic,innovative and yet conscious of the social context in which economic reform has to be carried out in India.

We have,in essence,put into operation what is contained in our manifesto.

May I add not just what is contained in our manifesto but also in the manifesto of the BJP and the NF.I have no hesitation in acknowledging these debts.

We are attempting on a larger scale what Jyotibabu has been trying in West Bengal.

Vishwanathji has always talked about doing away with what he calls discretionary interventions in the economy and for making the system transparent.We have done precisely that.

The BJP talks about debureaucratising the economy.We have done exactly this.

Chandrasekharji has talked about the need to simplify and remove unnecesssary hurdles to growth.This is what we have done.

What we are proposing to do in industry is what we have done in agriculture.

In agriculture,we established infrastructure and created institutions as support mechanisms,while depending on the native genius and innovativeness of the farmer to provide an impetus to growth.The time has come to replicate this approach in other sectors as well.

Sir,my government believes that resources for basic needs will be forthcoming on the scale needed if and only if we insist on efficiency and competitiveness in all economic and production activities.

Social justice is not ensured by having a maze of controls and regulations and an army of bureaucrats trying to decide what is good for everybody else.

```
The ends of an economy in quest of social justice are best
attained in an environment where market forces blend
harmoniously with Government efforts to restructure the social
framework.It is this blending and marriage that we are
attempting to arrange.

Two additional points I wish to make before closing.My colleague
Prof.Kurien will shortly be tabling a policy statement on what we
propose to do to strengthen the small and tiny industry.This
segment is very important particularly from the employment angle.

Secondly,I wish to reiterate that in the process of economic
reform we will ensure that the legitimate interests of labour are
protected.

Gains cannot accrue only to managements while pains are borne by
workers.Labour has nothing to fear.This is a new opportunity for
all of us to grasp and exploit.Of course,no process of change is
painless.But the pain can be managed and alleviated.

    Sir,this set of initiatives comes in the wake of the reform
of the trade policy we had announced a few weeks back.It is an
indication that my Government means business.We are determined to
get India moving ahead once again.
```

The prime minister won the vote of confidence in the Lok Sabha on 15 July. After his widely-appreciated reply on the same day, the prime minister instructed us to get the cabinet note on industrial policy reforms ready. The Ministry of Industry prepared the note and the cabinet was to meet on 19 July to consider and approve it.

By now, I was beginning to get nervous about whether we would ever be able to get the industrial policy reforms through. I was not the only one to have doubts. On 6 July, *The Hindu* carried a headline, 'New radical industrial policy coming'. But on 19 July, the headline read, 'New industrial policy may not be radical'! This newspaper generally had its hand on the pulse of the government at the highest levels—so one certainly had cause for worry!

Expectedly, there were fireworks in the cabinet on 19 July. Many ministers objected both to the substance and style of the note on industrial policy reforms. Some felt that we were abandoning Congress' ideology while some others felt that a strong case had not been made for these far-reaching changes. The predominant view was that the cabinet note appeared too damning of the past.

That very evening, A.N.Verma called me to his residence and told me what had happened. He said that the prime minister had set up a Group of Ministers (GoM) to look at the proposals once again and that he wanted me to reshape and recast the cabinet note in a suitable manner. I asked A.N. Verma what 'a suitable manner' meant, to which his reply was '*tum jaano* (you'd know)'. When leaving, Verma told me that the prime minister wanted me to attend the GoM meeting the next day and answer any question that may be raised. After listening to the deliberations of the GoM, I was to redo the cabinet note and send it to Verma and the prime minister immediately—which meant on the evening of 20 July.

The GoM met the next day. Madhavsinh Solanki[57] was worried that the industrial policy reforms would hit the development of backward areas and said that tight controls had to be retained on industrial location policies. Arjun Singh[58] and M.L. Fotedar[59] were apprehensive that we had gone too far in relaxing MRTP controls. B. Shankaranand[60] was unhappy with the provisions for opening ourselves to foreign investment, that too in such an obvious manner. Balram Jakhar[61] and Rajesh Pilot[62] too felt that we were diluting the party's public sector ideology significantly. But the commerce minister, P. Chidambaram, defended the reforms proposals unequivocally, addressing every single concern raised in his own inimitable style. I mostly listened, intervening only once or twice to clarify some doubts raised by the ministers.

As the meeting ended, Manmohan Singh smiled at me on the way out and said, 'Now it is up to you, Jairam.' I was confused and completely at a loss about what needed to be done. Were we going to abandon industrial policy reforms or were we to go ahead? The prime minister himself had not said anything, and A.N. Verma wasn't sure what the prime minister expected of me. Besides, I had barely been given any time.

I tried to make sense of the GoM meeting. It appeared that the political packaging of our reforms proposal was not right. It also appeared that the cabinet note, considered by the cabinet on 19 July,

---

[57]Madhavsinh Solanki was external affairs minister in Narasimha Rao's cabinet.
[58]Arjun Singh was human resource development minister in Narasimha Rao's cabinet.
[59]M.L. Fotedar was health and family welfare minister in Narasimha Rao's cabinet.
[60]B. Shankaranand was petroleum and natural gas minister in Narasimha Rao's cabinet.
[61]Balram Jakhar was agriculture minister in Narasimha Rao's cabinet.
[62]Rajesh Pilot was communications minister in Narasimha Rao's cabinet.

lacked historical context. I spoke to the finance and commerce ministers, and they orally gave me some formulations to mull over. I took about two hours to think them through and draft a longish preamble to the cabinet note. I showed it to A.N. Verma and he liked what he read. He dispatched it to the prime minister and asked me to go home.

A little while later, Verma called me and said that Narasimha Rao was appreciative of what I had done and felt that, with the preamble, we might still be able to get the industrial policy reforms through. Moreover, the prime minister had made some additions after consulting the finance and commerce ministers. The actual content of the cabinet note, however, remained unchanged.

The preamble read thus:

Policy Objectives:

Pandit Jawaharlal Nehru laid the foundations of modern India. His vision and determination left a lasting impression on every facet of national endeavour since Independence. It is due to his initiative that India now has a strong and diversified industrial base and is a major industrial nation of the world. The goals and objectives set out for the nation by Pandit Nehru on the eve of Independence, namely the rapid agricultural and industrial development of our country, rapid expansion of opportunities for gainful employment, progressive reduction of social and economic disparities, removal of poverty and attainment of self-reliance, remain as valid today as at the time Pandit Nehru set them out before the nation. Any industrial policy must contribute to the realisation of these goals and objectives at an accelerated pace. The present statement of industrial policy is inspired by these very concerns and represents a renewed initiative towards consolidating the gains of national reconstruction at this crucial stage.

In 1948, immediately after Independence, Government introduced the Industrial Policy Resolution. This outlined the approach to industrial growth and development. It emphasised the importance to the economy of securing a continuous increase in production and ensuring its equitable distribution. After the adoption of the Constitution and the socio-economic goals, the Industrial Policy was comprehensively revised and adopted in 1956. To meet new challenges, from time to time, it was modified through statements in 1973, 1977 and 1980.

The Industrial Policy Resolution of 1948 was followed by the Industrial Policy Resolution of 1956 which had as its objective the acceleration of the rate of economic growth and the speeding up of industrialisation as a means of achieving a socialistic pattern of society. In 1956, capital was scarce and the base of entrepreneurship was not strong enough. Hence, the 1956 Industrial Policy Resolution gave primacy to the role of the State to assume a predominant and direct responsibility for industrial development.

The Industrial Policy Statement of 1973, inter alia, identified high priority industries where investment from large industrial houses and foreign companies would be permitted.

The Industrial Policy Statement of 1977 laid emphasis on decentralisation and on the role of small-scale, tiny and cottage industries.

The Industrial Policy Statement of 1980 focussed attention on the need for promoting competition in the domestic market, technological upgradation and modernisation. The policy laid the foundation for an increasingly competitive export base and for encouraging foreign investment in high-technology areas. This found expression in the Sixth Five Year Plan which bore the distinct stamp of Smt. Indira Gandhi. It was Smt. Indira Gandhi who emphasised the need for productivity to be the central concern in all economic and production activities.

These policies created a climate for rapid industrial growth in the country. Thus on the eve of the Seventh Five Year Plan, a broad-based infrastructure had been built up. Basic industries had been established. A high degree of self-reliance in a large number of items—raw materials, intermediates, finished goods—had been achieved. New growth centres of industrial activity had emerged, as had a new generation of entrepreneurs. A large number of engineers, technicians, and skilled workers had also been trained.

The Seventh Plan recognised the need to consolidate on these strengths and to take initiatives to prepare Indian industry to respond effectively to the emerging challenges. A number of policy and procedural changes were introduced in 1985 and 1986 under the leadership of Shri Rajiv Gandhi aimed at increasing productivity, reducing costs and improving quality. The accent was on opening the domestic market to increased competition and readying our industry to stand up on its own in the face of international competition. The public sector was freed from a number of constraints and given a large measure of autonomy. The technological and managerial modernisation of industry was pursued as the key instrument for increasing productivity and improving our competitiveness in the world. The net result of all these changes was that Indian industry grew by an impressive average annual growth rate of 8.5% in the Seventh Plan period.

Government is pledged to launching a reinvigorated struggle for social and economic justice, to end poverty and unemployment and to build a modern, democratic, socially prosperous and forward-looking India. Such a society can be built if India grows as part of the world economy and not in isolation.

While Government will continue to follow the policy of self-reliance, there would be greater emphasis placed on building up our ability to pay for imports through our own foreign exchange earnings. Government is also committed to development and utilisation of indigenous capabilities in technology and manufacturing as well as its upgradation to world standards.

Government will continue to pursue a sound policy framework encompassing encouragement of entrepreneurship, development of indigenous technology through investment in research and development, bringing in new technology, dismantling of the regulatory system, development of capital markets, [and] increasing competitiveness for the benefit of the common man. The spread of industrialisation to backward areas of the country will be actively promoted through appropriate incentives, institutions and infrastructure investments.

Government will provide enhanced support to the small-scale sector so that it flourishes in an environment of economic efficiency and continuous technological upgradation.

Foreign investment and technology collaboration will be welcomed to obtain higher technology, to increase exports and expand the production base.

Government will endeavour to abolish the monopoly of any sector or any individual enterprise in any field of manufacture, except on strategic or military considerations, and open all manufacturing activity to competition.

The Government will ensure that the public sector plays its rightful role in the evolving socio-economic scenario of the country. Government will ensure that the public sector is run on business lines as envisaged in the Industrial Policy Resolution of 1956 and would continue to innovate and lead in strategic areas of national importance. In the 1950s and 1960s, the principal instrument for controlling the commanding heights of the economy was investment in the capital of key industries. Today, the State has other instruments of intervention, particularly fiscal and monetary instruments. The State also commands the bulk of the nation's savings. Banks and financial institutions are under State control. Where State intervention is necessary, these instruments will prove more effective and decisive.

Government will fully protect the interests of labour, enhance their welfare and equip them in all respects to deal with the inevitability of technological change. Government believes that no small section of society can corner the gains of growth leaving workers to bear its pains. Labour will be made an equal partner in progress and prosperity. Workers' participation in management will be promoted. Workers' cooperatives will be encouraged to participate in packages designed to turn around sick companies. Intensive training, skill development and upgradation programmes will be launched.

Government will continue to visualise new horizons. The major objectives of the new industrial policy package will be to build on the gains already made, correct the distortions or weaknesses that may have crept in, maintain a sustained growth in productivity and gainful employment, and attain international competitiveness. The pursuit of these objectives will be tempered by the need to preserve the environment and ensure efficient use of available resources. All sectors of industry, whether small, medium or large, belonging to the public, private or cooperative sector, will be encouraged to grow and improve on their past performance.

Government's policy will be continuity with change.

In pursuit of the above objectives, Government have decided to take a series of initiatives in respect of the policies relating to the following areas.

A. Industrial Licensing

B. Foreign Investment

C. Foreign Technology Agreements

D. Public Sector Policy

E. MRTP Act

A package for the Small and Tiny Sectors of Industry is being announced separately.

What the preamble did was provide a political context to technocratic text, with the clincher being the line 'continuity with change' at the very end! To use Narasimha Rao's own words (enunciated in another context), the preamble was a lesson in how to facilitate a desirable U-turn without it seeming to be a U-turn! This was my first major lesson in political packaging and marketing, and I would have numerous occasions to use this lesson on crucial occasions over the next quarter of a century in public life.

The union cabinet met again on 23 July 1991 to consider the revised cabinet note with the preamble. Most of the original sceptics who had protested on 19 July felt reassured after reading the preamble. M.L. Fotedar, a political heavyweight, took the lead and said that had the original cabinet note come with such a preamble, there would not have been so much as a murmur. He concurred with the cabinet note, and after he had spoken, others followed suit. Thereafter, in a most unusual move, the larger union council of ministers met to give a seal of approval to what the cabinet had decided.

Narasimha Rao did not want to leave anything to chance. He convened a meeting of the CWC at 3 p.m. at his residence. The official minutes of this meeting that lasted ninety minutes read as follows:

> [...] at the permission of the Chair, Shri Manmohan Singh, Union Finance Minister, who was specially invited in the meeting apprised the Working Committee about present financial position of the country and the Industrial Policy of the Government. After hearing Shri Manmohan Singh, the Working Committee endorsed the Government's industrial policy in principle and made it clear that every effort should be made to remain within the framework of the Party's manifesto.

At this meeting, after having been warned by the prime minister that he was very much on his own, the finance minister quoted extensively from the Congress' 1991 Lok Sabha election manifesto.[63] Manmohan Singh read out some crucial portions that went thus:

> Restoring sound management will require priority attention to fiscal policy. The massive deficit in the budgetary system has created a serious fiscal imbalance. This will have to be rectified [...] The Congress will restore fiscal balance in the budgetary system by drastically reducing wasteful expenditure, rationalising non-developmental expenditure and expanding the revenue base of the Government, particularly through a leaner, more dynamic and profit-oriented public sector. [...]
>
> The Congress will tackle the problem of the present foreign exchange crisis by pursuing vigorous export promotion, effective import substitution, establishing an appropriate exchange rate mechanism and increasing productivity and efficiency in our economy. [...]
>
> The Congress will pursue a sound policy framework: encouragement of entrepreneurship, development of capital markets, simplification of the regulatory system, bringing in new technology and increasing competitiveness for the benefit of the common man. [...]

---

[63] Actually, even its manifesto for the 1989 Lok Sabha elections committed the Congress to bolder economic reforms of the type that got carried out in July 1991. However, because of the prevailing circumstances, the 1991 manifesto acquired emotional value as the last will and testament, as it were, of Rajiv Gandhi.

Foreign investment and technology collaboration will be permitted to obtain higher technology, to increase exports and to expand the production base. [...]

The Congress will endeavour to abolish the monopoly of any sector or any individual enterprise in any field of manufacture, except on strategic or military considerations and open all manufacturing activity to competition.

As Manmohan Singh was coming out of the meeting, his senior cabinet colleague, Arjun Singh told him: 'Doctor Saab, you have read the manifesto more carefully than all Congressmen.'

◆

The next day was really an anti-climax. I was imagining a big bang announcement of the industrial policy reforms, as were many others. Instead, at about 12.50 p.m. on Wednesday, 24 July 1991, about four hours before Manmohan Singh was to present his budget, P. J. Kurien, the minister of state for industry got up in the Lok Sabha and read out a brief statement: 'Sir, I beg to lay on the table a statement (Hindi and English versions) on Industrial Policy.'

That was it. A bland sentence to usher in a radical transformation of Indian enterprise. The occasion was made more ironic by the fact that the junior industry minister's heart was not in the revolutionary contents of the new industrial policy. Indeed, at various points of time, he and his officials had acrimonious disagreements and the finance minister ultimately had to tell him that he had to fall in line to avoid international embarrassment.

Perhaps, this tepid introduction had been provoked by a fear of protests from sections of Indian industry. In fact, I had reason to believe that lobbying by some prominent figures of industry—nervous about foreign direct investment—had delayed the approval of the new industrial policy.

On 26 July, at the prime minister's bidding and, if I my say so, at my suggestion, an unprecedented event took place. Manmohan Singh, Vijaya Bhaskara Reddy, Rangarajan Kumaramangalam, P.J. Kurien and P.K. Thungon (the other minister of state for industry) met the press *jointly* to explain the new industrial policy reforms package. The finance minister held centre-stage, but the presence of five ministers was meant to convey the impression that all were on board. Almost all the questions were on foreign investment, the public sector and the abolition of MRTP controls, and all of them were fielded by Manmohan Singh himself—and that too aggressively!

The most detailed news report that appeared about this unusual event was carried in the 27 July 1991 edition of *The Hindu* and gives the full flavour of what transpired there.

Industrial Policy Not Anti-worker: Manmohan Singh
From Our Special Correspondent
New Delhi, July 26

In an unusual move, the Government today fielded five senior Central Ministers to emphasise the point to the press that the new industrial policy neither meant a go by to socialism nor would be detrimental to the interest of workers.

Denying the charge that the policy would mean a shift towards capitalism on behalf of other Ministers—Dr. Manmohan Singh, Finance, Mr. K. Vijay Bhaskar [sic] Reddy, Law and Justice both with cabinet rank, Mr. P.R. Kumaramangalam, Law and Justice and Mr. P.K. Thungon, Industry with Minister of State rank—the Minister of State for Industry Prof. P.J. Kurien asked how could socialist goal be achieved without increasing production.

The centrestage at the press conference was occupied by Dr. Manmohan Singh who said the process of industrial and economic transformation did not mean reneging on efforts in the direction of poverty alleviation, reducing income and wealth disparities, unemployment or rural-urban disparities. He said, social objectives enshrined in the Constitution would remain and quoted Pandit Nehru to say that 'instrumentalities must be adjusted to changing circumstances'. While the effort would be to modernise without tears he said 'we are committed to protect the worker's interest and modernisation process would not be achieved by breaking their backs'. Besides referring the cases of sick companies to BIFR [Board for Industrial and Financial Reconstruction], the Government would also contribute Rs. 200 crores to the proposed National Renewal Fund, he said.

Regional balance: On ensuring regional dispersal of industries, while Prof. Kurien was trying to say that there should be no apprehension on that count as special incentives would be given to ensure it, Dr. Manmohan Singh was really blunt. He said the Government was not going back on its commitment to ensure regional balance. But the earlier policies regulating industries to go to backward areas just did not work, he remarked, citing Bihar. Bihar had lots of industries but it still remained backward. There was no point in compelling capital to move in a particular area where its contribution to the local population in terms of quality jobs was minimal. Stressing the need for a positive and promotional approach, Dr. Singh recounted the example of Eastern UP to suggest that industries set up there did not create job opportunities matching the local skill. He felt the new policy was far superior to the old approach of regulating through industrial licenses. Under the new policy it would now be possible to effect substantial expansion by existing units even if it were at a new location.

Again Dr. Manmohan Singh rescued Prof. Kurien when pointed questions on foreign investment were raised. According to him the proposed Special Empowered Board would negotiate with multinational corporations (MNCs) as they had the technology. To a query on BHEL which was languishing for lack of orders and as to whether the entry of MNCs would not hit it further, Dr. Singh said, 'In these areas if somebody wants to come, we will discuss. But it should be understood that they (foreign investors) also wanted to make money,' he said and asked, 'why should they put their money here otherwise. If BHEL had no orders where will it be for these chaps.' A correspondent told him they came in under bilateral arrangements. But Dr. Singh said in an open environment, they would have to compete. 'It will be good for BHEL to compete and earn its living by being cost and quality efficient'.

On the entire gamut of foreign investment, Dr. Singh said three routes were open to them namely 51 per cent equity in 34 high priority industries eligible for automatic approval, 51 per cent foreign equity in trading houses and anything outside it to be approved by the Government. It was in the fourth category, though not mentioned per se in the policy, the Empowered Board would discuss with big companies abroad and consider their proposals on a case by case basis. Dr. Singh said, 'You can't operate the economy rigidly. It has to be transparent as there are areas about which neither of us know and it would be better to negotiate.' There was unease among businessmen in Hong Kong about their fate once the island rejoined China. 'Now if the MNCs want to come here, we would be willing to look at them.'

Foreign banking: Asked about the reported violation by Pepsi, he said, 'Let us not create unnecessary scare. India is not a small country and this excessive fear of foreigners might have been okay at the time of Independence. But in the last 40 years the country has created a new class of entrepreneurs, new confidence, new technical/ managerial skill and therefore this foreign bashing is not good for the morality of Indians.' He said, 'Look at Singapore, it has thousands of MNCs but when the Singapore Government sometime back expelled *Wall Street Journal* and *Time* magazine, the US swallowed it. It is the lack of self-confidence which is not justified here.'

As for the rationale behind increasing FERA limit from 40 per cent to 51 per cent, he said, 'If we are really in the game of getting foreign investment and technology, then we will have to address ourselves to the legitimate fear of foreign investors about possible leakage of technology and their consequential demand for management control. I do not see anything wrong in it.' This fear was perhaps the reason for India not getting top technology in the past. Further, he felt the country today was in a different ball game especially in a situation where capital was scarce and a new entrant like Soviet Union [was] offering 100 per cent foreign equity.

In a significant observation, he said that though present rules did not allow 100 per cent foreign equity outside EOUs and Foreign Trade Zone, the Special Empowered Board may consider even such cases if latest technology could be brought to India in the national interest. While the Government has allowed automatic clearance for CG imports up to the value of Rs. 2 crores because of tight foreign exchange position, this limit could be raised and eventually abolished if the BoP position showed substantial improvement. Dr. Manmohan Singh said 70 per cent of the cases came under this category.

However, the most interesting part of the press conference was provided by Mr. Vijay Bhaskar [sic] Reddy who announced that provisions in the MRTP Act relating to unfair/restrictive trade practices would now be extended to even the public and cooperative sector. Since existing law did not have such a provision, he was informed that he had made a policy announcement while Parliament was in session. Immediately, his deputy, Mr. Rangarajan Kumaramangalam corrected his senior to say, 'The MRTP Act does not cover public sector and we are examining where it can be changed without destroying the harmonious relation between consumers and the Act.' As for the assets criterion, he said though his Ministry would now be concerned with only post-entry rather than pre-entry problems of the MRTP companies, a legislation would be introduced to abolish chapters 3 and 3A which covered the asset limit, dominance, acquisition and mergers.

What about privatisation and disinvestment of public sector shareholdings? Dr. Manmohan Singh said, 'Life is not a linear path and in public life the best can easily become the enemy of the good, though there may be legitimate fears.' As regards the difference in expression used in budget speech and the industrial policy on disinvestment of public sector equity among mutual funds, financial institutions, workers and general public (stated in the industrial policy while the expression 'general public' was missing in budget) Dr. Singh said the Industrial Policy statement was a more authoritative text.

◆

Subsequently on 6 August 1991, P.K. Thungon laid a thirteen–page statement on the table of the Lok Sabha titled 'Policy Measures for Promoting and Strengthening Small, Tiny and Village Enterprises'. This was politically very important and perhaps in retrospect should have come first. In any case, this detailed statement helped provide a broader vision to the Rao government's approach to industry.

Rakesh Mohan and I succeeded in introducing the idea of a Limited Partnership Act to enhance the supply of risk capital to the small-scale sector. But both of us were quite disappointed that we were unable to push through our ideas on the de-reservation of items reserved for manufacture exclusively by the small-scale sector—the scope of which had expanded hugely when the Janata government was in power. Besides, what this reservation had done, as both of us had been arguing, was kill India's chances of emerging as a global supplier of consumer goods, garments, sports goods, toys and many electrical and electronic items—all of which became areas of China's manufacturing leadership in the 1980s and thereafter.

A few days after the announcement of the new industrial policy, S.K. Birla, the then president of FICCI, publicly expressed his apprehensions about a red carpet being offered to welcome foreign companies. The view of large sections of Indian industry was articulated by a young Anand Mahindra (today chairman, Mahindra Group) at a FICCI seminar in late 1991, where he argued for faster internal liberalization first and external liberalization thereafter. I recall it was the noted academic Mrinal Datta Chaudhuri (who passed away recently) who rebutted Mahindra by saying that this distinction did not hold so clearly in practice and, in any case, when the economy needed to revive, the start-up costs associated with external liberalization were much lower. I also recall telling the dapper industrialist that he sounded very much like a young JNU (Jawaharlal Nehru University) student![64]

---

[64]Sometime later in mid-1993, an informal group of industrialists that included Hari Shankar Singhania, L.M. Thapar, Ashok Jain, Keshub Mahindra, S.K. Birla and Rahul Bajaj met at the Belvedere Club at the Oberoi Hotel in Bombay (as it was called then). The group for which Rahul Bajaj emerged as the sole spokesperson welcomed industrial liberalization but voiced concerns regarding welcoming foreign investment and import duty cuts. The phrase made popular by this group—which has earned a place for itself in history as the 'Bombay Club'—was 'level playing field', which came to be seen as a euphemism for protection from foreign competition. The club actually met only once formally and submitted a five-page memorandum to the finance minister.

16

Dr Singh's Day Out: The Budget of 24 July

Dr Manmohan Singh had directly helped prepare seven budgets in the 1970s. But the 24 July 1991 budget would be the first that he would not only conceive and write (most of it at least), but also actually present. While in India's history, the May 1957 budget—bearing in some ways the imprint of one of Manmohan Singh's teachers, Nicholas Kaldor, and presented by T.T. Krishnamachari;[65] and the March 1985 budget—bearing the imprint of Rajiv Gandhi and presented by V.P. Singh[66]—have been heralded as milestones, the 1991 budget must rank among the most historic of all.

Normally, budgets are written by the mandarins and then touched up by the finance minister. Unfortunately, in July 1991, the two key officials in the Finance Ministry were not exactly on the same wavelength as the finance minister. Both the finance secretary, S.P. Shukla and the chief economic adviser, Deepak Nayyar, had been opposed to the IMF route and were not the most ardent champions of liberalization. Shukla had been appointed by Chandra Shekhar at

---

[65]T.T. Krishnamachari—TTK for short—presented a watershed budget, which made the first attempt to distinguish between active income (salaries or business) and passive income. However, his introduction of expenditure tax, high rates of income tax, wealth tax and estate duty earned him the sobriquet 'Tax, Tax and Kill'.

[66]The March 1985 budget shortlisted industries for delicensing, announced measures to deepen the stock market, proposed setting up the BIFR to deal with sick industrial units, and promised to formulate a long-term fiscal policy.

the behest of his finance minister, Yashwant Sinha, while Nayyar had been brought in by V.P. Singh when he was prime minister. Both were extremely diligent and meticulous. Both had fine reputations. But it was a fact that they did not see eye-to-eye with the prime minister's principal secretary and with the finance minister himself.

As it happened, Manmohan Singh turned to one of India's most versatile economists, Ashok Desai, to replace Nayyar. But Desai could join the Finance Ministry only in December 1991, although he had been offered the assignment in June 1991 itself. For bureaucratic reasons, he was designated chief economic consultant—and not chief economic adviser, as Nayyar had been (and before him Manmohan Singh himself, between 1971 and 1974). As Desai himself quipped to me, 'I stepped into Deepak's room but not into his shoes.'

I could see that Manmohan Singh was distinctly uncomfortable with this pair, but he was always proper, dignified and correct in his dealings with them—as they were with him. It was an extraordinary situation—the entire reforms programme was conceived and executed without the full and active participation of the finance secretary and the chief economic adviser. As for myself, like the finance minister, I had excellent personal relations with both these gentlemen but knew that they were not entirely supportive of what we had embarked upon. They, along with the foreign secretary, Muchkund Dubey, shared greater intellectual sympathy with the statement of the thirty-five economists than with the note issued by the quartet.[67]

Thus, the 24 July 1991 budget must be said to bear the personal imprimatur of the finance minister himself. Manmohan Singh delivered a deeply moving speech. Its contents, of course, marked a huge paradigm shift in economic thinking and charted out a course for the country that has remained steady for almost a quarter of a century. It also revealed a hidden side of the always serious-looking finance minister's personality—his fondness for Muhammad Iqbal's Urdu poetry.

Singh ended his budget speech by saying:

> I do not minimise the difficulties that lie ahead on the long
> and arduous journey on which we have embarked. But as Victor

---

[67]See chapter 9, 'Statements: Right and Left'.

Hugo once said, 'No power on earth can stop an idea whose time has come.' I suggest to this august House that the emergence of India as a major economic power in the world happens to be one such idea. Let the whole world hear it loud and clear. India is now wide awake. We shall prevail. We shall overcome. With these words, I commend the budget to this august House.

I recall Bimal Jalan[68] flashing the thumbs up signal to me in the Officials Gallery after Manmohan Singh had finished his speech.

◆

The 24 July 1991 budget was, without doubt, unusual. What happened the next day was even more unusual. Normally, officials of the finance ministry have a detailed press meet a day after the budget is presented. But on 25 July 1991, the finance minister himself made an unscheduled appearance at the press conference to ensure that the message of his budget did not get distorted by less-than-enthusiastic officials. The prime minister was happy that the finance minister had done so.

The finance minister explained his budget—calling it 'a budget with a human face'. He painstakingly defended the proposals to increase fertilizer, petrol and LPG prices. He also announced that with the full budget having been presented, the government would seek another emergency IMF loan, in addition to the US$220 million it had received on 22 July. In the context of today's concerns, it is worthwhile to recall that on 25 July 1991, the finance minister spoke extensively on the anti-black money scheme introduced in his budget.

The budget met with its predictable quota of bouquets and brickbats. The prime minister's friend, Nikhil Chakravartty—who had tried hard to dissuade him from taking the IMF route in early-June—wrote in his column in *Mainstream* on 10 August 1991:

Dr. Singh had begun with fairly plausible credentials. As the Secretary-General of the South Commission he was known to be

---

[68]Bimal Jalan, finance secretary in V.P. Singh's government, had been appointed chairman of the Economic Advisory Council to the Prime Minister by Chandra Shekhar and continued for a few months under Narasimha Rao as well.

trying to sensitise world opinion about the fearsome dimension of Third World debt, about the expediency of the Uruguay Round in tackling world trade imbalance and the negative character of the IMF with its conditionalities. Ironically enough, the very week that saw Dr. Manmohan Singh present his Budget—preceded by the announcement of the new industrial policy—that very week found Julius Nyerere, the head of the South Commission in New Delhi, on his way back from Beijing.[69] One wondered if the Chairman of the South Commission could convince himself with equal felicity about the line of consistency between the Commission's views and Dr. Singh's prescriptions for our country's economic ailment.

Along with such censure from a few influential and respected personalities, what was also immediately apparent was the extreme unease within the Congress, especially about the subsidy cut proposals. The prime minister asked me to gauge the sentiment amongst the MPs. I spent time in the Central Hall of Parliament talking to various Congressmen and came to the conclusion that we had a mini-revolt on our hands. It was a double whammy. Many MPs were apprehensive about the 'bonfire we had made of industrial controls' (a phrase that had been used earlier by both I.G. Patel and Jagdish Bhagwati), and on top of that, urea prices had increased by a whopping 40 per cent— the first time this was happening in a decade. While the increase in petrol and LPG prices was also under attack, it was the increase in fertilizer prices that was the particular target of the ire of a wide cross-section of Congress MPs.

I am sure the prime minister had got similar feedback from his floor managers, the most prominent of whom were Ghulam Nabi Azad, V. Narayanasamy[70] and Rangarajan Kumaramangalam. Rao looked grim when I reported my findings to him on the mood of Congress MPs. His only comment to me was, 'You people must learn to function in a political system.' He went on to add, 'Manmohan should have been more careful'—forgetting that as prime minister he had listened

---

[69]Julius Nyerere had, in fact, met the prime minister on 15 July 1991.
[70]V. Narayanasamy was a Rajya Sabha MP and secretary of the CPP.

to and approved of the budget being read out to him by his finance minister before it was presented.

Criticism of the budget from within the Congress mounted when the debate started in both houses of Parliament. Clearly, we were on the defensive and even the normally unflappable A.N. Verma looked distraught, blaming me at one stage for excessive zeal. I wondered whether he was reflecting the prime minister's views, but chose not to probe him further on the subject. The finance minister was also a bit rattled with the intensity of reaction within the Congress to some of his budget proposals.

It was then that the prime minister decided to allow Congress MPs to vent their spleen freely. A meeting of the CPP was called on 1 August 1991, in which the finance minister defended his budget. The prime minister stayed away and allowed Manmohan Singh to face the flak on his own. This was followed by another set of meetings on 2 and 3 August, in which Narasimha Rao was himself present throughout. Thereafter, three meetings of the CPP took place on 27, 28 and 29 August, in which the discussions focussed on agriculture—the main concern of the Congress MPs. The CPP meeting on industrial policy itself only took place on 16 December 1991—long after the industrial policy reforms had been fully digested and understood.

It would not be an exaggeration to say that barring in Jawaharlal Nehru's time, the CPP had not been as active or interactive as it was in August 1991. This was undoubtedly the prime minister's way of allowing the MPs to have their say, while reserving the right to have his way at the end. Of course, he did not put it across that way, but it seemed to me that this was smart politics—something neither the finance minister nor I fully appreciated then, but which we understood in our own ways in subsequent years as the finance minister became prime minister, and I, an MP and cabinet minister.

In the CPP meetings, the finance minister cut a lonely figure and the prime minister did nothing to alleviate his distress. He had no support whatsoever for his proposals to cut subsidies. Only two MPs were fulsome in their backing of the finance minister's budget—Mani Shankar Aiyar, the newly-elected MP from Tamil Nadu and one of Rajiv Gandhi's closest aides; and Nathuram Mirdha, the veteran farmer leader from Rajasthan. In view of his later opposition to what Manmohan Singh stood for, the support from Mani Shankar Aiyar would appear very surprising. He has justified his stance at the CPP as the outcome of his inside knowledge of the esteem that Rajiv Gandhi had for Manmohan Singh and his conviction that the late ex-prime minister would have approved of the 24 July budget given the extraordinary circumstances in which it had been prepared and the catastrophe that awaited India had such a budget not been presented.

In the CPP meeting of 2 August, when Mani Shankar Aiyar spoke of how the 24 July 1991 budget conformed to Rajiv Gandhi's beliefs on what needed to be done to stave off financial doom, his views were immediately challenged by R.K. Dhawan—who had also been an aide to Indira Gandhi and Rajiv Gandhi—on the grounds that it was impossible for anyone to know the late prime minister's opinion. Soon, the agriculture minister, Balram Jakhar, and the communications minister, Rajesh Pilot, went public against the proposal of their own cabinet colleague. Ironically, even the minister of state for chemicals and fertilizers, Chinta Mohan, expressed his disquiet, and mobilized several farmer organizations to protest against the cut in fertilizer subsidy.

Subsequently, fifty Congress MPs under the aegis of the Farmers' Parliamentary Forum signed a letter to the finance minister, critical of the budget proposal. The signatories made a strange grouping. The chairman of the forum was Prataprao Bhosale, a senior MP from Maharashtra believed to be close to the prime minister,[71] and one of the signatories was Murli Deora, the MP representing South Mumbai whose proximity to industry circles was known. To add to the tension, several opposition parties threatened to move a cut motion[72] against

---

[71]In December 1991, Bhosale was to chair a eleven-member Joint Committee of Parliament on Fertilizer Pricing, a step taken by the prime minister to assuage persistent political concerns on this issue. The committee submitted its report in August 1992. Most of its recommendations—like decontrol of pricing, distribution and movement of phosphatic and potassic fertilizers and a 10 per cent reduction in consumer prices of urea—were accepted.

[72]A cut motion is a powerful veto power given to MPs in the Lok Sabha to express

the fertilizer price hike. With the prevailing mood across the political spectrum, there was every prospect of the cut motion being passed, which would have spelt disaster for the government.

Moreover, another cut motion had been threatened on an announcement contained in the budget—a grant of ₹100 crore to the newly-created Rajiv Gandhi Foundation. The prime minister and the finance minister may have felt that they would be pleasing Congress MPs and the Congress as a whole, but, in point of fact, the move boomeranged badly. It was criticized both by Congress MPs and the opposition. The foundation's trustees led by Sonia Gandhi had not even asked for it and, in fact, wanted its withdrawal. Wisely, the finance minister scrapped the idea on 6 August in the Lok Sabha.

◆

The finance minister had proposed, as part of his budget speech, a 40 per cent increase in the prices of fertilizers to contain the subsidy bill. However, given the barrage of criticism he was subjected to from all political parties, including his own, he bowed to the pressure, and on 6 August 1991 announced in the Lok Sabha that the increase would be lowered to 30 per cent. However, even this did not pacify members, including Congress MPs. While the protests were still on, Manmohan Singh went ahead and announced that small and marginal farmers—who had about 76 per cent of the operational holdings, 29 per cent of the area under cultivation and accounted for 30 per cent of the fertilizer consumption in the country—would be totally exempted from the price hike. He did not roll back the increase in LPG and petrol prices but his concession on fertilizer prices silenced his critics, particularly within his party. I was a bit puzzled about how a dual pricing system would work in actual practice but kept my reservations to myself because it seemed to me that this was a huge

their opposition to proposals contained in the budget presented by the government. If the MPs oppose a cut in the fertilizer subsidy, for instance, they can move a motion seeking to reduce the allocations for the Ministry of Chemicals and Fertilizers or the Ministry of Agriculture by any specified amount, including just one rupee. If admitted, such a cut motion will have to be put to vote and if the government loses the vote it has to resign.

political victory for the prime minister and the finance minister. Within a few months, though, the idea's unworkability became apparent.

Behind the scenes, what had happened was this. The Cabinet Committee on Political Affairs (CCPA) had met informally on 4 August, and then again the next day on 5 August, in response to persistent pressure from Congress MPs from all states—including the prime minister's home state—and had decided the statement that Manmohan Singh would make on 6 August in the Lok Sabha on this matter.

Normally, no press statements are issued after CPP meetings. But this time, a statement was indeed released by the party spokesperson and MP, Professor C.P. Thakur, after the CPP meeting of 3 August which formed the basis of the CCPA deliberations. The statement dropped the idea of a roll-back which had been demanded over the past few days, but now spoke of protecting the interests of small and marginal farmers and—in what can only be described as classic Rao-Singh language—stated: 'The deliberations indicated clearly the bridging of the gap between political concerns of the members and the unfortunate economic realities that the Government has inherited.'

Both sides had won. The party had forced a rethink, but the fundamentals of what the government wanted—the decontrol of prices of fertilizers other than urea and an increase in urea prices—had been preserved. This was political economy at its constructive best—a textbook example of how the government and the party can collaborate to create a win-win situation for both.

Thereafter, there was one issue on fertilizer subsidies that had Narasimha Rao worried for a brief while. The former prime minister, V.P. Singh had written an article in *The Hindu* on 5 August arguing that farmers were being penalized for wrong investment decisions made by the government and that the technology we had selected was substandard. The prime minister asked me for my comments on the article. I knew something about the subject and assured him that the energy consumption of the gas-based fertilizer plants along the Hazira-Bijaipur-Jagdishpur pipeline was on par with global best practices. I added that while competitive bidding had not been resorted to for eight of the ten urea plants and the fertilizer pricing system needed an overhaul, the allegation of the former prime minister that the new generation of plants was energy-inefficient was not borne out of facts. Narasimha Rao seemed relieved that the V.P. Singh article could be countered were it to be raised in Parliament. As it turned out, the matter did not come up.

17

The First Review by the Finance Minister

By 14 August 1991, much of what we had set out do on 21 June had been accomplished. The devaluations had happened. Bold trade policy changes had been put in place. Dramatic reforms had been introduced in industrial policy. A watershed budget had been presented. After some initial foot-dragging at the official level, the Narasimham Committee on the Financial System had been announced on 14 August 1991.

I think it was on 15 August at the Red Fort that I suggested to the finance minister that he call key officials to review where we were and to identify the steps to be taken after the first round of policy changes and announcements. This meeting took place just one day later—after, I am sure, the finance minister had got the go-ahead from the prime minister. I kept notes of that meeting which are reproduced below:

Today, Finance Minister took a meeting with Principal Secretary to PM, Finance Secretary, Industry Secretary and Commerce Secretary.

The following are the main points that emerged from this meeting:

(i) Department of Industrial Development and Ministry of Commerce would put together a document on the economic changes that have taken place in the last few weeks. This would be written in simple language and would be meant for distribution to foreign audiences including embassies abroad, leading newspapers etc.

(ii) The Press Note on foreign investment would be got ready by today or tomorrow.

(iii) It was agreed that the Board on Foreign Investment Approvals would be compact and comprise of Principal Secretary to PM, Finance Secretary, Secretary (ID) and Commerce Secretary. Other Secretaries would be coopted as and when necessary. Principal Secretary would explore the possibility of having the Secretariat of this Board located in PMO to begin with.

(iv) Finance Minister suggested the appointment of special envoys of PM to travel to major countries like USA, Japan and Germany to explain our policies and interact with senior officials. Names mentioned in this regard were Shri M. Narasimham to East Asia, Dr. I.G. Patel to some western countries, Shri V. Krishnamurthy to West Germany etc. Principal Secretary to PM would get PM's approval for this concept.

(v) Finance Minister also desired that influential people from abroad, whether politicians, intellectuals, bankers, industrialists or academics be invited to come to India. This would be part of a marketing strategy.

(vi) On the follow up to negotiations with IMF and World Bank, it was decided that a Steering Group would be set up for monitoring the implementation. This group could consist of Principal Secretary to PM, Finance Secretary, Commerce Secretary, Industry Secretary and Secretary (PE). The inclusion of Secretary (Labour) and Secretary, Planning Commission could be considered as necessary. Finance Minister would take necessary steps in this regard.

(vii) Principal Secretary to PM mentioned the need to explore economic relationships with countries other than USA, Japan and Germany. In this regard, he mentioned Singapore and Taiwan and other countries in the East which have sizeable population of Indian origin and could be sources of investment.

(viii) Finance Minister drew attention to the need for follow up on many of the initiatives proposed in the Budget. These initiatives involve many ministries, other than the Finance Ministry. Finance Secretary proposed that the monitoring of these initiatives be taken up in the Steering Group under Pr. Secretary to PM.

(ix) Finance Minister suggested that the services of Shri S.K. Jain, former DDG in the International Labour Organisation be utilised in connection with the National Renewal Fund.

(x) The Law Ministry has expressed reservations on the SBI Bonds that have been proposed in the Budget. Principal Secretary to PM and Finance Secretary would have the matter clarified with Law Secretary so that the bonds could be issued soon.

(xi) Finance Minister suggested that he use his reply on the Budget as an opportunity for announcing concrete initiatives regarding NRI investments. Some initiatives have already been announced as part of the Budget. Some further initiatives were discussed including dual nationality for NRIs and use of exim scrips for remittances. Commerce Secretary mentioned the need to amend FERA also.

(xii) Finance Secretary would have the matter on import of edible oil from USA under Title III Grants examined.

(xiii) Secretary (ID) would take follow up action on the proposals to set up a Tariff Commission as contained in the Budget.

Finance Minister suggested that such a meeting could be held once a week to exchange ideas and review implementation of various policies.

Jairam Ramesh
16.8.91

◆

A day prior, the prime minister's traditional Independence Day speech had been a sombre affair. The high point of the speech was the sharp reference to the public distribution system—or PDS, as it is known in government circles—which is the nationwide network of over 4.5 lakh ration shops.

One of the key officials in the PMO was an Andhra Pradesh–cadre IAS officer, K.R. Venugopal, who was an acknowledged authority on PDS. He had much to do with what the prime minister said on the subject that morning. The prime minister announced his intention to restructure the PDS through which essential commodities like rice and wheat are distributed. Subsequently, such a restructured PDS was introduced, focussed on 1,700 of the poorest and most backward blocks of the country.

Besides PDS, Narasimha Rao spoke about rural development[73] and included a reference to the modernization of land records, an initiative launched in 1988 by Rajiv Gandhi, and with which Sam Pitroda and I had been involved. Unfortunately, the modernization and continuous update of land records is still far from complete and remains a pressing need.

◆

---

[73]It is generally not known that in addition to industry, Narasimha Rao kept the rural development portfolio to himself. He held on to the latter for four years, the second-longest tenure ever. He secured for rural development a huge increase in outlay in the Eighth Five-year Plan. To execute his priorities, he appointed another Andhra Pradesh–cadre IAS officer, B.N. Yugandhar as secretary, rural development. In the recent past, Yugandhar has been known as the father of Satya Nadella, the CEO (chief executive officer) of Microsoft, as has K.R. Venugopal as the father of Mrs Nadella. It was at Narasimha Rao and Manmohan Singh's insistence that a new Employment Assurance Scheme (EAS) was launched in October 1993 in 1,778 of the most backward and ecologically-stressed blocks of the country. This was based on Maharashtra's Employment Guarantee Scheme, which had—at Defence Minister Sharad Pawar's suggestion, and following a study group of Congress MPs headed by Mani Shankar Aiyar—been recommended for nationwide adoption. I had assisted the group of Congress MPs. The EAS was one significant milestone on the road to the Mahatma Gandhi National Rural Employment Guarantee Act (MGNREGA) passed by Parliament in September 2005.

A day after stock-taking, the finance minister met all trade union leaders. It was a long meeting, with labour representatives cutting across the political spectrum, highly critical of the industrial policy reforms and of the budget as well. Their arguments were predictable—a sell-out to the IMF, the opening of doors to multinationals, the death of the small-scale sector, backdoor privatization and freedom to retrench.

The finance minister, in turn, made his points without yielding much, but promised regular interactions with trade unions. He reiterated that there were no plans to privatize public sector companies and drew attention to the National Renewal Fund announced in his budget.

The labour leaders were clearly not satisfied but felt happy that the prime minister invited them over to his residence when their meeting with Manmohan Singh ended. The prime minister gave two assurances—no privatization and no exit policy talk, of which there had been some discussion.

At times, listening carefully and attentively itself earns dividends. And this is what happened that night.

18

The Prime Minister's Gorbachev Goof-up

I had seen Mikhail Gorbachev once, fleetingly, at the prime minister's residence on 19 November 1988. Rajiv Gandhi had asked Sam Pitroda to make a presentation to the visiting Soviet leader on new technological and economic directions that the Indo–USSR[74] bilateral relationship could take. Pitroda had roped in Ashok Ganguly, then chairman of Hindustan Lever, and V.S. Arunachalam, then scientific adviser to the defence minister. The four of us put together a presentation. Pitroda, Ganguly and Arunachalam made the presentation to the two heads of state (with 35mm slides since this was a pre-PowerPoint era), while aides like me sat in the adjacent room.[75]

Fast-forward to 19 August 1991—the day Gorbachev was ousted (temporarily, as it turned out) in a coup. When I reached the office on the morning of 20 August, I was inundated with phone calls from all sorts of people. The most concerned was the finance minister himself who asked me whether I knew why the prime minister had said what he had the day before, which had been reported on the front page of the *Hindustan Times*. No other newspaper had given the prime minister's remarks on the coup in Moscow any prominence except for this daily, in a news-item that went thus:

---

[74]The dissolution of USSR (Union of Soviet Socialist Republics) was formally enacted on 26 December 1991.

[75]Sam Pitroda has a more detailed account of this meeting in his forthcoming autobiography.

PM: It is a warning to reformers
New Delhi, Aug 19 (UNI, PTI)

Prime Minister P.V. Narasimha Rao today said the ouster of Soviet President Mikhail Gorbachev was a warning that any leader who chalks out plans for the future should take each step cautiously.

Mr. Narasimha Rao took note of the political developments in Soviet Union while addressing a national convention of the Youth Congress workers here on the occasion of the 48th birth anniversary of Mr. Rajiv Gandhi.

He recalled the close friendship between Mr. Gandhi and Mr. Gorbachev and in this connection mentioned their respective contributions for the improvement of the lot of their people.

The prime minister's statement was a dynamite. A.N.Verma, on learning what had transpired, was worried about the implications of Rao's comments, much like the finance minister. Would this put economic reforms in jeopardy, the two of them wondered when I met them to discuss the statement. Finally, I thought it best to ask the prime minister himself. The prime minister, on his part, really did not elucidate or enlighten, except to say that every country must choose the pace of change suited to its 'genius'. He also recalled the disastrous impact of the Shah of Iran's modernization programme[76] and then said something to the effect that we must be careful and cautious.

Meanwhile, the minister of state of external affairs, Eduardo Faleiro, had also given out a statement which was, once more, Mandarin-speak. He said: 'India is watching the situation. It is an internal development of the Soviet Union.'

On 20 August, Madhavsinh Solanki, the external affairs minister, spoke in the Lok Sabha in further detail and said:

---

[76]Mohammad Reza Pahlavi, the Shah of Iran (1941-1979), undertook a radical modernization programme in his country, the 'White Revolution', encouraging land reform, developing complex infrastructure and extending suffrage to women. However, some analysts suggest that the pace of change was so rapid that in 1978 a revolution broke out that forced the Shah of Iran to flee the country the following year.

Sir, India attaches the highest importance to its relations with the USSR which are based on the universally accepted principles of conducting inter-state relations and are reflected in the Indo-Soviet Treaty of Peace, Friendship and Cooperation. It was because of the importance that both countries attached to the Treaty that very recently they jointly announced their intention to extend it by a further period of twenty years. The above events in the Soviet Union are thus of vital interest to us and indeed to the whole world. The Government of India is, therefore, constantly and carefully monitoring the situation there since receiving reports of the announcements and is maintaining close touch with the situation in this regard.

But the damage had been done. It was the prime minister's remarks that held sway. In the Lok Sabha, Jaswant Singh, later to become external affairs and finance minister under Atal Bihari Vajpayee, pilloried the prime minister thus:

The Government responded to a situation of grave importance. Indo-Soviet relations were involved and the Government did respond with ineptitude blinkered with timidity. It responded in a situation where it appeared that the Government's response was grooved in yesterday's clichés. We have there on record not just that statement but an observation by the Prime Minister filled with unnecessary homilies, that reformists must be careful [...]

It was a baffling day which flummoxed all of us who were working with the prime minister. He had—as I told his principal secretary and the finance minister—'thrown a googly', the impact of which would be felt in the days and months to come.

As I tried to reconstruct the sequence of events that led to the prime minister's observations, it turned out that the Youth Congress had arranged a massive rally. Reports reached the prime minister that the crowd was restive, with speakers arguing vociferously both in favour of and against Manmohan Singh's policies of liberalization. The special protection group (SPG) advised the prime minister against going there, given how charged the atmosphere was. The prime minister, however, disregarded this advice and, in the words of someone who had worked closely with him for over a decade, 'phrased his own domestic concerns—and those of many in his audience—in an international metaphor that was as elusive as it was effective.'

Whatever the context may have been, there is no question that Narasimha Rao's elliptical remarks cast a shadow on our bilateral relationship with the Soviet Union and evoked a sharp response from the foreign policy establishment. One of Rao's own colleagues, K. Natwar Singh, who was minister of state for external affairs under him in Rajiv Gandhi's government, blasted him in a letter made public on 25 August, which pretty much summed up what most people were thinking:

> You are not unfamiliar with international affairs and have rightly earned a reputation for using words carefully. It is therefore a matter of surprise that you should have expressed the views you did on the current events in the Soviet Union. Those dealing with foreign affairs at high levels should think twice before saying anything. On the removal of Mr. Gorbachev, you, the External Affairs Minister Mr. Madhavsinh Solanki, the Minister of State Mr. Eduardo Faleiro have made different pronouncements. This has caused a lot of confusion and become a subject of adverse comment in Central Hall of Parliament and among senior journalists. It is possible to make a good case for each of these statements. It is equally true that each can be demolished with effortless ease. What worries me is that taken collectively they add up to an incoherent management of our foreign policy. Such a fragmented and piecemeal approach to momentous decisions is fraught with danger.

India was caught flat-footed by the Soviet coup attempt. Indeed, in an interview to the journalist Shekhar Gupta on 'Walk the Talk', broadcast on NDTV on 8 May 2004, roughly seven months before he passed away, Narasimha Rao allowed himself a rare admission of a mistake, saying, 'I blurted out something which perhaps wasn't proper at that particular moment.'

It wasn't just Rao who seemed to have egg on his face. The CPM fared no better. Harkishan Singh Surjeet had issued a statement on 23 August that the coup was a natural corollary to the policies followed by Gorbachev. There appeared to be considerable jubilation in the CPM camp (with the CPI showing less happiness) at the prospect of the permanent departure of Gorbachev from the political scene. *The Hindu* went on to report:

> Speaking with the authority of a man who had first-hand knowledge of the events in Moscow, Mr Surjeet claimed that the coup had the support of the people, and had not been imposed from above as the men behind it were party leaders who had been involved with the reforms initiated by Mr. Gorbachev.[77]

It is difficult to estimate the impact of the reactions of Rao and Surjeet on USSR's policies towards India. The Soviet ambassador in New Delhi, Vladimir Isakov, did meet with the prime minister on 23 August and Gorbachev himself wrote to the prime minister a few days later. But the fact remains that some unease crept into the bilateral relationship. Perhaps as an immediate fallout, on 6 December 1991, for the first time, USSR voted for a proposal sponsored by Pakistan and Bangladesh at the United Nations for creating a nuclear-free zone in South Asia.

---

[77]'More on Communist Reaction', *The Hindu*, 23 August 1991.

19

The Last Week of August 1991

The last week of August 1991 involved a lot of housekeeping. On 22 August, the establishment of a Foreign Investment Promotion Board (FIPB) was announced. Rakesh Mohan and I had prevailed upon a more-than-willing A.N. Verma that the FIPB should be small and compact, and the 'P' in FIPB should stand for 'promotion' and not 'processing'. This was a victory of sorts for the two of us because a view had gained ground that the FIPB would be a large bureaucratic body meant largely to facilitate quick clearances. Much against the wishes of the cabinet secretary and others, we had managed to convince the principal secretary to have the FIPB in the PMO itself, since its credibility needed to be projected speedily.

One of the very first proposals that came on the FIPB's agenda was a joint venture between IBM and the Tata Group. Ratan Tata and senior IBM executives, led by Kailash Joshi, met with the principal secretary to the prime minister and—thinking that this should get the widest publicity—I called up Reuters and gave them a briefing. Shortly thereafter, there was a news-item in the *International Herald Tribune* saying that India meant business and was welcoming foreign investment. But I think some complaints reached the prime minister about my private enterprise, and the principal secretary told me that the principal information officer ought to be doing such briefings.

◆

On 26 August 1991, the prime minister made a hard-hitting speech in the Lok Sabha while replying to the demands for grants for the Ministry of Industry. He was somewhat like the boxer Muhammad Ali that day—a jab here, a jab there, floating like a butterfly, stinging like a bee.

The BJP welcomed the 24 July industrial policy reforms on the grounds that they were a total repudiation of Nehruvian policy that had run its course. Narasimha Rao, however, emphasized the continuity aspects of the reforms and how they were not deviations in any way from the vision of India's first prime minister.

The Left and some other parties like the Janata Dal, on their part, attacked the 24 July industrial policy package as not just an abandonment of Nehru's vision but as something that would erode national sovereignty and lead to greater unemployment. To these critics, the prime minister stressed the change aspects of the package and spoke eloquently of the need to give up shibboleths of the past when confronted with new challenges.[78]

The exchanges were sharp and the prime minister kept getting interrupted. However, he more than stood his ground:

> Prime Minister: Coming to technology, Nirmal Babu has told us something about appropriate technology. If you have a washing machine, how many people are you throwing out of employment? The only thing is, if you have a lakh washing machines being made, to how many people you are giving employment on the other side? (*Interruptions*)
>
> Nirmal Kanti Chatterjee (West Bengal; CPM): How many?
>
> Prime Minister: Let us calculate. And what kind of employment are you giving, what kind of employment are you diversifying... (*Interruptions*)
>
> Nirmal Kanti Chatterjee: Those resources which are utilised for

---

[78]More of this gets elaborated in the chapter, 'A Final Word', in Narasimha Rao's unpublished self-portrait titled *Two Crucial Years: India under Shri P.V. Narasimha Rao's Stewardship*.

producing washing machine could be utilised for other purposes…
(*Interruptions*)

Prime Minister: That is the point. If you take that as the criterion
then you will remain a country of maid-servants only. This is the
point… (*Interruptions*)

Nirmal Kanti Chatterjee: That is your idea… (*Interruptions*)

Prime Minister: You are condemning our women folk to life of
drudgery permanently. This is where diversification is necessary.
That is why, we have not given them any education so far. Let
her be educated. She will refuse to do the washing, the moment
you educate her. Today, we are talking of a society which itself
is fast changing. And if you do not admit that this change is
coming, you will be overtaken by events. This is what I would
like to say. It is very simple to say that 'you are throwing people
out of employment'. But what kind of employment? (*Interruptions*)

This sparring went on, and towards the end, in an unusual turn of
events, one of Rao's ministers from West Bengal, Ajit Panja, joined
the fray.

Ajit Panja: Sir… (*Interruptions*)

Basudeb Acharia (West Bengal; CPM): Sir, how can a Minister
seek a clarification from the Prime Minister? (*Interruptions*)

Ajit Panja: I want to know from the Prime Minister whether
he is going to send a team of CPI-M members to Moscow, as
they say they do not appreciate our policy, for studying the New
Industrial Policy… (*Interruptions*)

Somnath Chatterjee (West Bengal; CPM): Sir, I would like to
know the Prime Minister's reaction to this flippancy on the floor
of the House… (*Interruptions*)

Prime Minister: Sir, there is another forum to discuss this. Do
not worry. […]

Ram Naik (Maharashtra; BJP): Sir, my point of order is this. It is a collective responsibility of the Cabinet. If the Minister wants any explanation, he can ask the Prime Minister in the Cabinet. This is not the forum where any Minister can ask any explanation or any information from the Prime Minister... (*Interruptions*) [...]

Speaker: I uphold your point of order...

Prime Minister: Sir, I understand my Minister perfectly. It was not for an explanation. It was a little provocation... (*Interruptions*)

It was parliamentary debate at its cut-and-thrust best.

◆

On 29 August 1991, the Committee on Tax Reforms under the chairmanship of Dr Raja Chelliah, India's pre-eminent expert on public finance, was announced. I had enjoyed a close relationship with Chelliah in the Planning Commission, of which he had been a member during 1985–89. He would insist on speaking to me in Tamil and I had to keep telling him that it was my wife who was a true-blue Tamilian and not me.

When Manmohan Singh had asked Abid Hussain (another member of the Planning Commission) and me to prepare an agenda for industrial policy reforms in September 1986, he had asked for a similar agenda on tax policy reforms from Chelliah. But like the industrial policy proposals, the tax reforms proposals went nowhere and died a natural death, only to be resurrected in Chelliah's speeches once in a while.

The Chelliah Committee set up by the finance minister made far-reaching recommendations; these formed the backbone of the budget proposals on both direct and indirect taxes presented in February 1992 and 1993.

◆

On 31 August 1991, the prime minister addressed a well-attended session of the All-India Kisan Congress, which was chaired by the senior Congress leader Ram Chandra Vikal, who was also a member of the CWC. Vikal attacked the government's policy strongly and was joined by many others, including Ram Naresh Yadav, a former chief minister of Uttar Pradesh.

The prime minister heard all of them patiently and then spoke his mind out for over an hour. He defended the budget and the industrial policy reforms, giving a background to why they were necessary. He admitted that two years of mismanagement of the economy had forced India to go to the IMF, but reassured the audience that there was no question of being defeated or capitulating to the Fund. He also ruled out going back on what had been done. Further, he exhorted those present to actually spread the message of his government's enterprise at averting a grave economic crisis and at giving a new direction to the economy consistent with Indira Gandhi's vision.

It was a typical Narasimha Rao performance, but his audience was still sullen and refused to be mollified. Their main grouse remained the hike in urea prices.

20

And That's It!

2 September 1991, a Monday, began, as always, with my being at my desk in South Block at 8.30 a.m. After about an hour, A.N. Verma called me into his chamber. After exchanging pleasantries, he asked me for an update on what I had been doing, since he had been away for a few days. I told him that just two days back the prime minister had separately met delegations from the three national industry associations—the Confederation of Engineering Industry (CEI, later to become the Confederation of Indian Industry [CII]), FICCI and ASSOCHAM—for which I was also present. The meetings were very useful and a number of suggestions had been made by the various captains of industry and business. I gave Verma a run-down of these suggestions. While several industrialists had wholeheartedly supported the policies announced in July 1991, some of them were still a bit hesitant about the big opening up to foreign investment. Verma listened to me patiently and asked for a set of action points for him to follow-up.

After about ten minutes or thereabouts, the principal secretary coolly dropped a bombshell—that the prime minister wanted me to be 'transferred' to the Planning Commission. I was shocked beyond words and asked him whether anything was amiss. Verma was at pains to point out that Narasimha Rao had specifically asked that I be designated as officer-on-special-duty to the deputy chairman of the Planning Commission and showed me official communication to that effect. He said that the prime minister had praised my contribution and wanted me in the Planning Commission to give shape to the Eighth Five-year Plan which was under preparation. The principal secretary told me repeatedly that he had himself lauded my work on more than one occasion and that the prime minister had agreed with his assessment.

I was convinced that I was being sacked. What baffled me completely was that just forty-eight hours back, the prime minister had asked me to attend his meetings with the three national industry associations—meetings that, in fact, he had asked me to organize. After the discussions were over, he had not given any indication that he was about to jettison me—asking me, instead, to follow-up on the meetings. His decision was (and remains) inexplicable to me.

Hence, I sought time from the prime minister and he saw me in the afternoon of that very day at around 4 p.m. He told me, in no uncertain terms, that he appreciated my work and what I had done in the initial days of his tenure when things were so grim. He went on to repeat what Verma had already told me—that the main objective of his getting me into the PMO had been achieved, and that he now believed that I could assist Pranab Mukherjee in the Planning Commission. I kept asking the prime minister whether I had done anything to invite his ire and wrath, but he kept denying that he was shunting me out—which I insisted he was. When I persisted, he said that I would continue working with him since he was the chairman of the Planning Commission and that he would depend on me for various issues. I took leave of the prime minister after about an hour, and his parting words to me were that I should keep sending him notes regularly so that he'd receive unvarnished feedback. I was extremely downbeat but managed to wish him all the best before leaving. A few days earlier, I had hoped to join Narasimha Rao on his maiden foreign visit to Germany as prime minister. That was not to be.

A little later, I called on the finance minister, who was visibly taken aback when I informed him of my shift to the Planning Commission. He hoped that this did not portend the prime minister's slackening interest in economic reforms. He added that I could meet him any time and that he would continue to count on me. Manmohan Singh can be philosophical at times, and this moment was no exception. His closing words were, 'Life is a learning experience,' and that I was young enough to take a setback in my stride and move on. He expressed confidence in my ability to bounce back and recalled fondly how he had recruited me personally into the Planning Commission along with Rakesh Mohan and Arvind Virmani, another eminent economist, in August–September 1986, overcoming the objections of the bureaucracy that people in their early thirties were being given senior positions.

After I left the PMO, I continued to have access to the prime minister and could speak to him on the phone whenever I wanted. I used to call on him now and then, and we would have general discussions on political and economic matters. During one of these conversations, he recalled his admiration for Swami Ramanand Teerth, a firebrand Congressman who fought the last Nizam of Hyderabad aggressively for over a decade and was also a noted educationist. But never once, during these freewheeling conversations, did I muster up the courage to ask him why he had shifted me out in September 1991. Even when I spent considerable time with him on a couple of occasions, long after he had ceased to be prime minister, the topic of his moving me out never came up.

Interestingly, after he retired, A.N. Verma mentioned that he could not understand why I had been told to leave so abruptly. I asked him whether he had theories or hunches, but his response was that the matter was beyond his comprehension. He did reveal one nugget of information, though—a couple of days after I had left the PMO, the prime minister and Verma had discussed the possibility of my joining the Indian embassy in Washington as minister (economic), but as it turned out, nothing came of that, and it was just as well.

Various theories did the rounds to explain my sudden exit. One wag acerbically commented that while I had failed to get an exit policy included in the industrial policy reforms, I had succeeded in attracting an exit policy for myself. Some said that I was too open and accessible and could not function self-effacingly; this was not entirely untrue.[79]

---

[79] R.D. Pradhan writes of my exit in *My Years with Rajiv and Sonia* (New Delhi: Hay House India, 2014). He says: 'With his journalistic attitude he [Jairam Ramesh] could not work in anonymity, so essential for working in the PMO.'

Still others speculated that Chandraswami[80] had never been happy with my presence since he had wanted his aide Pinaki Misra in the PMO and I had beaten him to it. A few were convinced that I was too close to a number of Congress leaders and that the prime minister resented this proximity. In fact, Farooq Abdullah, the erstwhile chief minister of Jammu and Kashmir, in a lunch hosted by the industrialist R.P. Goenka, went to the extent of loudly saying, 'PV will not stomach anyone who he thinks were Rajiv's boys.' But knowing the ebullient Kashmiri leader, I did not believe that charge one bit.

◆

Upon leaving the PMO, I worked very closely with Pranab Mukherjee in the Planning Commission and he involved me with the various activities of the Congress particularly. On 19 September 1991, at the first meeting of the new Planning Commission, the prime minister took the deputy chairman and me aside during the lunch break and told Pranab Mukherjee, 'I hope you are keeping Jairam more than busy!'

The prime minister also gave me some special assignments. In early 1993, Rajesh Pilot, with Rao's approval, requested me to assist him in his new post as minister of state for internal security and focus on the economic development of Jammu and Kashmir. I travelled extensively across the state with Wajahat Habibullah and subsequently, in collaboration with Haseeb Drabu, now the finance minister of the state, launched a number of new initiatives during my ministerial career between 2006 and 2013. But this is another story altogether.

In the meantime, Rao's political secretary asked me to help draft the resolutions for the March 1993 session of the All India Congress Committee (AICC) in Surajkund, Haryana, and the June 1994 session in New Delhi. When the Dunkel Draft[81] became a serious political issue in late-1993—creating in the process a strange alliance of Murli

---

[80]Chandraswami, a controversial Indian godman, was believed to have been Narasimha Rao's spiritual adviser.

[81]The Dunkel Draft was prepared by Arthur Dunkel, then director general of GATT (General Agreement on Tariffs and Trade), for further trade liberalization; this was to later form the basis of the World Trade Organisation (WTO).

Manohar Joshi (BJP), Ashok Mitra (CPM) and George Fernandes (Janata Dal)—the prime minister told me to prepare a detailed briefing document in easy-to-understand language for party workers. I did so and he liked my effort. Even so, the first year was a difficult period of adjustment, as it took some time to put the events of 2 September behind me.

◆

The last time I had a substantive conversation with Narasimha Rao was at the Congress' plenary session in Bangalore (now Bengaluru) in March 2001. Earlier, Rao had called me after a column of mine had appeared in *India Today* on 16 October 2000, titled 'Rao Doesn't Deserve This', in which I had expressed anguish at his travails in relation to various court cases in which he was embroiled. He had expressed happiness that I had written in his support at a time when he was battered from all sides.

At the Congress' plenary session, Sonia Gandhi had given Rao a prominent place on the dais alongside her. Rao saw me after a while and asked me to accompany him to a quiet place. He then proceeded to vehemently criticize the Vajpayee government's policy on the privatization of public sector companies, and especially the news that Air India would be sold off, as would other companies in the aluminium and telecommunications sector. He told me that this was never part of the reforms agenda of his government[82]—a matter, he added, that I would doubtless be aware of since I had been with him at the very beginning. That Rao would remember my small role was

---

[82]It was only in June 2015, thanks to Narasimha Rao's son, P.V. Prabhakar Rao, that I was able to see a paper written by Narasimha Rao himself titled 'Liberalisation and the Public Sector'. Apparently, he had prepared it for the AICC plenary session in March 2001. But he had not spoken at the plenary and so the paper was not circulated, although the economic resolution adopted reaffirmed the Congress' commitment to the public sector as a key differentiator from the BJP. The Narasimha Rao paper finds echoes in the conversation I had with him on the sidelines. Because it gives great insights into his thinking, and because of its contemporary relevance as well, I have included it in this book (Annexure 9).

gratifying and helped assuage the wound that I was carrying even after a decade. Rao kept returning to the 'middle path' approach he had advocated as prime minister and said that it merely was an extension of Nehru's model of a 'mixed economy'. I asked him why he hadn't written a book on the reforms period but he said he was tired and that it was up to youngsters like me to do so. That I was forty-seven and could still be called a youngster amused me no end.

◆

Much was to happen after the reforms blitz of July 1991. Manmohan Singh presented four more regular budgets, each hugely significant in their own way but none to match the sheer courage and boldness of the 24 July 1991 one. The economy did poorly in 1991-92 but that was expected. The finance minister had warned the country that the turnaround would take at least two years and indeed, it did. Growth momentum and investor confidence returned gradually, and from 1993-94 onwards, the economy was on a roll. When they left office in May 1996, the Rao–Singh duo had left behind foreign exchange reserves equal to five months of imports and three consecutive years of +7 per cent rate of GDP growth—something that had never happened before.

Success made new believers of old sceptics. What had started out as a matter of compulsion soon became a matter of conviction, and nothing epitomized this metamorphosis better than the attitude of the prime minister himself. He became increasingly assertive and started taking full credit for the emergence of a new India. I did not begrudge him that one bit, but felt the pre-1991 roots of the post-1991 successes were not being given adequate credit. I wrote about this in 1994 in *Business Standard*, only to invite rebuke from the establishment and from some neo-converts.

One issue on which I publicly differed with Rao and his administration was the Enron power project. Indeed, he was quite irked when L.K. Advani issued a press statement in early 1995 quoting my opposition to that power project and voicing his party's criticism as well. When the Shiv Sena-BJP government came to power in Maharashtra in early-1995, it cancelled the contract, but after a while took the project forward. In May 1996, the thirteen-day Vajpayee government gave the project its stamp of approval—offering a 'sovereign' counter-guarantee—just as the vote of confidence was being debated in the Lok Sabha.

21

A Final Word

So, at the end of it all, what do I make of Narasimha Rao? There is no need to revile him—as indeed he has been—or render him with a halo—as is being done to fight today's political battles. What is important is an objective assessment, a frank appraisal, something that the Chinese do but we seem to be incapable of. After all, Mao was officially declared 70 per cent right, 30 per cent wrong. And Mao himself had said that 'we consider that out of Stalin's ten fingers, only three were bad.'

There is no doubt that Rao was navigating India through a most troubled period, and that he had inherited a number of encumbrances. He was not in the best of health. He headed a minority government—a government that won a vote of confidence because many parties had walked out. Rao came to power against the backdrop of the brutal assassination of a young leader of immense charm and charisma, a man of great energy and exuberance—all qualities that he himself lacked in abundance. Even while the party he headed was in a state of shock, he had to stave off a leadership challenge from one of his colleagues, who he went on to accommodate in his cabinet as defence minister.[83]

At the same time, Rao was buffeted by all sorts of problems. A senior oil industry executive had been abducted in the Kashmir

---

[83]Sharad Pawar was the defence minister in Narasimha Rao's cabinet.

Valley—which was in ferment—and was kept in captivity for fifty-five days.[84] Punjab was in a state of tumult.[85] The abrasive chief election commissioner was giving the government a hard time.[86] Rao's party's government in Karnataka, a traditional bastion, was tottering. Another ally ruling in Tamil Nadu had started giving him huge headaches by her theatrical actions on the Cauvery river waters issue.[87] The principal opposition party had resumed its shrill campaign for building a Ram Mandir in Ayodhya.[88]

To make matters worse, Rao was under immense pressure to implement the hundred-day agenda mentioned in the party's manifesto, even while the economy was in the doldrums—gold continued being hypothecated to the Bank of England; foreign exchange remained at dangerously low levels; and inflation was running at over 16 per cent. As though this weren't bad enough, Rao had appointed somebody from outside the world of mainstream politics as his finance minister.

Without doubt, Narasimha Rao confronted huge challenges. Yet, in the very brief period I saw him at the closest of quarters, I have to say that he was simply magnificent. A lifetime of circumspection

---

[84]Indian Oil Corporation's executive director, K. Doraiswamy, was abducted by activists of the Ikhwan-ul-Muslimeen in Srinagar on 28 June 1991, and was released on 20 August in exchange for the liberation of four terrorists. The year 1991 saw the government plagued by several such incidents of kidnapping in the Kashmir Valley.
[85]Troubled by an armed separatist movement, the tense state of Punjab witnessed the killing of at least eighty train passengers near the city of Ludhiana in June 1991. The attacks came less than five hours after polling closed in the national elections.
[86]T.N. Seshan, the then election commissioner—known to have said, 'While I am here, it is I who will decide how elections are to be held; politicians have got away with nonsense for far too long'—had several run-ins with Narasimha Rao.
[87]The Cauvery river water dispute hit the headlines once J. Jayalalithaa succeeded M. Karunanidhi in 1991 as chief minister of Tamil Nadu. She secured an interim award from the Cauvery Water Dispute Tribunal—Karnataka was ordered to release 205 tmcft each year to Tamil Nadu, which Karnataka decided to challenge in the apex court. Subsequently, Jayalalithaa went on a four-day fast in 1993, demanding the release of the Cauvery waters.
[88]L.K. Advani, then the president of the BJP, had, in 1990, undertaken a rath yatra from Somnath to generate support for a Ram temple in Ayodhya, which was to be his final stop. In 1991, the BJP intensified its campaign, which would eventually spiral into the demolition of the Babri Masjid.

gave way to courage. From the outset, Rao proved everybody wrong. A man who famously remarked, 'Even not taking a decision is a decision,' was remarkably decisive in the initial months. Indeed, one of Narasimha Rao's closest aides, who worked with him when he was union minister and prime minister, but who prefers to be anonymous, says: 'I don't believe he [Rao] was indecisive; he was deferential to authority or to positions where the ultimate responsibility for decisions lay, but where he was assured that the position was his to hold, he was quick to decide. He crafted the National Policy on Education in May 1986 within eight months of taking charge of that [human resource development] ministry, and directed its modification, as prime minister, six years later.' The aide went on to say, 'I think he [Rao] was confident that the public postures of pressure to which he appeared subject would never, at that point in time, translate into actions that would threaten his government or indeed—and this was crucial and borne out in his private conversations with those who pressured—thwart the essential pace of reform.'

Would anybody else in his place have done differently in the initial months? It's hard to tell, but undoubtedly, Rao brought some unique characteristics. For one, by surprising everyone and ensuring that quick decisions were taken, by being exceedingly crafty as well as bold, he propelled change; critics could carp about the state of things, but they, too, knew in their heart of hearts that what he was doing was inevitable. Rao did not have the image of being pro-business and pro-industry, but to be fair, that could be because he had never served in an economic ministry earlier. This further meant that if he was championing liberalization, there may well have been something of value in it for the nation. Moreover, Rao had been around in Parliament for over a decade and hence, his voice did command respect. His reputation was that of a scholar who had been given a lot of importance by Indira Gandhi and Rajiv Gandhi and hence, when he spoke, he was heard intently, even if, more often than not, what he said appeared metaphysical and complicated.

For the most part, Rao was the author of whatever he spoke and wrote; he may have received inputs from here and there, but like Nehru before him, he was an original and crafted his own speeches.

Reading them now after a gap of so many years is truly an education. His interventions in Parliament were also mostly extempore with, of course, notes and points prepared by his aides, which mostly remained in the folder in front of him.

Undoubtedly, Narasimha Rao, self-effacing at one level, was a man acutely conscious of his own capabilities, without ever projecting a machismo of any kind. He could certainly not be accused of Narendra Modi's style of arrogance; rather, in him, one could see a strong sense of self-awareness. His was not the in-your-face conceit of his current successor but the self-pride of an intellectually superior person—of one who knows that he knows. This is evident in what he himself said of his succession, in a fascinating unpublished forty-six-page self-portrait he left behind titled *Two Crucial Years: India under Shri P.V. Narasimha Rao's Stewardship*:[89]

> Two years ago, when the young and dynamic Shri Rajiv Gandhi was martyred in the cause of the nation's unity and integrity, veteran freedom fighter Shri P.V. Narasimha Rao was called upon to make up his unfinished task. At that time the country was half-way through a mid-term parliamentary election. Nearly half the constituencies had already gone to polls, and Rajiv Gandhi was on the last leg of his cross-country campaign, when he was felled by a "human bomb". On May 29, 1991, the Congress Working Committee asked the scholarly Narasimha Rao to lead the party at the hustings in the remaining constituencies. The Congress once again emerged as the largest single party in the country; although it was still short of a majority, it had allies and supporters. The Congress Parliamentary Party elected Shri Narasimha Rao as its leader and accepted the President's invitation to form the government. With a long administrative experience he had served in almost all key ministries at the centre, except finance, and had been a close associate of both Shrimati Indira Gandhi and Shri Rajiv Gandhi, both in office and opposition. Another reason why he was regarded as a natural successor to

---

[89]This was made available to me by P.V. Prabhakar Rao, Narasimha Rao's youngest son, for which I'm indebted to him.

Indiraji and Rajivji was that he was not only acquainted with their thinking but had also been involved in the formation of their new ideas on how to carry the country to a new stage in its development.

When Indiraji returned to power in 1980, she had to devote herself to the difficult task of pulling the country out of the morass in which the 1977-79 Janata interregnum had landed it, and return it to the path of national advance which it had taken under the leadership of Mahatma Gandhi and Jawaharlal Nehru and which had been endorsed by the nation in successive general elections. But she had also come to realise from her long experience at the helm of the nation that having reached the stage and level of development already, the country needed fresh thinking and innovative practice. That is where Narasimha Raoji's sagacious advice proved useful and she did initiate some new ideas and measures. The young Rajivji pursued these ideas and practices with youthful boldness and greater vigour, and elaborated his thinking in terms of concrete time-bound measures in the election manifesto for the 1991 mid-term poll. Narasimha Raoji has helped him in drawing up the manifesto and has come to realise in the period since the Congress went out of office, the economic situation in the country has so deteriorated that immediate remedial measures were needed.

The national finances were in a particularly bad shape. Narasimha Raoji felt that he needed an expert to handle it. That is why, even before the cabinet was sworn in, he invited Manmohan Singh, one of the country's foremost economists with a long experience at home and in international organisations to take charge of the economy and immediately begin formulating measures to reverse its decline. Naturally, the new policy had to update the basic approach to national development written into the second and third five year plan documents by Jawaharlal Nehru and carry forward the new thinking initiated by Indiraji and pursued by Rajivji. But the BJP, which has emerged as the main opposition party, mistook the innovative measures suggested by Manmohan Singhji as abandonment of the Nehruvian approach. Partly taken in by the BJP propaganda, but largely because of their inability to free themselves from the hold of their dogmas, which in any case had proved mistaken, the Left Front parties also were critical of the new economic measures. They, however, had no alternatives to suggest. If the BJP hailed the measures for toning up the economy for wrong reasons, the Left Front's criticism lacked rationality. Now, of course, the BJP too has become critical of the economic policy, and is talking in terms of certain old concepts whose definitions have to be changed with the changing times [...]

It is the sagacious leadership of Shri Narasimha Rao which has enabled the [Congress] party to survive all threats to the government at the centre in and outside Parliament. At times, inner-party developments have created doubts about the survivability of the government. But by combining inner-party democracy with discipline, Narasimha Raoji has belied such doubts whenever they have arisen.

Narasimha Rao's own description of himself and how he came to be where he was in June 1991 cannot be bettered. It reveals much of the man and how he thought of himself.

Indeed, it wouldn't be an exaggeration to say that Narasimha Rao actually was a man of many parts. Unfortunately, many of his personal accomplishments have remained hidden. That he was a polyglot was quite well known—fluent in Telugu, Marathi, Hindi, Sanskrit and Urdu; familiar with Arabic and Farsi; able to give interviews in Spanish; and capable of writing in French. What is less well known is his computer-savviness, which was next only to Rajiv Gandhi amongst politicians then. He was personally operating desktops in the late-1980s and was amongst the very first to start using laptops. I recall, he once saw a Taiwanese laptop with me, assembled in India by Zenith, and asked me to get two sets for him—he kept one and gave the other to Jitendra Prasada. What also isn't well known is that he was a tennis buff, with the Spaniard great, Manuel Santana, apparently being one of his favourites!

My abrupt exit from the PMO was not pleasant—at least not from my point of view. For quite some time I seethed in rage, even while keenly aware of the helplessness of my position. Yet, I could not but admire the man who was responsible for my expulsion, and who, in some ways, was the Chinese revolutionary Deng Xiaoping's counterpart in India. Both were old men. Both had their ups and downs (more downs than ups). But when the moment came, they seized the opportunity to leave their imprint—Rao did it in June 1991, and Deng did it first in 1978 and then, more famously, in 1992. In the case of Deng, it was a complete U-turn—moving away from Mao's hard-line policies, and combining the Communist Party's socialist ideology with a practical adoption of economic reform. In Rao's case, although he changed the paradigm of economic policy, the paradigm itself had been chopped away bit by bit for well over a decade, with the blueprint for change having been debated and discussed for a number of years.

Notwithstanding his many talents, it must be admitted that Narasimha Rao was a most puzzling man. Winston Churchill, the British premier, said of Clement Attlee, his successor, that he was 'a modest man, who has much to be modest about'. Similarly, it could well be said of Rao: he was a much misunderstood man and he may well have done much to be so misunderstood—especially by his own colleagues.

Rao was a complex personality, not at all easy to comprehend, and he made no effort whatsoever to make people want to understand him—except when he was on the back-foot. I was simply in no position to know what went wrong between him and his own party—a party he had served with distinction for almost half a century. I was an anguished witness to a most painful event on 24 January 1998 which showed how remarkably friendless Narasimha Rao had become within the Congress. The occasion was the release of the Congress' manifesto for the 1998 Lok Sabha elections. I was seated on the dias when, in response to a question, the Congress president, Sitaram Kesri, emphatically declared that his predecessor would not be put up as a candidate in the upcoming polls. It was a most jarring moment, and coming from someone who had been personally selected by Rao as a successor made it even more unpleasant. The manifesto sank without a trace as the only news to hit the headlines was the former prime minister's humiliation.

Narasimha Rao was indisputably a loner, a man who didn't do much to cultivate and build relationships. To borrow a phrase from Michael White's biography of Isaac Newton, Narasimha Rao was above all 'a secretive man, a man coiled in upon himself'.[90] Moreover, his relationships with the sleaziest of characters—Chandraswami being the most notable of them—which I saw at close quarters, were inexplicable and did no justice to a man of such erudition and learning. At one stage in the early days of his prime ministership, Chandraswami had convinced Narasimha Rao that India could easily tide over its immediate financial crisis because the godman's buddy, the Sultan of Brunei, had agreed to extend a line of credit to India at the most concessional terms without any questions asked. That the prime minister took this suggestion seriously is borne out by the fact that a plane was ready to fly the finance minister to meet the Sultan! Thankfully, Manmohan Singh managed to convince his boss at the last minute that this would be a foolhardy adventure.[91]

Some months after I had left the PMO, Madhavan Kutty, the veteran Malayali journalist drew my attention to a devastating article titled 'The Great Suicide' which had appeared in *Mainstream Weekly* in January 1990. The author was identified as a 'Congressman' and was described as a senior leader of the Congress (I). Madhavan Kutty was convinced—and told me it was everybody's view—that the real author was none other than Narasimha Rao himself. That Nikhil Chakravartty was the prime minister's close friend made me believe what I was being told. I have checked with a few others, and everyone, after reading the article, has ascribed its authorship to Narasimha Rao, although Mani Shankar Aiyar says that the possibility of the author being Siddhartha Shankar Ray, the erstwhile chief minister of West

---

[90]Michael White, *Isaac Newton: The Last Sorcerer* (New York: Fourth Estate, 1998).
[91]Some hilarious stories revolving around Chandraswami have been recounted by K. Natwar Singh in *Walking with Lions: Tales from a Diplomatic Past* (New Delhi: HarperCollins, 2012) and *One Life is Not Enough* (New Delhi: Rupa Publications, 2014). When asked about his friendship with the self-styled godman in an interview with Prabhu Chawla of *The Indian Express* on 8 July 1991, the prime minister said, 'I know the gentleman. He belongs to Hyderabad from where I also come. That's about all.' He was being disingenuous, to say the very least.

Bengal, had also been suggested when the article had first appeared. As far as the article itself was concerned, the very title said it all. It was a highly critical analysis of the Rajiv Gandhi era and Rajiv Gandhi himself—whose style of functioning was panned as brash, self-destructive and immature—and examined the reasons for the severe drubbing the Congress received in the 1989 Lok Sabha elections. The article amazed me no end because it highlighted Narasimha Rao's frustration with his late leader, a kind of exasperation that did not quite fit the image I had (or for that matter, anyone else had) of their relationship. I had heard nothing but encomiums from Narasimha Rao for Rajiv Gandhi in June, July and August 1991 when I had been at his side. But evidently, the very same man in 1990 deemed it fit to write bitingly about the then Congress president. Maybe it was a knee-jerk reaction to an ignominious defeat. Maybe, as Mani Shankar Aiyar has pointed out, it was the result of being sidelined. There is no clinching or conclusive evidence that Narasimha Rao was indeed a 'Congressman', but if he was, as he is widely suspected to be, there is reason to reassess the man and his relationship with his mentors.

Rao's problems truly started with the Harshad Mehta securities scam that first came to light in April 1992, and thereafter, with the demolition of the Babri Masjid on 6 December 1992, an event that many of his own party colleagues believe he helped orchestrate, or allowed to happen or, at the very least, knew of as it unfolded, without intervening decisively. Almost the entire Congress believes that he wanted the masjid out of the way so that a permanent solution to the imbroglio at Ayodhya could be found. I had called Rao around 4 p.m. that fateful Sunday before leaving for Mumbai with Pranab Mukherjee, only to be told that the prime minister '*andar hain* (is inside)'. Rao has offered an elaborate defence of himself in his book[92] that came out

---

[92]P.V. Narasimha Rao, *Ayodhya: 6 December 1992* (New Delhi: Penguin, 2006). Not surprisingly, Rao's media adviser P.V.R.K. Prasad's memoirs has much more information on Narasimha Rao's thoughts on Ayodhya and his actions than the prime minister provided in his account. See *Wheels Behind the Veil* (Hyderabad: Emesco Books, 2012). Other 'participant' accounts of the events leading up to 6 December 1992 are Arjun Singh, *A Grain of Sand in the Hourglass of Time* (New Delhi: Hay House, 2012) and M.D. Godbole, *Unfinished Innings* (New Delhi: Orient Blackswan, 1996). Godbole was

two years after his death. That defence cannot be ignored. There were many circumstances that did preclude him from imposing President's Rule in Uttar Pradesh in October or November 1992. But there is no doubt that the responsibility for ensuring that 6 December 1992 never happened was his and his alone, even if there may be different views on his culpability with regard to what transpired that day.

If Rao still remains compelling of our attention, even commendation, it is for the truly transformational leadership he demonstrated at a most precarious time in India's economic history. Of course, it could be argued that he had no choice and the alternative would have been to go down in history as the prime minister who presided over a default—but that would be tantamount to cavilling. Rao did not put a foot wrong forward in the initial months, and displayed both political maneuvering and statesmanship of the highest order.

Moments sometimes produce men (and women). Narasimha Rao is an outstanding example of this.

◆

Narasimha Rao's masterstroke was the appointment of Manmohan Singh. One of his closest aides later recalled to me that even as a cabinet minister, Rao always felt that a prime minister should always have one source of senior, substantive and non-political advice, especially in those areas where the prime minister is weak.[93] The aide also recalled Rao citing the precedent of D.R. Gadgil, who was deputy chairman of the Planning Commission between 1967 and 1971.

In Manmohan Singh, Narasimha Rao found a tailor-made bulwark. It is true that Rao had told his finance minister right at the very beginning, 'Manmohan, if things go wrong, your head is on the chopping block; if we succeed, the credit will be ours.' Notwithstanding this warning, and despite the enormous pressure and criticism he faced, Rao backed his finance minister to the hilt, allowing him full

---

union home secretary at that time.
[93]Interestingly, Narasimha Rao did not make Singh a member of the CWC—something that was done by his successor, Sitaram Kesri.

freedom, even when his instincts told him not to.

I have always believed that the personality of the finance minister has much to do with the degree to which economic reforms seem palatable in the initial months and years. Manmohan Singh made the years of liberalization appear acceptable, largely because he defied ideological labels, and could, if anything, only be called moderately left-of-centre. He was personally very close to politicians and economists of the left; Jyoti Basu treated him with enormous respect and, as I was to discover many years later, so did Harkishan Singh Surjeet. While the archpriest of the Left establishment during Indira Gandhi's era, P.N. Haksar[94] was one of his staunchest allies, Haksar's colleague, P.N. Dhar, who was generally considered right-of-centre, was also his trusted friend.

Besides, the credibility Manmohan Singh had across the political spectrum was obvious. While S.K. Goyal from the Chandra Shekhar era was his intimate associate, the debates in Parliament of those times reveal that Atal Bihari Vajpayee, L.K. Advani and Jaswant Singh, too, held him in the highest professional and personal esteem.

At critical moments, what is said and done might matter; but what truly counts is the person who is talking and how he presents his case. The finance minister may have lacked political standing, but he had unparalleled moral authority, apart from unsurpassed intellectual gravitas. His phenomenal personal reputation for simplicity and his non-threatening style helped sell the bitter pills of devaluation, gold sales, subsidy cuts and whole-scale industrial deregulation.

Manmohan Singh's integrity has always been unimpeachable and what better example than what he did after he and Rao had taken a decision to devalue the Indian rupee? Manmohan Singh was worried that his personal rupee balance, born out of modest dollar savings from his South Commission stint in Geneva during 1987–90, would swell with the proposed changes in the rupee–dollar exchange rate. Therefore, he informed the prime minister that the 'windfall' gains would be deposited in the Prime Minister's Relief Fund.

Would I.G. Patel have been unlike Manmohan Singh had he been

---

[94]P.N. Haksar was also Prime Minister Indira Gandhi's principal secretary.

finance minister? Substance-wise, decidedly not; but perhaps in style, here and there. Both I.G. Patel and Manmohan Singh had studied with distinction at Cambridge University. Both had doctorates in economics. Both had served in international institutions—IG at the IMF and the UNDP (United Nations Development Programme), and Manmohan Singh at UNCTAD (United Nations Conference on Trade and Development). Both had held key positions in the finance ministry; had been governors of the RBI;[95] and had served as part of academic institutions—IG at the London School of Economics and Singh at the Delhi School of Economics. Moreover, both were sensitive to political realities—with IG being a product of the Nehruvian 1950s and very early 1960s, and Singh being a product of the 1970s when he first came into contact with Indira Gandhi. The only difference between the two was that IG was considered to be more market-friendly and Manmohan Singh a little more state-friendly. It was only a nuance and nothing fundamental separated the two.

Two other appointments Narasimha Rao made proved to be very shrewd. Unfortunately, the same could not be said of his other appointments, especially in key infrastructure ministries. His choice of P. Chidambaram as commerce minister—although not at the full cabinet level but one notch lower—ensured that far-reaching trade policy reforms got executed very quickly. Although Chidambaram had not served in a mainstream economic ministry earlier, he took to the Commerce Ministry instantly and provided a bold thrust. More importantly, the finance minister found in him a very articulate ally to champion the cause of economic reform both at home and abroad.

The appointment of A.N. Verma as principal secretary was also fortuitous. Verma had wide experience both in the Commerce and Industry Ministries, commanded respect in the bureaucracy, had a low-key but effective style, and was able to execute the prime minister's instructions well.

◆

---

[95]Morarji Desai and H.M. Patel appointed I.G. Patel as governor of the RBI in 1977, and Indira Gandhi appointed Manmohan Singh to the same post five years later.

There is a Tolstoyan perspective of history which holds that individuals are irrelevant and circumstances create events. Another view is that individuals matter and do decisively shape the course of history. My own feeling is that what got accomplished in June–July 1991 was inevitable, if our goal was to avoid the opprobrium of default.

The Rao–Singh duo happened to be at the right place at the right time. They had neither bargained nor lobbied for the responsibilities they found themselves with; but there they were, saddled with onerous tasks.

'*Carpe diem,*' wrote Horace in his immortal *Odes*. This is exactly what the Rao–Singh jugalbandi did—they seized the day. There was no guarantee of success, and certainly no likelihood of quick positive outcomes; indeed, the results of the reforms started becoming evident only after 1993. Consequently, theirs was a huge leap of faith. It was, in fact, a gamble of sorts. The most risk-averse of gentlemen took this wager only because the alternative—namely a default—was an anathema to both. Besides, they were men intent on carving a distinctive niche for themselves in India's political and economic history.[96] And let there be no mistake about it—they definitely did.

To borrow an analogy from Isaiah Berlin, if Manmohan Singh was the hedgehog who knew only one big thing and that is economic

[96]Yashwant Sinha starts his memoirs, *Confessions of a Swadeshi Reformer* (New Delhi: Penguin, 2007) with a chapter entitled 'The Original Reformer?' The question mark is misleading because he makes a self-serving case for himself to be considered so, on four counts: (i) he was the first to introduce the concept of a fiscal deficit as opposed to a conventional budget deficit; (ii) he was the first to talk about public sector disinvestment; (iii) he talked about rationalizing expenditure on subsidies, reducing allocations on major subsidies and better targeting of subsidies for the poor; and (iv) he stated his commitment to fiscal discipline in an unambiguous manner. He overstates his case. It is true that he was the first to suggest public sector disinvestment which was to be implemented by later administrations, but the Rao–Singh claim to fame is based on much firmer and larger grounds. The Chandra Shekhar government wanted to introduce trade policy reforms but didn't. The Rao–Singh–Chidambaram troika did that and earned a permanent place in history for that accomplishment. Sinha never even mentions industrial policy reforms; actually during a debate in the Rajya Sabha on 7 August 1991, he was very critical of the industrial policy reforms announced on 24 July.

reforms, Rao was the fox who knew many things. It is this fox-hedgehog combine that rescued India in perhaps its darkest moment. India in 1991 could well have mirrored Greece in 2015. That it didn't is due to the Narasimha Rao and Manmohan Singh combine.

June–July 1991 was a revolution, but it was an evolutionary one—some years in the making. There was, no doubt, a huge element of chance in what Rao-Singh did, but as Louis Pasteur said, 'Chance favours only the prepared mind.' Narasimha Rao's political astuteness and Manmohan Singh's economic wisdom brought India back from the very brink. Together, they demonstrated that a consensus can, on occasion, be created by tough executive action. They proved that sometimes, if you listen intently but do what you have set out to do unwaveringly, accord can emerge. They converted an unprecedented crisis into a not-to-be-lost opportunity. Of course, circumstances were ripe for a mindset change, but more than being lucky by being there at the right time, they were plucky—they challenged set minds.

The hand of destiny took me close to Rao and Singh as they began saving the country. And although I remained in their vicinity for an exceedingly short while, I was privileged to play a small role—in the words of one of Rao's closest aides—in setting history in motion.

A Note of Thanks

I thank Pranab Mukherjee, Dr Manmohan Singh and M.L. Fotedar for extended conversations.

P.V. Rajeshwar Rao and P.V. Prabhakar Rao allowed me to see their father's private papers and spoke to me about people and events of those months. I am grateful to them for allowing me to use two of Narasimha Rao's unpublished pieces.

Montek Singh Ahluwalia, Mani Shankar Aiyar, Naresh Chandra and a very close aide of Narasimha Rao who prefers anonymity, have been liberal with their recollections.

Daman Singh gave me easy access to all her father's academic papers, speeches and interviews. Her own delightful *Strictly Personal: Manmohan and Gursharan* (New Delhi: HarperCollins, 2014) has important recollections of Manmohan Singh on his tenure as finance minister.

Pramath Sinha gave me whatever papers A.N. Verma had left behind. Sumit Chakravartty was most helpful in locating his father's articles that appeared in *Mainstream*.

Vinay Sitapati—whose much-needed comprehensive biography of Narasimha Rao will be published soon—and I have had useful chats. Sanjaya Baru, who is also writing a book on Narasimha Rao, encouraged me to write this account saying, 'This is the least you can do for our Telugu PM, considering we Telugus sent you to the Rajya Sabha for two terms!' The persistent insistence of Ritu Vajpeyi-Mohan of Rupa made this recollection possible.

The originals of all the primary and secondary sources used or quoted in this book have been deposited with the Nehru Memorial Museum and Library.

I asked Naresh Chandra—amongst the most impressive of civil servants I have known over the past three decades and more—why he had not penned his memoirs after almost half-a-century of distinguished service to the nation. He said that he was against self-glorification and that any honest account must also include mistakes made. I hope I have avoided the first and have been candid about the second!

Finally, why this memoirs-of-sorts at this time? For two reasons, really. First, the twenty-fifth anniversary of the July 1991 reforms is approaching and I thought this would be an appropriate occasion to look back and place what I saw and knew in the public domain. Second, after the Congress' electoral debacle in 2014, I found myself in need of worthwhile things to do to keep myself intellectually busy. Therefore, after two books on my stint as environment and forest minister and on the 2013 land acquisition law, this one appears. I thought there was an interesting *story* to tell and that is what I have tried to do, without attempting 'to etch my name like a schoolboy on a small tree in the forest that is history'.[97]

---

[97]This phrase is borrowed from the introduction to H.Y. Sharada Prasad, *The Book I Won't be Writing and Other Essays* (New Delhi: Chronicle Books, 2003).

ANNEXURES

Annexure 1: A discussion paper on new industrial policy initiatives the author had been asked to prepare in September 1986 in the Planning Commission

Annexure 2: Note prepared by Pranab Mukherjee on the economic situation for a meeting of the Congress Working Committee on 19 February 1991

Annexure 3: Pranab Mukherjee's interview in *The Times of India*, given on 20 June 1991, the day before Narasimha Rao and Manmohan Singh were sworn in

Annexure 4: Two interviews of Finance Minister Manmohan Singh to Paranjoy Guha Thakurta in *Sunday*, 14-20 July and 4-10 August 1991, given as reforms were happening

Annexure 5: Statement issued by P.N. Dhar, I.G. Patel, M. Narasimham and R.N. Malhotra on 1 July 1991

Annexure 6: Statement issued by thirty-five 'left oriented' economists on 8 July 1991 and reprinted in *Mainstream*, 13 July 1991

Annexure 7: The West Bengal government's proposal to resolve the balance-of-payments crisis, made public on 4 July 1991 and sent to the prime minister and finance minister a few days thereafter; reprinted in *Mainstream*, 20 July 1991

Annexure 8: Cover of the booklet issued on Narasimha Rao's address to the nation on 9 July 1991, that is not included in his *Selected Speeches*, Volume 1

Annexure 9: An unpublished paper by Narasimha Rao titled 'Liberalisation and the Public Sector', prepared in February–March 2001, made available from his archives by his youngest son, P.V. Prabhakar Rao

Annexure 10: Interview of Dr K.N. Raj to *Frontline* in mid-July 1991 that greatly bolstered the confidence of the prime minister and finance minister

A discussion paper on new industrial policy initiatives the author had been asked to prepare in September 1986 in the Planning Commission

A DISCUSSION PAPER

ON

NEW INDUSTRIAL POLICY INITIATIVES

I.   Introduction

Over the past fifteen months, a number of initiatives have been taken to simplify the industrial policy framework. The focus of these measures has been to make it easier for entrepreneurs to obtain licences and approvals from the Central Government to invest or to expand. This is necessary, but not sufficient. A much broader and bolder thrust is needed if industry is to move to a higher growth profile of 8-10% per year. This thrust would involve greater, not less reliance on planning; increased, not diminished state intervention.

II.   Investment Levels

2.   The stagnation in industrial growth after the mid-1960s has been attributed, among other things, to a slowdown in public investment. It is true that public investments recorded low growth rates during the Annual Plan and Fourth Plan periods. However, since then public investment has increased substantially in absolute and relative terms. Public investment has increased over the past decade from 7.7% of GDP in 1971-74 to 11.7% in 1981-84. The composition of investment has also changed in a manner designed to alleviate critical bottlenecks to industrial expansion. The Table below portrays the change in public investment during the last decade :-

Average Annual Public Investment

(percentages based on 1970/71 prices)

	Percent of GDP			Percent of Investment			
	IV Plan	V Plan	VI Plan	IV Plan	V Plan	VI Plan	VII Plan (projected)
1 Agriculture	0.9	1.1	1.1	12.2	12.0	12.2	12.7
2 Manufacturing	1.4	1.9	2.2	18.8	21.0	15.4	12.5
3 Energy	1.4	2.0	2.9	18.9	22.1	27.2	30.5
4 Transport + Communications	2.0	1.9	2.0	27.5	20.7	15.9	16.4

3.   As will be observed because of the rising ratio of public investment to GDP, none of the major sectors has actually experienced a significant decline in public investment relative to GDP over the past decade. However, three

aspects of public investment policies requiring attention need to be highlighted :-

(i)   although the energy sector has not been starved of essential invest-
        ment as it was in the late 1960s and early 1970s, within the energy
        sector itself imbalances have arisen. For instance, investments
        in establishment of new and modernisation of existing transmission
        and distribution facilities have severely lagged behind investments
        in power generation facilities. The Department of Power should
        prepare a system-wise analysis of the reasons why T&D facilities
        have not expanded at a pace required and identify measures to
        accelerate this pace;

(ii)   increases in investment levels have not been accompanied by com-
        mensurate increases in efficiency of utilisation. This is particularly
        so in the power and coal sectors where the scope for improving
        capacity utilisation and enhancing productivity is still substantial.
        It has been over a year since the Power Rehabilitation Fund was
        established. The Department of Power should prepare a review
        of how this scheme is working so that plant-level constraints to
        higher capacity utilisation are better appreciated. Similarly, the
        BICP report on the Coal Industry of 1983 had identified measures
        to enhance capital productivity in the coal mining industry. The
        Department of Coal should prepare a note highlighting the extent
        to which the recommendations of the BICP study, as also that
        of subsequent studies relating to increasing productivity, have
        been implemented;

(iii)   the high priority given to the energy and manufacturing sectors
        over the Fifth and Sixth Plan periods has implied a corresponding
        decline in the share of public resources allocated to public invest-
        ment in transport and communications during the last decade as
        compared to the preceding decade. The overall rate of public invest-
        ment in transport and communications has barely been maintained
        at about 2% of GDP. This sector not only provides essential infra-
        structural inputs to industrial expansion but also serves as a source
        of demand for Indian industry.

4.   Thus, while in the macroeconomic perspective, the increase in the
levels of investment is impressive, it has still not kept pace with what is required. Power, railways and communications are three outstanding examples
where this situation prevails and where a step-up in the levels of investment
would be called for. In the case of power and communications, there would
be a strong case for premitting private investment as well. A clear policy in
this regard needs to be announced and conditions under which private corporate

investment would be permitted made public by the concerned administrative departments. Private entrepreneurs have expressed an interest in power and telecommunications. A final view on the proposals already submitted to Government should be taken by the CCEA over the next one month.

5.   Having said this, it must be admitted that substantial further increases in the share of public investment in GDP would be very difficult to attain. Raising the level of public investment in GDP is, of course, possible through higher borrowing rates. Suffice to say here, this option would present its own problems, not the least being the risk of generating inflationary pressures. Thus, in the overall to expect significantly larger proportions of public investment would be unrealistic. This applies particularly to the energy sector where the increases in investment witnessed in the past decade would be difficult to sustain in the next. In this context, it becomes imperative to look at the energy-intensity of our development strategy. By making deliberate choices of technology and location in agriculture, industry and transport, it is possible to reduce the pressure on the energy system without implying any sacrifice in terms of growth objectives. The Advisory Board on Energy should be asked to conduct a detailed sectoral analysis of energy-intensity and efficiency and come up with a programme of action designed to reduce the energy-intensity of the economy. Since a lot of information is already available, it should be possible to complete this exercise in about two months time.

III.   Agriculture–Industry Link

6.   Another factor influencing the rate of industrial growth is the rate of growth of agriculture. It has been estimated that a 1% growth rate in agriculture can, by itself, generate a rate of growth of 0.5% in industry. This is a strong influence considering that industrial growth is not totally dependent on what happens in agriculture. The present note does not discuss this issue specifically. There are hopeful signs and far-reaching developments taking place, notwithstanding the fact that foodgrain output has growth at a trend rate of 2.5% per annum between 1967/68 and 1983/84, which amounts to a modest but positive trend growth of 0.25% per annum in per capita terms. However, a higher trend growth of 3.4% per annum in foodgrain output between 1978/79 and 1983/84 - the last two record harvests - and the quite modest production shortfall in the severe 1982/83 drought are positive indicators. In addition, some backward areas are developing fast. Growth in fertiliser consumption, a good index of growth agricultural prosperity, is no longer a localised phenomenon and substantial increases have taken place in States like UP, West Bengal, Karnataka and Gujarat which were earlier regarded as laggards. Output growth and fertiliser use growth in Haryana may now be comparable with that in Eastern UP, even though the surplus per worker is still low. This opens up new

opportunities for Indian industry to market goods and services, opportunities that have to be systematically identified and exploited. However, it must be admitted that Indian business has, for the most part, not shown either the inclination for or exhibited any great expertise in rural marketing. This will have to change.

7.   It also hardly bears reiteration that mere acceleration in the rate of agricultural output would not result in expansion of industrial output. More important is the creation of incomes. A large proportion of demand for industrial products still originates from a narrow segment of the population. This is one factor that could militate against sustained increase in industrial output. National Sample Survey statistics indicate that the top 10% of the rural population accounts for 38% of the rural consumption of industrial goods. This appears to have remained more or less at this level over several NSS Rounds. How the bulk of increments in agricultural incomes should be prevented from being appropriated by a few, is an issue that leads to an examination of broader issues relative to terms of trade, fundamental structural features of our agrarian structure and institutional frameworks. It is not just agricultural incomes that matter. Perhaps, we should now consciously plan for increasing incomes from off-farm activities also, the potential for which is considerable. For example, we have really not exploited the potential that economic activities like afforestation, and agricultural residue processing have to offer not only for generating employment but also for creating new wealth on a dispersed basis. All these issues relating to the agriculture-industry nexus need to systematically analysed. The Department of Agriculture should arrange for this to be carried out in consultation with other Departments like the Development Commissioner, Small Scale Industries, Department of Rural Development and the Department of Non-Conventional Energy Sources. A discussion note should be ready in about two months time.

IV.   Important Policy Initiatives

8.   Before identifying certain critical areas requiring policy intervention, it is necessary to highlight the total inadequacy of the industrial information system. The Index of Industrial Production, the most widely quoted indicator of industrial growth, is definitely misleading in terms of the magnitude and sometimes even the direction of growth, even for the registered manufacturing sector of Indian industry. The problems that plague the Index have been well-documented but efforts to rectify the lacunae have not been forthcoming in full measure and in a speedy fashion. The bulk of official effort has been directed towards changing the base year of the Index from 1970 to 1980/81. This task itself has taken well over five years and is still not complete. Even so, with the change in base year, the Index would still not be representative of

the entire Indian industrial economy and would impart a downward bias to industrial output. A thorough overhaul and revamp of the Central Statistical Organisation is called for, for as it is presently structured, staffed and funded, it is unlikely to provide a true leadership role and deliver meaningful information on time. A High-Level Committee should be appointed and asked to report in three months time on measures required to completely modernise the management and organisation aspects of the CSO's functioning. Meanwhile, it is imperative that between the CSO and the Ministry of Industry, the structural problems that persist with the Index relating to coverage and returns be addressed on a time-bound basis.

9.   Apart from the Index itself, the information system to monitor impact of various policy measures is also inadequate. The data available readily relates mainly to letters of intent, licences, registrations, collaborations. It is well known that historically less than a third of these entrepreneurial intentions to invest have actually been converted into projects that expand job opportunities and increase output. And where they have, the gestation period is not less than three to four years. Admittedly, the establishment of such an information system that provides access to field-level impact is a difficult task since it would involve interaction with various agencies and institutions at the Central and State Government levels. But a beginning has to be made somewhere. The Ministry of Industry should consider engaging the services of a professional consultancy company that would examine this in detail. This examination could also include an analysis of how the various "single windows" set up by the States to expedite project implementation are actually functioning in practice.

10.   Some important areas for future initiatives in the field of industrial policy directly that would lead to an acceleration in the rate of output growth are discussed below. The discussion is necessarily selective and is confined to a few critical issues. Not discussed are issues relating to procedures and the day-to-day manner in which the new industrial policies are being implemented. There is still great scope for simplification and streamlining of procedures. This should be under constant review.

    (i)   **Market Structure :** Competition and the progress of liberalisation is still judged in terms of number of companies, number of licences, number of registrations, number of new entrants. This is misguided, to say the least. It is a mistake to think that competition arises only when there are 20-30 companies producing a product. It is not really the extent of competition as much as the nature of competition that is going to determine whether objectives relating to cost reduction and technology upgradation are going to be met. this swing from one extreme of controls and regulations to the other extreme of permitting a 'free for all' in many technology-intensive industries has resulted in fragmentation of capacities, that would, in turn, only result in high costs. An appreciation of market structure would involve acceptance of an oligopoly in many technology-intensive industries. This simply means that a few (between 5-8) procedures would control the market and would aggressively fight it out for establishing their market share. Competition can also be ensured through appropriate tariff policies. For instance, the world over in industries like synthetic fibres and telecommunications, four to five large companies control the market and there is intense technological competition among them. We should not fight shy of saying that in sectors like synthetic fibres, telecommunications, TVs, automobile components and electronic components, Government policy would be to encourage only a few parties establishing production facilities at truly efficient scales of plant. In selected items of consumer electronics, for example, production at international scales could reduce prices by as much as 60%. Demand growth for output of the most recent products at international costs would be rapid. The trend, unfortunately, has just been the opposite. Where fragmentation has already taken place, we must now remove all barriers to expansion by the top four or five firms and actively encourage them, through fiscal mechanisms, to effect speedy mergers, amalgamations and takeovers. The Ministry of Industry should be asked to prepare a paper to review what changes would be required in the MRTP and Companies Acts to facilitate this.

In these technology-intensive industries, the approach should be to invite composite proposals from entrepreneurs that would encompass capital goods, technology, location and other factors. The applications should be invited simultaneously so that Government is then in a position to take a final view in the matter of which parties should be permitted to produce. An approach of this kind has been attempted by the Ministry of Industry in the field of VCRs. This is an approach worth adopting in other areas as well. The Ministry of Industry should now be asked to identify a few sectors where fragmentation has taken place and work out detailed schemes to ensure that only the truly efficient plants come up. This exercise could start with EPABX where some 40 licences have already been issued.

A second aspect of market structure that should be of concern is in regard to policies that discourage growth of companies. Our policy today is to allow a company which has a cement plant to set up one TV facility, to set up one VCR facility, to go into fertilisers, to go into refineries and so on. While horizontal dispersion is being encouraged actively, there are severe barriers that have been put on companies to grow in size in the same field of activity. From a technology point of view, a company that is horizontally diffused will hardly have any incentive to invest in any meaningful R&D. We should be actively allowing a large company to grow.

For this major modifications will have to be introduced in the MRTP Act to permit large companies to become truly international giants. The Ministry of Industry should have this matter studied.

A third aspect of market structure emanating from the inevitability of monopolies (both in the public sector and private sectors) and oligopolies in some sectors is the need to have a new approach to the concept of monopoly control. A much more vigorously enforcible restrictive trade practices approach is needed. Such an MRTP Act should control the abuse of dominance and size power. Since this has major political ramifications, we should consider constituting a High Level Committee, broad-based in its composition, that would redefine and redesign the MRTP Act ab initio so as to also provide for an effective Restrictive Trade Practices Act embracing all classes and sizes of enterprises.

(ii) **Market Development :** Major policy initiatives are required to give a boost to demand and consumption to complement the supply-side liberalisation that is taking place today. The focus of such initiatives should be to enable a faster growth of efficiently produced mass consumer goods so that within a reasonable period, every household is provided with the necessities of life at the cheapest possible price with the best available technology in the world. The prime example of this is textiles. It is possible to double the production of textiles in India by roughly halving the prices so that Indian textile prices approximately match international prices during the next eight to ten years. The country will be able to supply the raw cotton required. The prices of hydrocarbon feedstock and that of intermediate inputs will need to be rationalised and reorganised. Existing producers will be required to reorient scales and costs of production. The threat of imports will have to be used judiciously to push them in that direction. The performance of private sector textile industries will need to be monitored and if, as is possible, the private sector does not respond, investments may have to be organised on a joint sector basis. The Bureau of Industrial Costs and Prices should be asked to examine this example of textiles further and suggest a detailed input and intermediate price rationalisation scheme that would result in a reduction of consumer prices. A similar exercise can be carried out in other areas like plastics, which have enormous potential for use in our economy.

In some sectors, demand stimulation would come about not just by fiscal reforms, but by legal changes, for instance. A good example of this is the cement industry, which is dependent on a major spurt in housing activity. Housing is required in itself, but its growth has been stymied on account of restrictions on transfer of land in urban areas and rent control legislations. Once these reforms are made, with better taxation policies and easier flow of institutional finance, the expansion of housing can be very rapid. Proposals in this regard for treating housing as an industry have often been made, but a final decision has yet to be taken. This should be expedited. It is also time to take a whole new look at our construction industry and see whether there is scope for introducing new technology without adversely affecting prospects for labour absorption. This would, incidentally, be of great relevance to hydel project planning as well. The Ministry of Works and Housing should set up a group to examine this issue further and report back in three months time.

Some important industries like tractors and commercial vehicles are credit-driven. A large part of the demand in these industries is dependent on the flow of institutional finance. However, there has been no stable policy in this regard. This has led to sluggish market conditions. There is need for more liberal and stable credit policy, apart from the fact that the use of manufacturers themselves as intermediaries in financing would also give a fillip to sales. Another aspect of demand stimulation particularly in the commercial vehicle industry has to do with the role of the private sector in public transport. Since the same chassis is used for both freight and passenger transport and since the burgeoning demand for passenger services is unlikely to be met by State-run undertakings alone, both in qualitative and quantative terms, the entry of the private sector in this field would not only boost off-take but would also fulfil a vital public service. This is an issue that has been discussed in the draft automotive sector policy document prepared by the Ministry of Industry which requires urgent consideration.

In some sectors like aluminium the country is going to be in a surplus shortly. But insufficient attention has been paid to market development. In the particular case of aluminium it is unlikely that the rapid increase in market penetration would result with our existing policy of restricting the entry of primary metal producers into other areas. For instance, primary producers are now allowed to manufacture semi-fabs upto 50% of metal capacity (not production); semi-fabs are taken to include electrical rods and wirebars. This needs review by the Department of Mines.

Yet another instrument of demand stimulation that has to be used is procurement policy. This has particular relevance in the capital goods industry. For instance, the railways and the defence industries are going to be larger purchaser of machine tools worth over Rs. 300/400 crores in the next 3-4 years. Unless there is a definite procurement policy and unless orders are placed in advance, domestic industry is not going to grow and demand is going to be met through imports. This would have a detrimental impact. It goes without saying that a procurement policy has to be a part of the overall policy encompassing an appropriate tariff regime that provides adequate and fair protection to Indian manufacturers. Today, the tariff regime is weighted heavily against domestic manufacturers and it is reflected in the growth patterns. For instance, the non-electrical machinery sector grew by 0.5% in 1985/86, whereas it is projected to grow by about 8% in the Seventh Plan period. The Ministry of Industry has recently prepared a detailed note outlining a comprehensive policy package for the Indian Capital Goods Industry. This needs to be considered and implemented expeditiously. Also, special consideration needs to be given to measures required for effecting a more permanent and mutually supporting linkage between investment planning in the defence sector and the non-defence sector. A Committee should be constituted by the Ministry of Defence and the Planning Commission to study this matter and report back in three months time.

(iii) **Raw Material Prices :** Indian industry cannot sustain a high growth rate and also be internationally competitive at the present prices of domestically available raw materials. We should take four or five major raw materials that are critical to the industrial economy and undertake a major exercise in seeing how their prices can be brought down to domestic producers. This initial list could include steel, aluminium, copper, naptha and gas. In the case of aluminium, decontrol is an option to be considered seriously. In the case of steel, it is possible to lower steel prices by about 20% immediately by abolishing various levies and duties. In the medium and long-term there appears to be no alternative except to supply Indian industry with raw materials and components at international prices, particularly in situations where it is confronted with competition from imported supplies. A number of studies have demonstrated that the competitive disadvantage of Indian firms in many items of manufacture in the capital goods industry, for example, arise out of in-built disadvantages from the fact that they pay over two times more for raw materials and components than their international competitors. In terms of conversion costs Indian industry appears to be, by and large, competitive. The BICP should be asked to prepare a specific plan for rationalisation of price for the five basic raw materials mentioned above. A surcharge on imports may also have to be considered to keep any rationalisation revenue-neutral.

(iv) **Modernisation :** Modernisation must pay and be profitable to the firm undertaking it. With our existing credit, fiscal and labour policies, it will not. Hence, the lukewarm attitude towards modernisation in spite of its obvious need to reduce costs. The IDBI should be asked to carry out a comprehensive review of why in spite of various funds being available, the pace of modernisation has lagged behind. The example of the cement industry would be instructive in framing policies towards modernisation. It is only when cement units were allowed to generate resources internally that the process of modernisation received a boost. No amount of funds and soft loans are going to be lasting solutions; ultimately the firm has to be in a position to generate resources and plough it back for modernisation and new technology. The economic environment (e.g., prices, depreciation principles) has to be conducive to modernisation. The subsidy-approach to modernisation will not be tenable in the long-run.

In many resource-intensive industries, electronic instrumentation controls are beginning to make their mark in a big way. As an example, in the most modern electronically process-controlled factories, sugar conversion costs can be up to Rs. 1.50 per kg lower than in an inefficient unit. Microprocessor-based instrumentation can save up to a quarter of energy costs in energy-intensive industries like fertiliser and cement. It is necessary to have a detailed industry-specific perspective prepared to see how modern technologies can be utilised in the most of traditional of industries to cut production costs and thereby prices to the final consumers. To begin with, we could consider microprocessor-based systems and applications—specific integrated circuits. The Department of Electronics should be asked to take a few important industries - sugar, textiles, leather, paper, transport, power stations - and to prepare a detailed investment plan for the introduction of such technologies.

Even the most traditional and backward of industries can be modernised effectively and made competitive if an opportunity is given to introduce technologies that are now commercially available to cut production costs and diversify into new lines. The jute industry, for instance, could be effectively modernised if its capacity were used for extrusion to manufacture HPDE/PP woven sacks. This should be studied further by the Department of Chemcials and Petrochemicals in consultation with the Department of Textiles and the State Government concerned.

(v) **Infrastructural Bottlenecks :** The dimensions of infrastructural bottelnecks, particularly in regard to power, are well understood at the macro-level, but it is at the micro-level that it has to be tackled. Five States in the country - UP, Karnataka, Haryana, Tamil Nadu and Bihar - that account for about one-third of national manufacturing output, face energy shortages of well over 10%. These shortages are not likely to be alleviated over the next five years. The problem is particularly acute in the States of Haryana and Karnataka. In most industrially advanced States like Maharashtra and Gujarat, the problem is less one of base-load shortages than one of peaking shortages. In some States like Orissa, which in the aggregate contributes just about 2% to national manufacturing output, the issue of power is particularly important because of the strategic nature of the user industries. Already a production loss of about 140,000 tonnes of saleable steel has been reported in the first two months of 1986/87 on account of power shortages of Orissa. In the short and medium-term, there appears to be no alternative to the use of hydrocarbon fuels as sources of peaking power in some States and as a source of base-load power in States like Haryana and Karnataka. This would mean a postponement of investment decisions in regard to petrochemicals, for the same product that can be used as feedstock can also be used as fuel. But such conscious choices have to be made because in the ultimate analysis, petrochemicals are tradable commodities, whereas power is not. Specific proposals for hydrocarbon fuel-based utility power generation in Haryana and Karnataka have been waiting a decision by the Centre for quite some time now. These need to be expedited. This would be far better than sanctioning individual diesel generating sets as we are doing today.

The States play an important role in providing infrastructure and support facilities for industrialisation. However, not much planning is being done for the efficient provision of such infrastructure. We know of areas within States where drinking water is scarce but water for industrial use is available. States compete with each other to provide such facilities to attract industries. The real question lies in another direction. If the available resources for infrastructure are to be stretched to the maximum, power-intensive industries must locate close to the sources of cheap power, water-intensive industries and processes close to plentiful sources of water and so on. We neither give industry the proper signals nor follow appropriate pricing policies which would then give the correct signals to prospective entrepreneurs. In many cases regions which are well-endowed with resources are classified as backward areas and pricing policies which do not reflect resource endowments discriminate against such resource-rich areas. The point is that industrialisation perspectives should be related to local resource bases, instead of industries being "attracted" to any region without considering resource and environment costs. This issue is discussed later. Suffice to say here, each State must have an industrial location policy of its own - a policy that is clear in terms of the types of industries it wants to attract and how these should be dispersed within the State. Perhaps, a special meeting of the National Development Council should be convened to discuss this and catalyse the States into formulating and implementing dispersal policies.

(vi) Investment Patterns : While the industrial investment climate is certainly buoyant, certain key sectors are not attracting investment either for modernisation and technology upgradation or for new production facilities. The bulk of proposed corporate investment is in the consumer electronics and petrochemical areas. Foremost amongst those that are not attracting new investment on the scale required is the engineering industry which accounts for a weight of over 30 in the Index of Industrial Production. If this industry is not going to grow and become competitive, overall growth rates are going to be brought down. A mix of tariff, procurement, fiscal and credit policies will be needed to attract investment, sustain profitability and ensure continued growth of the engineering industry. Recent policies changes, however, militate against this. The lack of adequate and fair tariff protection, the continuation of the project imports scheme, the continued import of second-hand machinery, the growting use of turn-key offers and the discontinuation of the the Investment

Allowance Scheme would all dampen the growth of the engineering industry. In response to a directive from PM, the Ministry of Industry has recently prepared a note suggesting steps to create a healthy growth environment for the capital goods sector. This needs to be considered and decisions taken quickly.

The emerging imbalances also point to the need to move away from the generalized across-the-board liberalisation that has been attempted so far to a more detailed sector-specific liberalisation and policy reform. This has already been done in the case of electronics, sugar and textiles, although only in the case of sugar and to a far lesser extent electronics, can reform be considered "successful" so far. The electronics sector presents a case study of phenomenal output growth, falling prices in some areas like computers but little domestic value-based and less-than-desirable indigenisation levels. This must be avoided by the rigid enforcement and constant monitoring of stricter phased manufacturing programmes and import duty rationalisation to force a shift away from screw-driver operations. There are many other important industries in need of policy change - capital goods, automotive components, pharmaceuticals, alcohol being some examples.

(vii) Capital Market : The growth in the capital market over the past three years has been very impressive. Still, certain basic issues need to be addressed if further growth is not to be choked and if industry is to raise increased resources from the investing public, as it must. First, the question of pricing of shares : with proper pricing at least 50% more capital can be raised from the public. Second, the question of development of the secondary market in shares and debentures particularly outside outside the four metropolitan cities : in the absence of such a market, potential investors are turning to other investments like fixed deposits, real estate and gold. Third, the question of stability : institutional reforms like the establishment of a Securities and Exchanges Commission are needed to inspire confidence in new investors and to ensure that the stock market will grow in a healthy manner. The Finance Ministry should set up an Expert Group to examine these three and other related issues and come up with a CCEA note by the end of 1986.

(viii) Small-Scale Industries : A more aggressive policy towards small scale industrialisation linked with organised industry needs to be implemented. Such growth does not necessarily come from "reservation" but from improved local planning, infrastructure and technology support policies. It is in this context that the whole issue of ancillarisation and sub-contracting as a means of developing the small-scale sector assumes importance. In response to a suggestion made by PM, the Ministry of Industry is setting up a Group to examine what policies are required to accelerate the process of ancillarisation and sub-contracting in Indian industry. This Group should submit its report by the end of 1986. This should form a valuable input into the planning process for the future growth of small-industry.

In response to a directive from PM, an exercise has already been initiated in the Ministry of Industry to identify those items reserved for the smallscale sector for whom the asset limit could be raised from Rs. 35 lakhs to Rs. 75 lakhs - Rs. 1 crore. This needs to be done to enable the small entrepreneurs to invest in technology modernisation (including quality control) without fear of losing fiscal concessions. This exercise needs to be expedited and a list of industries should be announced soon.

Since 1972 there has been a justifiable demand for introducing a Limited Partnerships Act in India along the lines in vogue in UK and Japan. This would expand the equity base of small enterprises and increase the availability of risk capital necessary specially for technology-based new ventures. The Finance Ministry should be asked to examine the feasibility of introducing such an Act in the 1987/88 Budget.

Use of modern cybernetics and communications technologies are opening up new patterns of industrialisation of relevance to India. It affords an opportunity for us to leapfrog. Computer-integrated manufacturing (CIM) is a nifty way of allowing manufacturing capacity to be spinkled lightly across the country, instead of being concentrated heavily in targeted areas. Flexible manufacturing plants are ideal not just for industrial giants but even more so for the tens of thousands of tiny workshops. The full implications of this are still being understood even in countries like USA. The Planning Commission in consultation with the Ministry of Industry, should commission a conceptual study to understand the full implications of this revolutionary change in technique, on scales of production and location as applicable in the Indian context.

No discussion on the small-scale sector would be complete without a reference to village and cottage industries. It would not be wrong to say that in spite of having had a number of committees examine this subject and having established a number of institutions, a definite strategy for the development of village and cottage industries is still lacking. The number of those seeking a living in this sector is dwindling. The statistics show that whereas the absolute number of those employed in the village and cottage industries sector is falling, the employment has certainly increased in some fields involving further provision of primary products and basic materials (for example garment making). On the other hand, employment in the primary production sectors like handlooms, knitting and leather has fallen. There are new lines of employment developing in this important sector. If we simultaneously seek to improve every industry, we shall flounder badly and will be able to cover non satisfactorily. Out of the large number of industries, it should be possible to select those which at present engage a large number of artisans. It would also be necessary to select from the present experience the new fields of growth where the production can be vastly improved and marketed. Sericulture, Tassar culture, Lac culture, garment-making, jewellery and stone-ware appear to be fields with potential. The Sivaraman Committee had suggested that emphasis be laid on industries like food and tobacco products, edible and non-edible oils, beverages, textiles, footwear, non-metallic mineral products and carpentary in addition to the fields identified above. The Committee had also pointed out that there is a tremendous lack of organisation and technical expertise in most of the village and cottage industries. A committee has been constituted by the Ministry of Industry to review the functioning of KVIC. This Committee would, no doubt, make a number of recommendations to make KVIC's role more effective, and broad-based going beyond the preoccupation with Khadi alone. However, this in itself would not be sufficient and some fundamental rethinking is necessary.

Our rural industrialisation programme has not had the desired impact. A far more technology-intensive approach that integrates on-farm and off-farm activities in a mutually supporting manner is required. To begin with, IDBI and NABARD should take a few districts where dryland agriculture predominates and experiment with such an approach. A lot of piecemeal activity is going on presently. The Department of Rural Development should coordinate the setting up of a Group that would review these activities and suggest a more effective long-term approach to rural industrialisation.

(ix)   Location : An element of selectivity has to be introduced in our locational policies in deciding which industries to disperse and where to disperse. Industries with low backward and forward linkage, coefficient and capital-intensive industries should come up in such locations where, from an economic point of view, their cost would be the lowest. What would need to be guarded against when approving their location is that they do not pose any kind of a hazard through the risks of pollution or accidental leakages of poisonous substances.

In regard to industries which continue to be subject to industrial licensing, efforts will no doubt continue to make them go to the areas and districts which are less industrialised than others, but a number of questions will have to be faced. Is it really desirable that medium and large scale industries (as distinct from small-scale, village and handicraft industries or delicensed industries which choose them of their own accord) should be located in every district of India? Even in the most highly industrialised countries, there are vast green areas where people live on agriculture and allied activities, including agro-based and small-scale industries which have no large industries belching smoke or polluting the water. Many of our hill stations make good incomes out of tourists.

Some positive developments relating to dispersal have taken place. There were only 35 industrial centres employing 25,000+ workers in the non-household manufacturing sector in 1971. This went up to 57   in 1981. If we can double this number in this decade and have new centres with 25,000+ jobs created in backward regions, a sustained process of structural change would have been initiated. Manufacturing employment of 25,000+ means a city size of 1.5 lakh, and the essence of viable strategy of regional development is to concentrate on viable development with minimum size. Such developments will need coordination of policies between the Centre and the States and are not just a question of licensing, but active promotional policies. Following the work of the Shivaraman Committee, about 60 centres can be identified in the existing backward areas, in which the target of industrialisation in each would be an additional manufacturing employment of 30,000-50,000 workers over the next 5-10 years. The selection of these centres should be done in a manner such that the cost of provision of the essential infrastruture by the States is minimised in relation to local resource endowments.

So far, the issue of new location has been raised. Equally import is the issue of relocation. The classic example of this being the Bombay Textile Mills who could generate all the resources required for their modernisation if they are allowed to relocate to less congested areas. There are obvious political overtones but we should explore some practical way of such decongestion which is politically acceptable as well. The Ministry of Industry could be asked to prepare a discussion paper on these alternatives.

(x) **Technology Development :**   Recently, Government has announced policy measures to accelerate the process of technology absorption in Indian industry. This is a long-awaited move and must be monitored vigorously by the DGTD. However, many more issues remain. First, in regard to specific technology missions in the industrial sector, the Ministry of Industry in consultation with the Planning Commission, must finalise in all respects a set of crucial technology missions. There must be three types of missions - technology application missions where the focus is on the rapid acquisition of commercially available technology from whatever source and its introduction into key industries to cut costs and enhance productivity, technology development missions where the focus is slightly over a longer period to develop technology ourselves in areas where technology suitable to our needs is not easily available and futuristic missions where the focus is on building up a strong indigenous R&D infrastructure in key areas that are going to be important in the next fifteen to twenty years. This exercise must be complete by the end of 1986 so that we are in a position to launch them early next year.

A Committee has already been constituted to review the functioning of CSIR. The Committee's recommendations, it is to be hoped, would cover measures required to forge a more effective and durable linkage between the research and production systems. A similar Committee needs to be established to examine the nature of linkages that should be fostered betwen the DRDO (Defence Research and Development Organisation) and the production system.

A number of incentives are needed to promote not just R&D but also the successful commercialisation of indiginous R&D. These incentives would relate to licensing policy liberalisations and fiscal policy measures like weighted tax benefits and accelerated depreciation. The Ministry of Industry should come up with a CCEA note in about a months time detailing a package of incentives to give the proper signals to Indian companies in regard to R&D. An important element of our R&D strategy should be the development of engineering design companies. A large base has been built up over the years particularly in the field of petrochemicals, refining and thermal power. Yet we lack a clear policy on how to improve the quality of work and how to enable these companies to emerge as international giants selling not just man-hours but also technology. In consultation with the Departments of Petroleum, Department of Science and Technology, and other Departments, the Ministry of Industry should prepare a policy paper identifying initiatives needed to strengthen Indian engineering companies to upgrade the quality of their work and to foster their linkages with financial institutions, R&D laboratories and production enterprises.

A major review of an technology acquisition strategy is also overdue: In many areas, it is unlikely that we are getting the "best" technology or are taking full advantage of the presence of multinationals. An example of the former is the whole question of NRI investments which have not really resulted in the flow of contemporary technology into India. A case in point of the latter is the pharmaceutical industry where in spite of a liberal policy environment, we have not been successful in getting the most modern technology from foreign firms. Obviously, a sector-specific approach is called for, which identifies the technologies we want and the channels through which they should be acquired. Many innovative arrangements are possible. In some cases, we might be better off buying companies abroad to keep abreast of contemporary developments. In some cases, joint R&D ventures could be considered between Indian and foreign companies. all this requires examination. A few critical areas could be taken - pharmaceuticals, microelectronics, biotechnology, for instance - and an approach to aquisition worked out. The Department of Science and Technology in consultation with the DGTD, should take the responsibility for this.

V.   Administrative Action Points

11.   This note has discussed some important areas for policy intervention to accelerate the rate of industrial growth. The objective is to generate debate and discussion and not to provide definitive solutions. Subsequent notes will deal with issues not highlited here - like industrial employment, linkages between industry and educational institutions, and industrial restructuring. Meanwhile, the administrative action points emanating from this note are summarised below:

i)   Department of power to prepare a system-wise analysis of the reasons why power transmission and distribution facilities are not being modernised and expanded at the required pace and to suggest measures to accelerate this pace;

ii)   Department of Power to prepare a review of the functioning of the Power Rehabilitation Fund.

iii)   Department of Coal to prepare a note detailing steps taken to improve productivity of capital in the coal mining industry.

iv)   Departments of Power and Telecommunications to announce a clear policy in regard to the entry of the private sector in the fields of power and telecommunications respectively. A final view on pending proposals to be taken by the CCEA over the next one month.

v)   Advisory Board on Energy to conduct a sectoral analysis of energy-intensity and efficiency and suggest specific strategies to reduce energy-intensity in agriculture, industry and transport.

vi)   Department of Agriculture to coordinate preparation of a paper on the agriculture-industry nexus covering measures needed to increase farm incomes, to increase incomes from off-farm economic activities and ensure better distribution of such incomes.

vii)   Government to constitute a High-Level Committee to suggest measures to completely modernise and overhaul the management and organisation aspects of the functioning of the Central Statistical Organisation.

viii)   Ministry of Industry and Central Statistical Organisation to resolve structural problems persisting with the Index of Industrial Production on a time-bound basis.

ix)   Ministry of Industry to engage the services of a professional company to design a truly effective and up-to-date management information system to monitor the impact of various policy changes.

x) Ministry of Industry to examine ways and means of expediting project implementation in the private sector, covering also an assessment of the functioning of State-Level "Single windows".

xi) Ministry of Industry to identify important sectors where fragmentation of capacity has probably taken place (or is likely) and work out detailed schemes for ensuring that only efficient plants come up. Exercise could start with EPABX where some 40 licenses have been issued.

xii) Ministry of Industry to prepare a paper reviewing changes required in the MRTP and Companies Acts to facilitate speedy mergers, amalgamations and take-overs in industries characterised by significannt economies of scale and in which the balance of social costs and benefits favours such mergers, amalgmations and takeovers.

xiii) Ministry of Industry to insist on composite and complete applications from prospective entrepreneurs simultaneously in industries subject to licensing and involving high level of technology.

xiv) Ministry of Industry to review remaining barriers, policy and procedural, to expansion by large firms to become international giants.

xv) Government to set up a broad-based High Level Committee to review the MRTP Act ab initio to also provide for a vigorously enforcible Restrictive Trade Practices Act.

xvi) Ministries of Finance and Industry to consider fiscal policy initiatives required to boost demand in sectors where licensing policy liberalisations have taken place. The Bureau of Industrial Costs and Prices to suggest a detailed input and intermediate price rationalisation schéme to reduce consumer prices in textiles and plastics, to begin with.

xvii) Government to take a final view on pending proposals to boost housing activity in the country. These include better taxation laws, increased availability of institutional finance, treatment of housing as an industry, and review of rent control legislations and urban land ceiling Acts.

xviii) Ministry of Works and Housing to set up an Expert Group to examine how technologies in use in the Indian construction industry can be modernised without adversely affecting prospects for labour absorption.

xix) Ministry of Finance to establish a liberal and stable credit policy regime for industries like commercial vehicles and tractors; vehicle manufacturers to be used by banks as intermediaries in channelising credit for sales.

xx) Urgent consideration to be given to the automotive sector policy document prepared by the Ministry of Industry that, among other things, suggest ways to boost offtake of commercial vehicles by involving private sector in passenger traffic movement.

xxi) Department of Mines to review present plans for increased absorption of aluminium in view of the anticipated surplus and also review restrictions on expansion by metal producers.

xxii) Government to announce a definite procurement policy in regard to industries like capital goods.

xxiii) Government to expedite consideration of the policy package proposed by the Ministry of Industry to strengthen the indigenous capital goods Industry.

xxiv) Planning Commission and the Ministry of Defence to constitute a Committee to examine measures needed to effect a permanent and mutually supporting linkage between investment planning in the defence and non-defence sectors.

xxv) The Bureau of Industrial Costs and Prices to prepare a specific plan for reducing prices of steel, aluminium, copper, naptha and gas to the domestic consumer. Consideration to be given to the supply of raw materials and components at international prices to Indian industry when confronted with competition from imported supplies.

xxvi) IDBI to carry out a review of why in spite of funds being available, pace of modernisation has lagged behind in industries in obvious need of it.

xxvii) Ministry of Industry to explore alternatives to the subsidy-approach to modernisation and feasibility of extending the successful approach adopted in the cement industry to other industries in need of modernisation as well.

xxviii) Department of Electronics to coordinate the preparation of a detailed investment plan for the introduction of new technologies like microprocessor-based systems and applications, specific integrated circuits in traditional industries like sugar, textiles, paper, leather and power generation,

xxix) Department of Textiles and Department of Chemicals and Petrochemicals to examine the feasibility of utilising existing jute mills to manufacture HDPE/PP woven sacks also.

xxx) Government to expedite decisions on setting up of hydrocarbon-based utility power stations in Karnataka and Haryana. Consideration to be given to greater use of hydrocarbon fuels for peaking purposes. When choice between petrochemicals and power is involved, power to be preferred.

xxxi) The Ministry of Industry should review industrial location policies and evolve fresh guidelines to accelerate the industrialisation of backward areas and also induce each State to have a location policy reflecting local resource endowments.

xxxii) Generalised across-the-board liberalisation to be supplemented by sector-specific policy change. Specific sectors in need for a review include capital goods, automobiles (covering all types of vehicles and components) pharmaceuticals and alcohol.

xxxiii) DGTD and Finance Ministry to follow a policy of rigid enforcement and stricter monitoring of phased manufacturing programmes and import duty rationalisation to force a shift away from screw driver operations in sectors like electronics.

xxxiv) Finance Ministry to set up an Expert Group to examine issues relating to future growth of capital market covering pricing of shares, development of a wide-spread secondary market for shares and debentures and new institutional arrangements required to regulate the stock market and increase investor confidence.

xxxv) Ministry of Industry to expedite review of policies needed to accelerate process of subcontracting and ancillarisation in Indian industry.

xxxvi) Government to announce list of industries reserved for small-scale sectors where investment limit needs to be raised to facilitate investments in technology and modernisation.

xxxvii) Finance Ministry to examine feasibility of introducing a Limited Partnerships Act in the next Budget to expand the supply of risk capital for the small sector and new technology-based ventures.

xxxviii) Planning Commission and Ministry of Industry to commission a conceptual study to fully understand the implications of new technologies like computer-integrated manufacturing and flexible manufacturing plants on scales and locations in the Indian context.

xxxix) Department of Rural Development to coordinate setting up of a Group to review on-going activities, institutions and approaches to rural industrialisation and to suggest a more technology-initiative and effective long-term strategy for the development of village and cottage industries.

xxxx)   IDBI and NABARD to select a few districts where dryland agriculture predominates and mount experiments to integrate on-farm and off-farm activities in a mutually supportive manner so as to maximise impact of increased flow of funds.

xxxxi)   Government to adopt a new approach to industrial location emphasising concept of growth centres. 60 growth centres to be identified in backward area where target of industrialisation in each would be additional manufacturing employment of 30,000-50,000 workers over the next five-ten years.

xxxxii)   Government to adopt a more selective strategy in terms of industries to be dispersed. Industries with high employment potential to be prime candidates.

xxxxiii)   Ministry of Industry to prepare a policy paper on relocation of textile mills and other industries away from congested areas, so that industries can generate enough resources on their own for modernisation.

xxxxiv)   Planning Commission and Ministry of Industry to finalise in all details a set of technology missions in the industrial sector, covering technology application, technology development and futuristic technology missions.

xxxxv)   Committee set up to examine CSIR's functioning to also consider measures required to forge a more effective and durable linkage between the research and production systems. A similar Committee to be established to maximise spin-offs from the DRDO (Defence Research and Development Organisation).

xxxxvi)   Ministry of Industry to come up with a note for CCEA identifying licensing and fiscal policy change required not only to promote R&D but also for commercialisation of R&D.

xxxxvii)   Ministry of Industry to coordinate preparation of a policy paper identifying initiatives needed to strengthen Indian engineering design companies and to upgrade the quality of their work.

xxxxviii)   Department of Science and Technology to coordinate preparation of a policy paper reviewing our technology acquisition strategy in key sectors like pharmaceuticals, electronics and biotechnology. consideration to be given to new strategies like buying companies abroad and having joint R&D ventures between foreign and Indian companies.

Annexure 2:

Note prepared by Pranab Mukherjee on the economic situation for a meeting of the Congress Working Committee on 19 February 1991

ECONOMIC SITUATION

The Congress Working Committee notes with grave
concern the deteriorating economic situation since the
National Front Government came to Power. The country is
passing through a serious economic crisis. Positive developments like higher rate of growth, stable price situation,
steady Industrial growth and encouraging credit rates in
International Money Market witnessed during the whole
decade of eightees are no longer visible.

In the whole decade of eightees during the 6th
and 7th Five Year Plans Indian economy registered significant
achievements. The Indian economy has considerably changed
since the second oil shock in 1979-80. Perhaps it is now a
different economic entity compared to even a decade ago.
During the decade 1980-90 India's G.N.P. has increased from
150 billions US Dollars to 210 billions US Dollars (1 billion =
100 crores 1 US ⌀ = 14 rupees). The size of Industrial sector
is now about two times that of even in 1980. Compared to the
experiences of many other developing countries the experience of
India in the decade of eighties has been quite encouraging.
India's G.D.P. growth rate was 5.2 p.c. per annum compared to
the performance of other developing countries with 2.2
per annum during the same decade. Even compared to its own
earlier performance (with 3.5 p.c. G.D.P. growth per year
from 1951-52 to 1979- 80) the decade of eighties had been of
considerable growth. During this decade India's per capita
income increased at the growth rate exceeding 3 p.c. per annum.

The Industrial sector was the most dynamic with its
growth rate accelarating in the second half of eighties.
During 1984-85 to 1989-90 the Industrial growth rate was 8.5 p.c.
per year. Not only the growth rate was high, in fact it was one
of the highest since Independence but it also accompanied with
considerable changes in the structure of India's Industry with
the emergence of new and technology intensive industries. Yet
there has been a decoupling of Industrial and agricultural growth
rates. During the eighties the agricultural growth rate was
modest but this did not pose a constraint vis a vis the
Industrial growth. This was manifested in the drought year of

....2/-

1987-88. Even the severest drought of the century did not
dampen the pace of Industrial growth unlike the experiences
of earlier drought years.   This structural change has considerable
significance for the future growth prospects. As far as price
stability is concerned, the ~~arrangement~~ *average annual* rate of inflation in the
eighties has been 7.3 p.c. per year. Only twice during the decade
in 1980-81 as part of the legacy left by the Janata Party -
Charan Singh rule and in 1987-88 because of drought the rate
of inflation reached double digit figures of 16.7 p.c. and
10.7 p.c. respectively. In many of the developing countries
especially those of Latin America, the average rate of inflation
has been much higher. On export front though initially performance
in the early part of the eighties was not satisfactory, in the
later part particularly in the last three years of the Seventh
Plan the export registered a growth rate of 16-17 p.c. in US
dollar terms.   Another encouraging development has been
the considerable improvement in the use of capacities in the
infrastructural sectors such as Railways and Power that enabled
the economy to attain higher industrial growth rates. In
agriculture sector the growth was modest. However productions
in grains, sugar, oilseeds and pulses reached new peak levels.
Through efforts of technology mission the production of edible
oil has increased substantially and dependence on import
has been reduced correspondingly.

However in 1990 the scene has been changed dramatically.
Rate of inflation has already crossed double digit as on first
week of February the rate of inflation (EPI) is around 12 p.c.
on point to basis. Consumer Price index is also running parallel
and registering even annual rate of inflation around 12.5 p.c.
in December, 1990. In fact every week in the whole year of 1990
the price curve moved upwards without any break. Despite good
monsoon there is no respite in price front.

Balance of Payment situation is critical. India secured
I.M.F. loan of 1.8 billion US $/under Compensatory Contingency
Financing Facility (CCFF) to tide over the crisis situation
arriving out of oil imports and 0.78 billion US $/ for a stand by
arrangement available under a first credit tranche for three
months. The rate of interest for the loans is 9 p.c. and
repayment have to start in three years and three months spread
over a period of two years. India's foreign exchange reserves

...3/-

never came down below 487 millions SDR for as long as 8 years
till June 1990.   But from June 1990 situation started
deteriorating so fast that by September 1990 it came down to
nil level.

There was serious short-fall in revenue realisation.
According to the analysis of National Council of applied
Economic research (NCAER) in the first two quarters (April
to September, 1990) of the current financial year revenue
receipts slowed down. The combined revenue realisation was
6.5 p.c. against the budget estimates of 8.8 p.c. and the
previous year 1989-90) performance of 14.6 p.c.

The year 1990-91 witnessed heavy doses of taxation and
increase in administered prices. In the budget for the year
additional net taxation amounted to rupees 1790 crores and
rupees 1400 crores was raised by increasing prices of petrol
and petroleum products. In October additional levies were
imposed to the extent of Rs. 4600 crores for the full year and
Rs. 2300 crores for the remaining six months of the current year.
In December there was another bunch of taxation yielding
2000 crores of rupees for the full year and about rupees 400
crores for the remaining period of the current year. In short
in a single year additional resources ,obilisation through
taxation and increase in administered prices amounted to
rupees 5890 crores. This figure does not include the increase
in steel and coal prices and the increase in railway freight.
Despite this substantial resource mobilisation the likely revised
budgetary deficit is estimated to be around eleven to twelve
thousand crores of rupees against budget estimates of Rs. 7200
crores.

The slogan of 'empty coffers, raised by the Prime
Minister and Finance Minister of the Janata Dal after assuming
office led to a dangerous situation where even credit ~~rates~~ Rating
in the International money market dipped at a very low level.
No International Banker and financial institution is ready today
to advance loan to this country. Political instability has

.... 4/-

worsened the situation.

Eighth Five Year Plan is yet a non starter. Though in June 1990 the approach to the ighth Five Year Plan was approved by NDC, in the first year the country had no plan and the second year is also likely to be a virtual plan holiday. In a lengthy document of approach to eighth five year plan with 74 pages and 123 paragraphs there is no indication of the financial outlay of the plan and how to fund it. In the current years budget the actual plan outlay was stepped up in nominal terms by only 14 p.c. Lack of investable resources through plan has already made its mark in slowing down of Industrial growth. According to an analysis Infrastructure performance continues to be dismal showing a full in the production in three industries - coal, crude Petroleum, and refining. The production in other infrastructure sectors also remains much below the target and as a result the growth rate of infrastructual group as a whole has fallen to less than 2 p. c. during July-November compared to 5.7 p.c. in the first quarter (April-June). If these sectors have to reach the target; the coal production will have to rise by 31 p.c., electricity generation by 18 p.c., crude oil production by 23 p.c. and salable steel production by 21 p.c. in the remaining period which appears to be impossible. In this situation it is no wonder that "The Economist" (London) has expressed fears that the 'Hindu rate of growth' will return to Indian economy.

Long before Independence, Indian National Congress pledged to the people of this country to create a just and egalitarian social order (through peaceful means) which will be free from hunger, poverty and exploitations. Since 1951-52 till 1989-90 Congress had endeavoured to achieve this objective through seven five year plans and three annual plans. Before demiting office in December, 1989 Congress Government finalised the approach to Eight Plan. The following objectives were indicated in the document -

(1) Annual GDP growth rate of at least 6 p.c.;

(2) A sharper focus to reduce disparities and to ensure dispersed growth;

(3) International competiveness in an expanding range of manufacturing and excellence in

....5/-

select sectors.

(4) self realiance in technology, food, security and
resources for investment;

(5) greater resilience of the economy to adapt
to and take advantage of the changing
international sector.

Poverty alleviation and equity was given top priority
in the 8th Plan. It aimed at -

(i) reduction of poverty level to 18-20 p.c. at the
end of the 8th plan and to zero level by the end
of the century;

(ii) annual employment growth of 3 p.c., working
towards an employment guarantee to the poor;

(iii) clean drinking water for all by 1995 and
health for all by 2000 A.D; and

(iv) universalisation of elementary education and
eradication of illiteracy in the working age
population (15-35).

These lofty objectives could jave been realised but for
the drift in the economy in the recent months.

Immediate task before the nation is to put economy
back on rails. To achieve this, both short and long term
strategies are necessary.

The immediate task before the government is to remove
the sense of panic and frustration and to restore confidence
in the system. Government cannot and should not press panic
buttons. They should face the situation with courage and
fortitude.

To check unabated price rise demand and supply management
should be strengthened. Psychology of scarcity should be removed
and stringent measures are to be taken against hoarders, black
marketeers, smugglers and profiteers who want to exploit the
situation.

Impact of the Gulf crisis on Indian economy should be
assessed carefully and appropriate measures should be taken.
There is no doubt that the panic reaction of earstwhile Janata

....6/-

Dal Government and its failure to locate alternate sources
of one crude oil supply since the beginning of the Gulf crisis
created the dislocation in availability of diesel, kerosin
and Petrol. It is interesting to note that except for a
short while the prices of petroleum Crude remained at a
reasonably low level. Even after the out break of the war
in gulf regions the oil prices did not increase so sharply
as was projected. The majority of forecasts predicted that
within 48 hours of the out-break of war oil prices to shoot
up between 40 $/ to 100 $/ per barrel did not materialise.
In fact the oil prices in the last week of January fell in
International market by as much as 10 $/ a barrel.

It has come dowm to 16-17 $ a barrel. It may be temporary at
the present supply is strengthened by release from United States
strategic oil reserves. However as the end of Gulf War is
visible one may expect that for some time in near future
oil prices may not be as exorbitant as it appeared to be in
early August.

Congress Working Committee strongly feels that policies
initiated in the eighties should not be reversed. Temporary
problems of today should not shake our confidence in the
policies for changes necessary to build up a dynamic, vibrant
economy for the future.

Although in the growth rate terms, the performance in the
eighties/has been very dynamic it did create some major weakness
and structural imbalance. Mainly because of the failure of
public sector enterprises to generate adequate resources
and the increase of subsidies both direct and indirect the
investable surplus became considerably inadequate. Therefore
to maintain the tempo of development government's dependence
on borrowing increased substantially. Deficit in revenue
account increased from 0.6 p.c. of GDP in early eighties to
2.8 p.c. of GDP at the end of the seventh plan. This
distortion happened because three major non-developmental
expenditure could not be limited to planned targets. Increase

....7/-

services, defence expenditure

in debt and subsidies created this structural imbalance.
If contracting such very high debts was accompanied by increased
growth rate of exports and rate of domestic savings, the debt
level perse would not have been of much concern. Accelerating
growth through borrowing has been a classic strategy of many
dynamic economies. But unfortunately performance of economy in
both these areas was disappointing. During the eighties the
net savings in the economy as a percentage of net national
product declined from 15.1 p.c. in 1980-81 to 11.6 p.c. in 1987-
88. Similarly India's share in the world's market especially
in manufactured products did not increase as rapidly as the
world trade. These macro-economic imbalances were reflective
of (i) deterioration of international competitiveness of
India's industrial sector,(ii) the growing breakdown of
"development consensus" amongst various social groups. This
breakdown is particularly serious as it has led to the erosion
of public saving and investment as various subsidies made
growing demands on India's exchequer and thus reducing
government's ability to step up the public saving and private
investment.

These factors have made the growth process unsustainable
unless radical changes are made. The radical change in policy
will not only involve macro-economic policies but also major
overhaul of trade and industrial policies in micro-economic
reforms. Promotion of industrial structure that is internationally competitive will have to be the corner-stone
of this new strategy. This can only be done in an open
economy framework by actively seeking to increase the share
of foreign trade in the country's gross national product.
This would mean bringing domestic relative prices in line
with the international prices by removing non tariff barriers
and by launching tariff reforms. Hard budget decisions on
subsidies and distribution of national cake is inevitable
in this strategy.

In this strategy of radical reforms Public Sector enterprises
are to play a crucial role. Public participation in the public

....8/-

sector enterprises can be debated and a decision may be
taken at the appropriate time. What is urgently needed in
the better performance of the public sector enterprises.

With an investment of over Rs 103,000 ~~thousand~~ crores riding
on 248 Central Public Sector Enterprises, there can be no
two opinions about the compulsive need to improve the
performance of the public sector. During the 8th Plan period
envisaged that the public sector will generate around
Rs. 22,300 crores per year to support the planned development
of the nation. To achieve this target, public sector has to
gear itself up. The return on capital employed which has been
stagnating around 4.5% must show improvement. No longer
can the Government keep on providing funds to the
Central Public Sector Units both for their capital projects
and for meeting their losses on non-plan account.

An indepth analysis shows that out of the 118 profit making
public sector units, only in top 10 enterprises the ratio of
net profit to capital employed was 14%; in another ten
it was 8% and in the next 98, 2.3% to 4.3%. These 98
companies are definitely not earning their potential profit
and must show better performance.

A close look at the 101 loss making public sector units
shows that as many as 75 such units fall in the category of
competitive sector. Somehow our public sector has failed to
exhibit the quality needed to cope with the fast pace of
change. The quality of goods and services being produced
leaves much to be desired. As a matter of fact, there are
about 40 public sector units which have been showing losses
continuously for the last five years and now have a negative
networth.

In order to generate resources for development, Government
must join for radical economic reform in line with internation
trends of de-regulation, competition and decentralization. To
achieve national objectives and to tone up the functioning of
Public Sector, the following steps have now become necessary.

    i) The objectives of the public sector should be

redefined to include:

a) Self-reliance
b) Return on capital employed
c) Essential and infrastructural services

ii) Financially unviable units with low social
responsibility should be privatized through
formulated "exit policy".

iii) Greatest importance should be attached to performance,
improvement and the recruitment of top executives,
reward and punishment systems, and performance
evaluation systems should be redesigned to achieve
these objectives.

Congress Working Committee firmly believes that before
the end of this century this last decade of nineties can be
the decade of transformation for Indian economy — transformation from sluggishness to dynamism, transformation from
stagnation to growth and transformation from 'closed economy'
to 'open economy.'

Annexure 3:
Pranab Mukherjee's interview in *The Times of India,*
given on 20 June 1991, the day before Narasimha Rao and
Manmohan Singh were sworn in

BUSINESS ☙ TIMES

'Economy must be put back on the rails'

By R.K. ROY
Our Economic Editor
NEW DELHI, June 20.

Mr Pranab Mukherjee, a spokesman of the Congress, barely hides his impatience with the Janata Dal and BJP for projecting what he considers to be "non-issues" before the country. Both Mandal and Mandir propositions require a "one-time" settlement, but what thereafter, asks Mr Mukherjee, finance minister in Mrs Indira Gandhi's cabinet in the early eighties.

In his view, the new government will have to put the economic agenda high on the list of priorities that call for immediate action. The economy must be put back on the rails. Mr Mukherjee states in this interview held in Delhi on Monday that the key problems which are of concern to the people are the control of inflation, creation of new jobs and easing the inflow of imports.

The Congress has been projecting stability as the main issue to counter the equity and Ram cards of the principal parties opposing it. Has not your party given economic issues less importance than they deserve?

A: That is precisely the kind of distortion brought about by opposition propaganda of which I am critical. From the economic perspective, consider what the weakness of the government has resulted in.

Prices are rising and everyone knows that so long as a weak government remains in power, nothing will be done about this. Inflationary expectations cannot be dampened by equity or Hindutva. What is required is a stable strong government.

Take the recent sale of gold confiscated from smugglers. The mere fact of lodging bullion with banks (abroad) would have earned India a reprieve from the pressure of paying the debt servicing instalment — if only a stable government were in position in the country.

External pressures on patent or trade negotiations, Super 301, etc, have mounted because of the lack of stability of government.

The Congress wants to roll back prices. What is the targeted rate of price rise the party has in mind?

Inflation cannot be zeroed, but it can certainly be brought down from the current double-digit rate to 8 per cent or even lower that was the average in the eighties. I would start with this kind of a modest target.

As regards rolling back prices, the government has some fiscal manoeuvrability in this regard as, also administrative measures available to it. I would not like to amplify upon these now.

How do you propose to slow down inflation?

By acting on the fiscal deficit, of course. Subsidies which do not reach the target groups will be redesigned, rationalised. We will review the purpose of each subsidy, withdraw those that are not required.

To save expenditure, we will dismantle government organisations which serve no purpose.

What about raising tax revenues?

Well, we don't want to tamper with direct taxes for some time. We would also like to keep indirect taxes stable

Mr Pranab Mukherjee

for at least one year. The effort will be to improve tax collection by strengthening the tax administration. We would also like to widen the tax base.

By lowering the income tax exemption limit?

Not necessarily. We would like to bring the self-employed and traders (with taxable incomes) into the fiscal net.

The fiscal deficit requires to be brought down this year from 8.3 per cent of GDP to about 6.5 per cent.

This would mean a reduction of Rs 5,500 crore from the level of 1990-91 and by Rs 9,000 crore or so in 1991-92. The kind of measures you have indicated will hardly make the required impact on the fiscal deficit.

There are three other sources of revenues that can be tapped. First, the government must not allow any waiver or remission of dues to it. Second, rates of goods and services offered by government-owned departments and undertakings will be raised: rail tariffs, postal and allied charges, banking and insurance charges, for example. Prices charged by the public sector industries will take a hike.

What is the third source, privatisation?

Yes. We can raise revenue by selling a proportion of the equity of public sector undertakings to the Indian public.

What about sales to foreigners?

Well, let us say we could sell PSU equity to NRIs. The principal point you see is to get the eighth plan started. We are having a plan holiday for the second successive year.

You are talking about resuming the plan, but the IMF wants economic liberalisation?

We want planning and liberalisation. We must give room for play to the private sector. The public sector must vacate the areas in which the private sector has the capability to come in. The public sector must move into the difficult areas of advanced technology.

You are not averse to conditional assistance from IMF?

No. Actually the government (of Mr V.P. Singh) ought to have taken advance action in 1990. The conditionality would have been less harsh.

But surely the Congress government could have gone to IMF in early 1989?

You see, in 1989, the mix between short-term borrowings and the lines of long-term credits available to this country was fair. The proportion of short-term credit rose in 1990, before the Gulf war. If the Congress had been returned to power, we would have gone to IMF in 1990.

Fiscal correction will mean a tight budget. So how will you protect economic growth?

By consolidating past gains. Getting more out of the industrial and infrastructural capacity we have created over the years. By introducing competition we will get a larger output from existing as also additional investment.

Improved capacity utilisation will require intensive maintenance of plant and equipment. This will be one area of job expansion besides priority budgetary allocation for poverty alleviation programmes.

You see, Congress alone among the parties has thought out the economic strategy for getting the economy to move forward. In our thinking, stability holds the key. This rationale rules out a hung Parliament.

Annexure 4:

Two interviews of Finance Minister Manmohan Singh to Paranjoy Guha
Thakurta in *Sunday*, 14-20 July and 4-10 August 1991,
given as reforms were happening

COVER STORY

Sweat, toil and tears

Manmohan Singh is determined to rejuvenate the Indian economy

SUNDAY: It is not at all clear why the depreciation of the rupee was done in two phases. You have said that this was done to test the reaction of the market. It is believed that the governor of the Reserve Bank of India and the chief economic adviser both favoured a one-time devaluation. Why did you go in for a two-stage devaluation?

Manmohan Singh: We in this country live under certain illusions—economists have been responsible for it—that devaluation is something immoral, anti-national. You look around the world. Over the past year, both the Soviet Union and China have gone in for massive devaluation of their currencies. Our people—the economists, the journalists, the politicians—somehow believe that devaluation is sinful and dishonourable. It's nothing of the sort.

The exchange rate is just a price. If you are in the business of selling, your price has to be competitive. And who are our competitors? They include South Korea, the countries of south and south-east Asia and Pakistan. Look at what they have done. I think their exchange rate policies have been aggressive and designed to enhance their competitiveness. Now if in this situation we do nothing, our balance of payments, which is already precarious, would worsen further.

Q: But why was devaluation done in two stages?
A: To be honest, I had to test the reaction of the market, test the political reaction and prepare the country for

a bigger devaluation. That was why we launched a trial balloon. The initial reaction was favourable, the market took it calmly. But then on Wednesday (3 July) morning, a mischievous news item was published in a newspaper (*The Economic Times*) saying that the State Bank of India had defaulted. I realised that morning that people may get nervous reading the news, that there may be an unsustainable run on the rupee.

I had two options. I could have sat back and watched the country go down the drain. I thought that instead,

let us act aggressively and take the bull by the horns. I told the Reserve Bank governor that you have full authority to do what was ultimately done.

I believed that this would stop destabilising speculation. Everybody's been saying that India would be defaulting.

Q: What exactly happened? It is believed that though the State Bank of India's (SBI) New York branch may not have technically defaulted, certain payments got delayed by a few days.
A: We have an over-bureaucratised system. There was some problem between the MMTC (Minerals and Metals Trading Corporation) and the SBI. Some papers did not move on time and each tried to blame the other. There is no question of the SBI de-

faulting. But that mischievous news item could have created havoc when the markets opened that day. I, therefore, advanced what I was planning to do anyway.

Q: Did you go in for a sudden devaluation instead of a gradual one—say, spread out over a month—because time was running out?
A: A gradual kind of devaluation could not have been done in the present situation. Normally you have creeping devaluation which is not noticed. If I allowed a gradual slide,

> "Even if I fail in fulfilling a great cause—and I don't think I will fail—I will have done my duty to the nation. And I will thank Prime Minister Narasimha Rao for having given me an opportunity to serve the country at the fag-end of my career"

the rupee could have suddenly slumped. In this country and abroad, people were saying that the rupee was so weak that no government would be able to sustain its value. The ideal thing to do would have been to devalue at one go, but I had to prepare domestic public opinion, I'm grateful that the Prime Minister has understood the gravity of the problems.

Q: About the implications of devaluation, it is generally agreed that it will boost exports. But there's the other side of the coin. Our imports will become more expensive, especially oil imports. This means we will import inflation and people are worried about higher prices, especially at a time when there is seasonal pressure on prices. How will you tackle inflation?

A: The question that should be asked is: what would have happened if the rupee had not been devalued and the country defaulted on its obligations? You are talking about higher oil prices. But we would have been in a situation where we wouldn't even have had the money to import oil or fertilisers. If India is declared a defaulter, we wouldn't be able raise loans to import anything. Then there would be reckless inflation, reckless unemployment.

Having said that, I do agree that the costs of imports will go up. But I don't think this will affect the general price level in a big way. After all, we're not

such a large trading country. Imports comprise only eight-nine per cent of our gross domestic product (GDP) and exports are not more than five-six per cent of the GDP. So trade is not that big a part of our national income.

Yes, the prices of certain imports will go up, but not all imports. A lot would depend on international supply-demand conditions. But I'm convinced that if I have tight fiscal and monetary policies, the prices of some other commodities will decline. What we've done is to change the relative prices of imports and exports. Therefore, I don't expect the exchange rate correction to generate a generalised type of inflation. If the country accepts the kind of tight policies I have in mind for the next two years, then inflationary expectations will come down.

Q: If the oil import bill goes up by Rs 2,000 crores as it is expected to, then the promise made in the Congress manifesto about rolling back prices of diesel and kerosene will become impossible to implement.
A: I don't want to discuss these matters right now. You should wait till I present the budget.

Q: After the devaluation and the trade policy changes, what more needs to be done to contain the fiscal deficit?
A: We must reduce the fiscal deficit to sustainable limits. That means strict curbs on unproductive expenditure. We must also look at ways to improve our performance on the revenue side.

Q: That means higher taxes?
A: I can't discuss budget matters. But we must improve the efficiency of the public sector. As the Prime Minister has said, we cannot tolerate waste and inefficiency whether it is in the public sector or the private sector. I will reveal a comprehensive strategy about how we will bring about a credible improvement in the fiscal situation. But first we have to remove the underlying structural impediments to growth. If productivity of investment remains as low as it is, then short-term corrections will not help. We will go back to our bad old ways.

Therefore, it is absolutely essential that this opportunity for fiscal correction should be combined with large-scale structural reforms to utilise the

full potential of the nation. The cobwebs of controls, which do not serve any social purpose but which stifle enterprise and initiative, have to be removed, be it in the area of industry or foreign trade. We have to unleash the productive forces of the economy and create an environment in which investment, technical change and modernisation become profitable propositions. Obsolete enterprises must reform and, if they cannot, they must close down.

But the cost of reform should not fall on the backs of the working class and the weaker sections of society. This must be prevented. Also our obligations to the rural poor have to continue and leakages in anti-poverty programmes have to be plugged. The wealth of the nation must be used not for the benefit of a few, but for the vast majority who are poor.

If the living conditions in the rural areas improve, it will prevent premature migration to the cities which, in turn, will curb the growth of slums and reduce law and order problems in urban areas. We want to eliminate the rural-urban divide.

Q: What kind of loan are you seeking from the International Monetary Fund? How much money is expected to come and by when?
A: We haven't reached any agreement yet on the numbers or on the policy package. We are in an advanced stage of negotiations. I have heard from the managing director of the IMF and the president of the World Bank and they have publicly stated that they are appreciative of our efforts. I'm confident that things will work out. I don't buy the argument that these two institutions are out to exploit India. We have worked with them in the past and my feeling is that they are concerned about India's development.

I don't think these institutions will ask us to do something which is detrimental to our national interests. If we do get their money, it is not my intention to spend it on consumption. I intend using the money for strengthening our reserves and paying back some of the short-term loans which have piled up. The money won't be used to let the country go again on an import spree. We need their money today, we will need it for the next three or four years. But, ultimately, the country has to stand on its own feet, ultimately our strategy has to be one of maximum possible self-reliance.

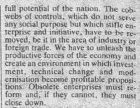

"I have heard Jyotibabu say that instead of going to the IMF, we should tap the thousands of crores of rupees that are supposed to be lying with NRIs. But today the NRIs, instead of bringing money into the country, want to take back the money they have kept here"

ASHOKE CHAKRABORTY

We will be grateful to our friends abroad who will help us. But we will use that help to launch a process so that in five years' time—if I'm still there to present a budget in Parliament—we can say we are now on our own feet. That is my vision. We have to critically examine why we have become flabby over the last 30 years. People say the world system exploits India. But I feel that the world has treated us quite well, particularly in relation to some other developing countries. Our terms of trade have not deteriorated to the extent certain other countries' terms of trade have.

Once the productivity of investments improves here, we can do away with dependence on concessional aid. I wish to welcome direct foreign investment. India should have something to offer to the world which is also mutually beneficial. Then the finance secretary can stop going around the world with a begging bowl. I see this happening five years from now.

Q: But will you have that much time? Comparisons are being drawn between you and former finance minister Sachin Chaudhuri who had to quit soon after he devalued the rupee in 1966. It is being said that after the dirty work has been done, you may be made a scapegoat. How do you react to such comparisons?

A: I'm not going to be like Sachin Chaudhuri. I consider it a privilege that the Prime Minister has appointed me to undertake structural reforms which are long overdue. If these reforms click—and I believe they will—then I think we in the government will get the backing of the entire nation. As I've already said, we don't believe in playing partisan politics with issues of national importance. Therefore, I don't fear that I will be made a scapegoat. And even if I fail in fulfilling a great cause—and I don't think I will fail—I will have done my duty to the nation. And I will thank Prime Minister Narasimha Rao for having given me an opportunity to serve the country at the fag-end of my career. But I think we are soon going to see the beginning of a glorious chapter in the history of India.

Q: How have you responded to Jyoti Basu's alternative economic programme, based on land reforms and expansion of domestic markets?
A: I have great respect for Jyoti Basu as a national leader and as a patriot. I have worked closely with him in the

past. Still, I must say that I have explained everything to Opposition leaders, including leaders of the communist parties. I have asked them: what is the alternative? I have heard Jyotibabu say that instead of going to the IMF, we should tap the thousands of crores of rupees that are supposed to be lying with non-resident Indians (NRIs). But the situation today is that NRIs, instead of bringing money into the country, want to take back the money they have here. NRIs are patriotic, but they also love their money. Therefore, it is simply not true that NRIs will come to India's rescue.

It has been stated that we imported

Subramaniam Swamy says that he thought Manmohan Singh was a leftist and is now surprised to see how much of a *laissez-faire* economist he has become. Singh, however, says that he still believes in certain plus-points of socialism

too much in the past. That's right. But this is not true any longer. In order to save the honour of the country, we have imposed the most savage cuts on imports. There is no alternative macro-economic strategy with the Opposition and I think they know it. As for land reforms, I do agree that there should be a positive movement in that direction.

Q: You have been described as mild-mannered and timid and people say there has been a sudden transformation in your personality since you became finance minister. Do you agree?
A: I don't think it is at all true that I have been timid. One day, when the country's archives are prepared, people will know the truth. What I'm saying now is what I've been saying ever since I came into the govern-

ment. It is true that I have lived within the system and that I have not been successful in changing the system's thinking earlier. Go through what I've written in the Sixth Plan and Seventh Plan documents—I'm saying the same things even today. Maybe I was not able to implement everything, but then I was just a small cog.

When I came to the finance ministry in 1971, I wrote a paper called 'What to do with victory'. I had written at that time that all these controls in the name of socialism would not lead to growth but would strangle the impulses for growth. I had said that these controls would not reduce inequalities but increase them. I have not been timid. I have spoken my mind freely and frankly. But I've also served as a faithful civil servant. Even if I have been overruled, I have carried out the orders of my political masters.

Q: In what ways have your economic views changed over the years?
A: I used to be in favour of gradual change. But I look around the world and realise that time is not on our side. There has been a complete collapse of the command economies of Eastern Europe. This country will be marginalised if we don't move forward at a breathtaking pace. I'm convinced that if there has to be structural change, it must be done quickly. That's how my views have changed. ●
Interviewed by Paranjoy Guha Thakurta/New Delhi

Sunday
August 4-10, 1991
p. 36-37

"I'm no prophet"

But Union finance minister Manmohan Singh is optimistic that his tough budget will not hamper growth

He sleeps barely three to four hours a day and seems possessed by a demoniac zeal. The transformation of academic-turned-bureaucrat-turned finance minister Dr Manmohan Singh into a political animal is complete.

Gone is the hesitancy of the economist in him when he admitted that the Congress(I) pledge to roll back prices of essential commodities was not a realistic one. Now, he defends his attempts to fulfil the promises made in the party manifesto with a vengeance. He's not saying: I'll try even if I can't. He actually believes he can. And that the Prime Minister will back him to the hilt.

Manmohan Singh has, of late, acquired the aggressiveness necessary for a politician to put down his rivals. Witness the dressing down he sought to give his predecessor Yashwant Sinha and BJP stalwart K.R. Malkani on Doordarshan's post-budget programme. Yet, despite a very long innings as a financial administrator, Singh is a newcomer to politics. He has been pitchforked to an exalted position at a time when the country is passing through one of its worst economic crises ever.

But can Manmohan Singh perform a veritable 'Indian rope trick'? Can he have a budget which is harsh but which does not hurt the interests of the poor, thereby making the International Monetary Fund (IMF) "amend its manual" of prescriptions for developing countries, wonders well-known economic journalist Swaminathan S. Anklesaria Aiyar. The answers to these questions will become known only after some time.

But the finance minister is optimistic and that is an essential qualification for his job. In a brief interview with SUNDAY, Singh explained why he feels his tough budget will not hamper the growth processes in the country. Excerpts:

SUNDAY: Your budget is said to be a deft balancing act, a tightrope walk. However, it is felt that the expenditure estimates made for the current year are unrealistic and that the full impact of devaluation has not been taken into account in a number of sectors, particularly defence.

Manmohan Singh: I have already said that some of these adjustments will be made later to the best extent possible. Only time will tell whether the expenditure estimates will be adhered to.

Q: But won't defence expenditure have to be cut a lot if your estimates are to be stuck to?
A: That is a conscious decision. I don't want expenditure (on defence) to run riot.

Q: Of the 81 broad heads of expenditure in the budget, over 80 per cent of the figures are identical to the ones given in the March 1991 vote on account. It seems there's an underestimation.
A: Why? What is wrong? It does not follow that there has been an underestimation.

Q: Like all your predecessors, you say that expenditure estimates have to be adhered to. But the bill invariably goes up at the end of the year.
A: I hope it doesn't go up. I will make a conscious effort to see that it does not take place.

Q: What about dearness allowance (DA) payments to government and public sector employees?
A: What we have said is that administrative ministries and public sector corporations will have to live within the constraints of the existing budget. If they wish to pay DA, they will have to cut somewhere else. No separate provision has been made (for DA payments).

Q: You are talking of austerity with growth. The austerity part is apparent, but the growth part is not all that clear in your policies.
A: Growth takes place as a result of the cumulative thinking of the people of India. If people think that this country is moving again, I think growth will take place. If everybody says that the coffers are empty, that the country is ruined, then there can be no growth in the future. The government (alone) cannot provide growth with the best of intentions.

Growth is the cumulative consequence of what the farmers of India do, what industry does, what labour does. All that the government can do is to create an atmosphere, a climate for growth. I think we have succeeded in doing that. What will be the eventual impact (of the new policies) only time can tell. History will judge.

Q: Let us consider the schemes you have initiated to unearth black money and use it for socially productive purposes. Will these measures suffer the fate of similar schemes introduced in the past? Do you think these schemes can make even a small dent in the country's parallel economy?
A: I'm no prophet. The proof of the pudding is in the eating. The Raja Chelliah Committee had made suggestions about having such schemes. It's also there in our election manifesto. Mr (Vasant) Sathe has been writing about it and saying that the huge amount of black money in the country should be used for socially useful purposes. I've given the holders of black money a chance to come clean.

Q: There is scepticism about whether the manufacturers whose products have been given excise duty reliefs will pass on the benefit to consumers in the form of lower prices.
A: There should be a strong non-governmental consumer movement in this country. The government can

> "There is this mentality here that the government can somehow take care of all problems. This attitude is at the very root of our problems. The people must learn to help themselves"

do only a limited number of things. There is this mentality here that the government can somehow take care of all problems *(laughs)*. You have a phenomenon like Mr Ralph Nader in the United States. He's a great national institution. I remember when I was in the US, the consumers' association would bring out books which would tell you what is wrong with various consumer products—in technical terms, whether they are priced rightly or not.

Q: But how can the consumer movement in India grow?
A: The people of India must learn to help themselves. The government can't take care of all their problems. This attitude (that the government should intervene) is at the very root of our problems.

Q: How much money from the IMF would you be happy with?
A: I've not discussed any numbers with them. Nor do I know what they will do. We haven't had any serious discussions yet. We will be doing that now.

Q: Was it a deliberate decision to announce the new industrial policy and the budget on the same day?
A: My expectations were that the industrial policy would be announced earlier. People wanted to be consulted. The Prime Minister wanted to consult the (Congress) Working Committee. It had to go through the Cabinet Committee on Economic Affairs. Then he (the PM) wanted it approved by the full Cabinet and the Council of Ministers. All these procedures took time.

Q: What is your personal contribution to the budget?
A: All credit must go to the Prime Minister. If there are any shortcomings, I am responsible. The Prime Minister is the source of inspiration for everything. I can't do anything without his guidance and his approval. Ultimately, he has to hold my hands. And he's backing me fully.

Q: Lately, you seem to have become quite aggressive. You told Yashwant Sinha on television that he had been sleeping on the job.
A: That is because he said there was no capital flight (during his regime). You look at the amount of money they borrowed from the IMF, add to that the reserves they had and see what the reserves were when he left. Obviously there was capital flight. All sorts of things were going on.
He did the worst thing in the history of India—the government withdrew its solemn obligation to present a budget. He ran away. What great purpose was served by not presenting a budget? They wanted to stay in office and thought that this was a way of prolonging the life of their government. Capital flight was a consequence of all that. The word of the Government of India was devalued. The fault lies not in the stars. It lies in the mess that was created in the last two years. It affected international confidence in our country in a big way. ●

Interviewed by Paranjoy Guha Thakurta/New Delhi

AGENDA FOR
ECONOMIC REFORM

India is confronted with the most severe financial crisis in her post-independence history. The task of steering the national economy towards stability and thereafter towards accelerated growth requires, above all, a political and social consensus and a national commitment to overcome obstacles. In this context, we welcome the broad framework of policy initiated by the Prime Minister in his first address to the nation, which has been elaborated further by the Finance Minister in his press conference and consultations with leaders of opposition parties.

The symptoms of the crisis are well known. Inflation has accelerated despite three bumper harvests and satisfactory growth in industrial production. Fiscal deficits have risen to unsustainable levels. The country's balance of payments situation is precarious. The level of reserves is at an all-time low. The high and increasing levels of current account deficits in the last several years have led to an accumulation of a large foreign debt and an increasing proportion of it on short-term commercial basis. Servicing this debt has presented a major challenge. The large macroeconomic imbalances that have presisted over a fairly long period are now set to push the economy into a situation where growth may be jeopardised, inflation may become uncontrollable and living standards of the vast majority of our people may suffer.

Simply stated, this situation has come about because, as a nation, we have got used to living beyond our means, our persistently high fiscal deficits and current account deficits are testimony to the firmly-grounded belief that social and economic irresponsibility carries no penalty. But history has no special favourites. We cannot afford the luxury of apportioning the blame.

The immediate task of achieving as rapidly as possible, a viable balance of payments position should be pursued alongside the aim of rectifying the major imbalances in a medium-term context. It is essential to address the underlying inefficiencies that constrain sustained growth and development. Behind the twin deficits lie structural deficiencies and rigidities which contribute to inefficiency and slow growth and ultimately, to slower improvements in the well-being of our people. We cannot therefore, ignore or postpone the structural reforms needed to tackle these problems. Adjustments now and reforms later is not a sound strategy. What we need is growth-oriented adjustment as growth cannot be sacrificed at the altar of adjustment.

Due to self-imposed constraints, productive forces in the economy are not allowed to generate more output and employment. If these constraints are not removed quickly and effectively, we will witness a succession of crises of increasing seriousness. The means for ending the present stalemate are at hand. There is inherent strength in our economy. We need to utilise this strength to build a better future.

The present crisis has to be met by a well-considered adjustment programme. The centrepiece of such a programme has undoubtedly to be restoration of the fiscal balance to contain inflation which is hurting the poorer sections particularly hard, and relieve pressure on the balance of payments. We should aim to reduce the fiscal deficit from its present range of 8.5 per cent to 9 per cent to below 4 per cent of GDP over the next three years. Only a comprehensive strategy that ensures fiscal propriety within a framework of structural reform will create confidence in the international community. It will facilitate the needed external financing for moderating the impact of corrective measures essential for restoring the health of our internal and external accounts. Without adequate levels of external financing, the burden of adjustment will fall in a disproportionate measure on the poor. In the immediate future, there is no alternative to going to the IMF for a substantial drawing of around SDR 5 to 7 billion.The conditionality of the IMF need not daunt us. We need indeed, self-imposed conditionality in the three major areas where the IMF also is likely to ask for reform, viz in correcting the fiscal deficit, in having an appropriate and competitive exchange rate and in moving towards and open economy.

A substantial reduction in government expenditure can be achieved through a phased programme of reduction in subsidies and rationalisation of plan expenditure. A sharp reduction in fertiliser subsidy is very essential. Food subsidies will have to be rationalised and targetted at sections of the population not protected against inflation so that the burden of adjustment on the poor can be minimised. Financial incentives for exporters should be provided through an appropriate exchange rate policy rather than through the budget. While these are the overt subsidies, there is a great deal of subsidisation in areas like power pricing, irrigation charges and higher education, all of which call for review and economies. Defence expenditure should be frozen in real terms and then reduced in the medium-term. Plan expenditure should be rationalised with a view to eliminating waste and focussed more on poverty removal and employment generation and completion of on going schemes. In the short run, those who have assured incomes will have to bear a larger share of the cost of adjustment. While expenditure control is important, we should guard against careless fiscal austerity in the form of cutting investment in essential infrastructure.

A sizeable reduction in revenue expenditure is essential for sustaining public investment in infrastructure and for increasing the access of the poor to health, education, nutrition and other poverty alleviation programmes. Investment in agriculture and energy sectors has to be sustained at a level that will generate an adequate rate of growth.

Additional revenue mobilisation is inescapable. The broad approach should be not to tinker with the tax rates, but to widen the tax base and rationalise the tax structure by eliminating exemptions and plugging loopholes and improving tax enforcement. It may not be possible to lower direct tax rates in the current year. However in coming years, income tax rates should be lowered from the present 56 per cent (including surcharge) to about 45 per cent without raising the minimum taxable limit. The indirect tax structure needs rationalisation and greater progress towards adoption of the VAT system.

While fiscal adjustment holds the key to the present balance of payments crisis, this as mentioned earlier, has to form a part of a medium-term structural reform. It is imperative that the concept of planning be refashioned. Pervasive state regulation and intervention, justified in the name of planning, has neither led to high growth and associated autonomous technological development nor made a significant contribution towards reduction of social and economic inequalities or improvement of the welfare of the poorer sections of our society. The next phase of development demands indeed compels, a fundamental change in the way we look at planning. The plan has to be formulated on an indicative basis with reference to market signals. Experience has shown that centralised planning produces waste, inefficiency and stagnation. The logic of reform flows from our national experience in this matter.

Moving towards a more open economy will, of necessity, be a process of well-sequenced and interconnected reforms in several sectors. In industrial policy, our objective should be to eliminate, as soon as possible, all industrial licencing subject only to laws relating to environment and industrial safety. While the small-scale, village industry and tiny sectors should be promoted, this should be done through fiscal measures on a time-bound basis and not, in any case, by product reservations. While the right of entry into industry should be liberalised, it is equally imperative that we liberalise the right of exit as well. Deregulation of industrial production is a pre-requisite for exposing the economy to international competition, bereft of domestic competition, the economy will be totally vulnerable to the onslaught of foreign capital.

A well-conceived policy for a freer induction of foreign investment can also be effectively deployed to stimulate domestic competition. Foreign investment can fill many existing gaps in our industrial structure and needs to be encouraged as a source of both finance and technology as long as it is foreign exchange neutral in its impact. It needs to be recognised that fears of foreign investment have been grossly exaggerated and a more welcoming stance is necessary to attract MNCs to invest in India . A target of $2 to $3 billion per year in the next few years should be both desirable and feasible. The paramount objective, however at this stage, is to promote domestic competition. The whole corpus of policies and regulations that today inhibit such competition has to be decisively and definitively swept away. As a step in that direction, the MRTP act should be drastically 'revised. Restrictions on growth of firm size should be removed. At the same time, the section related to restrictive trade practices should be further strengthened.

The public sector, which dominates the economy, should be made to follow rules that reward profitability and punish inefficiency. The budget, rather than public enterprises, has to take care of the welfare aspects. There is no social justification for the continuation of public sector enterprises that show losses year after year, nor is there any justification for public sector activity in areas where private entrepreneurs can do the job better. Unless the public sector is subjected to the test of competition and efficiency, there will be no accountability, nor any improvement in managerial performance. Reform and restructuring of the public sector entreprises is a task of national importance. It can no longer be postponed.

In the sphere of trade policy, the goal should be to replace quantitative restrictions by tariffs and to lower tariff levels to about 40 per cent in the next four to five years with a view to building an internationally competitive industrial structure. The loss in custom revenues should be made good by raising excise duties suitably. The incentive structure has to be fashioned to encourage exports and not, as now, high-cost import substitution. The exchange rate policy has an important role in giving signals to the economy. We should aim to have a liberal exchange rate regime with the object of making the rupee fully convertible in the medium-term and allow it to settle at a level which more truly reflects the relative scarcity of foreign exchange.

The financial and banking sectors are also in urgent need of reform. Greater autonomy, more transparency in accounts, adequacy of capital, elimination of behest lending and eschewing populist measures such as loan meals and loan waivers and a greater measure of competition are called for. The health of the financial system can only be ignored at the peril of weakening the entire economic edifice.

Movement towards a vibrant and competitive economy calls for new approach to industrial relations and exit policies. The issue is whether we can continue our present emphasis on overprotecting organised labour at the cost of the vast number of unorganised and unemployed labour. Our present policies are biased against the use of labour which is abundant and in favour of use of capital which is scarce. Wage policies and wage negotiations are distorted because of undue and unwarranted intervention by the state. We recognise that relaxation of labour market rigidities will take time, but we stress that a discernible movement for lowering such rigidities will lead to larger employment and output benefits for the economy. Closures of unviable units, with adequate provision for employment termination benefits and schemes for worker training are a sine qua non for a strong industrial sector. The present policy structure of providing fiscal and credit reliefs to sick units has been a costly, inefficient and wasteful form of protecting employment.

The state has to play a major role in absorption and adaptation of technology, not by imposition of unimaginative controls of one kind or another, but by providing the right fiscal signals to encourage domestic R&D and by coordinating corporate planning.

The process of creating conditions for a more open and competitive economy will thus call for simultaneous and concerted action over a broad array fiscal, trade, exchange rate, industrial and labour policies. Going about it in piecemeal or only in some sectors could be conterproductive but if done together, we could well find the whole being larger than the sum of the parts.

Our intention is not to furnish a detailed blueprint of reform. The main guiding principle is that within a framework of macroeconomic stability, which only the state can provide and nurture, decision-making in economic spheres should be decentralised to the maximum extent consistent with our basic socio-economic objectives.

The present crisis is an opportunity to learn and unlearn. There is no escape from the painful process of adjustment. The national economy has to be stabilised. The bitter medicine of fiscal austerity has to be swallowed if we have to have a change of recovering from our self-inflicted injuries. But having recovered, vigorous growth will not come from doing more of what we have done before. A bold programme of setting free initiatives and capabilities will have to be put in place. For this, resolution and courage are needed. But, more importantly, shedding of dogma is indispensable.

India is at crossroads. The colossal challenges ahead cannot be met by hesitant, faltering and half-hearted steps. The entire country must act with the courage of conviction that reforms are necessary to pave the way for making India a stable, strong and vibrant nation. All representative organs of our society, and above all, the Parliament must reflect that the nation is poised to grasp the future unitedly and with determination.

NEW DELHI, JULY 1,1991

Annexure 6:

Statement issued by thirty-five 'left oriented' economists on 8 July 1991 and reprinted in *Mainstream*, 13 July 1991

DEVALUATION AND IMF LOAN

Leading Economists' Alternative View

The following statement—"Structural Adjustment: An Alternative Viewpoint"—by leading economists from different parts of the country alongwith some academics and close observers of the economic scene was issued in New Delhi on July 8, 1991. It brings out a point of view on devaluation and the IMF loan that is radically different from the Government of India's approach. As such its exceptional importance is obvious. We are publishing the statement in full for the benefit of our readers.

           —Editor

To meet a financial crisis, the nature and magnitude of which have been shrouded in secrecy, the government has launched an all out effort to obtain a large loan from the IMF. Despite protestations to the contrary, it is now clear that domestic policies are being refashioned in keeping with the requirements specified by the IMF. In a peculiar effort at a two-stage devaluation of the rupee, its value has been reduced by around 20 per cent relative to most leading currencies. And judging by statements by government spokesmen, a major liberalisation of the trade regime, the financial structure and industrial policy, as well as a substantial reduction in subsidies on food and fertiliser are in the offing.

The implications of the devaluation are manifold. To start with, by rendering imports more expensive, it is inflationary. This would be so even if the government does not raise the administered prices of goods like oil which it imports. But that would mean an additional burden of expenditure on the government in a period when there is general agreement that the fiscal deficit should be cut. Further, the rupee cost of servicing external debt will rise in proportion to the depreciation, aggravating the fiscal crisis. So the net effect of devaluation will be higher inflation, worsening fiscal problems, greater recession, or a combination of these. Since the responsiveness of exports to the steady real devaluations of the 1980s has not been remarkable, it is not clear that the costs of this devaluation will be compensated by increasing exports, especially since export subsidies are to be reduced even as costs of production increase.

Some economists have argued that independent of the need for balance of payments financing from the IMF, policies of the type advocated by it are desirable in the Indian economy. This strategy achieves balance of payments adjustment within an open trade regime, essentially through domestic deflation via cutbacks in public expenditure and/or devaluation. Such a strategy is not merely recessionary, affecting industrial demand and employment, but also entails cuts in social and developmental expenditures, thus affecting both the growth prospects of the economy and the welfare particularly of the poorer sections.

Our perception is different. While there is definitely the need to reduce the fiscal and external imbalances, the mechanisms of ensuring this should include a more restrictive import regime, that corrects for the foreign exchange profligacy during the 1980s, a reduction in the revenue deficit of the government through increased direct taxes and rationalisation of expenditures and the provision of incentives in the form of tradable REP licences to those who earn hard currency through exports. This would improve government finances, while allowing some expansion in subsidies targeted at the poor, providing employment guarantees, raising expenditures on education, health, sanitation and drinking water and increasing capital expenditures aimed at raising the growth potential of the system.

In the short run, these measures must be accompanied by efforts to raise access to international liquidity. A gradual process of trade reform that helps enhance competitiveness without leading to closures and unemployment, a balanced approach to foreign investment and technology, special incentives to non-resident Indians and efforts at saving foreign exchange by cutting back on some mega-projects of doubtful value, could all play a role in this connection.

As opposed to this, there have been official declarations of acute financial stringency that makes IMF borrowing "inevitable", panic statements about the foreign exchange reserves position and talk of "floating" the rupee, all of which reduce India's bargaining position with the international financial institutions and in international capital markets. Instead, we strongly recommend a carefully modulated reform programme, wherein the highest priority is given to raising the productivity of all the Indian workers, through better education, while the system is debureaucratised and strengthened before subjecting it to international competition in a fundamentally iniquitous world system.

Signatories:

Prof Bhabatosh Dutta, Calcutta; Prof C.H. Hanumantha Rao, New Delhi; Dr Rajni Kothari, New Delhi; Dr Ashok Mitra, Calcutta; Dr Arun Ghosh, New Delhi; Prof G.S. Bhalla, New Delhi; Dr K.S. Krishnaswamy, Bangalore; Prof I.S. Gulati, Trivandrum; Dr R.C. Dutt, New Delhi; Prof C.T. Kurien, Madras; Prof Amiya Bagchi, Calcutta; Prof Moni Mukherjee, Calcutta; Prof Deb Kumar Bose, Calcutta; Prof Biplab Dasgupta, Calcutta; Krishna Raj, Bombay; Prof Krishna Bhardwaj, New Delhi; Prof Prabhat Patnaik, New Delhi; Prof Satish Jain, New Delhi; Prof Utsa Patnaik, New Delhi; Prof Atul Saram, New Delhi; Prof K.N. Reddy, New Delhi; Prof M.C. Purohit, New Delhi; Prof D.K. Srivastava, Varanasi; Dr Raghabendra Chattopadhyay, Calcutta; Balraj Mehta, New Delhi; Prof K.N. Kabra, New Delhi; Prof Venkatesh Athreya, Tiruchi; Dr K. Nagaraj, Madras; Dr Pulin Nayak, Delhi; Dr A. Majid, Delhi; Dr Kumaresh Chakravarty, Delhi; Dr Arun Kumar, New Delhi; Dr Abhijit Sen, New Delhi; Dr C.P. Chandrasekhar, New Delhi; Dr Jayati Ghosh, New Delhi.

The West Bengal government's proposal to resolve the balance-of-payments crisis, made public on 4 July 1991 and sent to the prime minister and finance minister a few days thereafter; reprinted in *Mainstream*, 20 July 1991

WEST BENGAL GOVERNMENT DOCUMENT

Alternative Policy Approach to Resolve BoP Crisis

The following is the "Note on an Alternative Policy Approach to Resolve the Balance of Payments Crisis" released by the West Bengal State Government on July 4, 1991.

—Editor

Confronted with the present severe balance of payments crisis, demonstrated by sharp downward adjustments in the rupee and reported negotiations of the Government of India for external loan from the IMF and other agencies, the following questions naturally arise: (a) What are the factors primarily responsible for this balance of payments crisis and this increasing need for the external loans including the IMF loan even after taking a massive quantum of loan from the IMF in 1981? (b) Who have suffered and who gained over this process of perpetuating the crisis? (c) How to guarantee that the past mistakes are not repeated and the country not forced into an international debt-trap?

In the following note, we shall try to answer these questions and suggest, in the interests of the common people, an alternative approach, both for short as well as the long run, to resolve to an extent the present balance of payments crisis.

This balance of payments crisis and the ever-increasing dependence on the external (particularly the IMF) loan are not an isolated phenomenon. These are inseparably connected with the very strategy followed by the Congress-I Government at the national level over the past several years, and particularly in the 1980s. This strategy begins by making no serious attempts at altering the existing unequal distribution of productive assets, particularly of land in agriculture and capital in industry. As a consequence, in this strategy, planning for production has tended to be viewed through the eyes of the landed gentry in agriculture and big industrialists in industry. As a result, given their interest, there has also been a tendency to adopt technology which is overly capital-biased and import-intensive with inadequate absorption of labour force in production, causing widespread unemployment. The stalled land reforms and the widespread

unemployment have been major factors behind inadequate purchasing power of the common people.

This inadequate purchasing power of the common people got further eroded by the increasing burden of indirect taxes (now reaching about 85 per cent of the total taxes, while the direct taxes falling to 15 per cent of the total) and continuous inflation, particularly fuelled by hikes of administered prices of essential commodities and inputs.

On the other hand, due to unequal ownership of land and industrial capital, and adoption of this overly capital-biased technology, there has been a selective increase in incomes of upper income classes. This erosion in purchasing power of the vast majority of common people coupled with selective income increases of the minority of upper income groups have distorted the entire scenario of industrial growth in the country—tilting it from the mass consumption goods to the selected elitish consumption goods industries which are known to be specially capital-biased and also import-intensive. This has further aggravated the problems of unemployment and lack of purchasing power of the masses, which, in turn, have restricted the domestic market and acted as a major bottlenek on the overall industrial expansion in the country.

Confronted with this situation of limited domestic market, salvation has been sought in the policy of the Central Government in terms of exports by ignoring the vast sections of domestic population. The data on foreign trade, however, indicate that exports have not increased in a significant manner. But due to adoption of capital-biased and import-intensive technology, particularly to meet the sumptuary aspiration of the upper income groups there has been a massive increase in imports—capital-goods imports now accounting for nearly 25 per cent of the import bill. The objective of

(Continued on page 34)

West Bengal Government Document
(Continued from page 4)

national self-reliance has in the process been sacrificed. Not only has there not been any *determined* policy towards oil-exploration*, with the result that our dependence on POL remains high (again nearly 25 per cent of the import bill); but even what can be produced within the country has not been produced. Domestic fertiliser plants, for instance, have been allowed to lie closed or underutilised while the import of fertilisers continuously increased, reaching almost three per cent of the total import bill. There has been in effect a deluge—an indiscriminate rush towards import liberalisation. And, this entire strategy was adopted when the IMF loan was taken in 1981. It was a strategy which was designed to make the vast majority of the common people suffer and only a minority of upper classes benefit, and open the door overly to imports, relating particularly to the needs of the richer sections and, in the process, worsen the balance of payments situation further. This was an overall strategy to make our country increasingly dependent over the years on the external loan. In fact, recourse was taken to indiscriminate and ever-increasing commercial borrowing, particularly during the years 1987-88—1989-90, and the external debt of the country increased sharply from around Rs 18,400 crores in early eighties to way over Rs 1 lakh crores now, with a severe accompanying balance of payments crisis.

◆

IN the midst of this crisis, we are alarmed to note that two sharp downward adjustments of rupee have been effected twice within two days! Facts and rationale of this move are not at all clear. In particular, this two-step nature of the move has raised genuine doubts in the minds of the people about its possible relationship with the IMF loan. Moreover, such a two-step move can itself lead to a wrong kind of Keynesian destablising speculative process. There are also reports about significant hikes of prices of non-ferrous metals and possibility of such hikes of coal prices. Moreover, there are now further policy announcements on hike of the banks' lending rates and on trade liberalisation. All

*From the experience of West Bengal, it has been noted, for instance, that our communications at the highest level regarding oil-exploration possibilities in the State have been left unattended even now.

these sudden and extraordinary steps are being taken just before convening the parliamentary session and also when the vote of confidence is so shortly due, and particularly at a time when the Government of India is reportedly negotiating external loan with the IMF and other agencies. The common people are being kept totally in the dark about the basic facts behind these extraordinary steps and their possible relationship with the IMF loan. We have therefore repeatedly demanded that at this moment of crisis the Government of India must come into the open and take the nation into confidence about the basic facts of the situation and all conditionalities of the IMF loan, so that the right course of action can be democratically decided both for the short run as well as the long run in order to protect the interests of the common people and priorities of our country.

In choosing the right course of action, we should learn from the past mistakes and must not repeat the same. The conditionalities of the present IMF loan negotiations are still not known to us. We are therefore considering only certain possibilities. It is possible, for instance, that the conditionalities may be directed towards domestic fiscal deficit reduction and structural adjustments. But, then, through which channels are the deficit reduction and structural adjustments being considered? If the fiscal deficit reduction and structural adjustments take the following course, namely, increase in the burden of indirect taxes, increase in administered prices of essential commodities and inputs, reduction in subsidies meant for poorer sections, particularly related to the public distribution system, dismantling of the public sector, relaxation of restrictions on the monopoly industrial houses, increase in the banks' lending rates and liberalisation of imports, then by following this course of actions, we shall only be repeating most of the past mistakes. For instance, increase in indirect taxation, onslaught of inflation through administered price hikes and erosion in public distribution system will not only pass on the burden of adjustment again to the poorer sections, but, what is equally worrying, all these steps, by unleashing further inflationary spiral, will discourage the growth of exports and become counterproductive in the present balance of payments crisis. Similarly, removal of monopoly restrictions will only worsen the existing market imperfections. Increase in the banks' lending rates will also put the smaller producers at a relative disadvantage vis-a-vis the larger houses, and again make the entire system less competitive. These moves towards further weakening the competitiveness are potentially inflationary and can discourage exports, and thus become once again counterproductive in the present context. Our experience also shows that liberalisation of imports, the argument of linking imports with export-oriented production notwithstanding, has always, on the whole, worsened the balance of payments situation.

As against this approach, which has been followed in the past and has been self-defeating, we are suggesting an alternative approach. Since available information is inadequate, this is not an exhaustive statement, but only the outline of an alternative approach. If full information is made available, then, on the basis of further interaction, this note can be made more exhaustive.

To begin with, for achieving any desired extent of domestic fiscal deficit reduction, inflationary methods based on indirect taxation and administered price hikes or curtailment of public distribution system are not the only means. The same quantum of fiscal deficit reduction can be achieved through an alternative and better policy package consisting of an increase in income tax (particularly for the upper income deciles), better enforcement of the collection from existing taxes, including arrears, unearthing of black money, selective non-priority cuts in non-Plan expenditure of almost all the Ministries without affecting interests of the poorer sections. While achieving the higher targets of resource mobilisation as well as economisation of expenditure, new possibilities of realignment in the Centre-State relations towards more decentralisation may be seriously considered.

◆

THE real advantage of this alternative package is that it can ensure the same quantum of deficit reduction without hurting the interests of the common people and without creating any inflationary pressure and, therefore, without having any adverse effect on exports. In this alternative package, it is again possible to achieve the same deficit reduction by retaining those subsidies which are directed towards the poorer sections, particularly the food subsidy in relation to the public distribution system or subsidies meant for small scale industries or common farmers. It must be clearly pointed out that subsidised public distribution acts as a countervailing force against inflation. By containing inflation, it tends to reduce the expenditure side of the budget and helps achieve fiscal deficit reduction

and also export promotion. Similarly, subsidies and reduced lending rates of the banks for small-scale producers can inherently increase the competitiveness of the system, and thus again have an inflation-containing and also potentially export-promoting effect.

So far as the working of the public sector is concerned, the approach should be one of combining its desired social orientation with drastic improvement in internal efficiency. Unnecessary bureaucratic delays should be systematically removed. All these can then be a part of expenditure reduction as well as growth (and also export)-promoting exercise.

Comprehensive import curtailment is an essential part of this alternative approach. By going through each item of the import bill, it is indeed possible to reduce a significant quantum of import of all items unless they are connected with mass consumption goods, essential production, infrastructural requirements or exports. In addition, it needs to be categorically pointed out that rather than uncertain and frequent adjustments in the rupee, a clear statement of facts may be made with a strong appeal towards the NRIs so that the NRI-capital flow can be favourably reversed.

This outline of an alternative approach thus indicates how, even in the immediately short run, it may be possible to narrow down the gap in the external balance of payments as well as in internal fiscal deficits, protecting at the same time interests of the common people at every step. In this regard, proposals of this alternative approach need to be contrasted with the policy measures self-defeatingly taken in the past as well some of the measures possibly being contemplated even now.

In the long run, however, this alternative approach has to be based on increase in the purchasing power of the common people, and on the concept of agricultural and industrial growth primarily on the basis of expansion of the domestic market, thus placing a significant emphasis on the much-important objective of self-reliance. For achieving all these, it is essential to begin with land reforms and with a wider dispersal in the ownership of industrial capital. We can then think of progress of a new kind of technology which will be both modern and yet be able to use and not displace labour and natural resources in a fuller manner. To sustain this long run alternative approach, there is of course the need for a different political process which can be developed on the strength of democratic movements of the common people across the country. ❑

Annexure 8:
Cover of the booklet issued on Narasimha Rao's address to the nation
on 9 July 1991, that is not included in his *Selected Speeches,* Volume 1

An unpublished paper by Narasimha Rao titled 'Liberalisation and the Public Sector', prepared in February–March 2001, made available from his archives by his youngest son, P.V. Prabhakar Rao

LIBERALISATION AND THE PUBLIC SECTOR

Five decades ago, India made a tryst with destiny. The most important ingredient of that tryst, taken from Mahatma Gandhi's well-known Talisman was simple: When you wish to know if anything you want to do is good or not, imagine the face of the poorest man in the land and ask yourself whether your proposed act will be of any gain to him . . .The Parliament of India endorsed the Talisman when the Lok Sabha declared: ***The basic criterion for determining the lines of advance must not be private profit but social gain, and that the pattern of development and structure of socio-economic relations should be so planned that they result not only in appreciable increase in national income and employment but also in greater equality in incomes and wealth.*** Neither the Parliament itself nor any political party has said anything opposed to this dictum so far. Private profit may have since entered our calculations more, but social gain has never been jettisoned.

To me this is not a mere cliche', howsoever mixed may have been the actual achievement. It is the essence of our tryst with destiny. When you call anything basic, you mean that it is unchangeable, as such. All that one can do is to try different methods and modes to reach that objective.

Those who entered the freedom movement were basically motivated by the <u>Talisman</u>. No leader recruited them. In fact, they, as young activists, chose their leaders, from out of many luminaries in the political spectrum. some of us chose to follow Nehru, whom none of us knew personally. Maybe we tried to understand what he stood for, and that appealed to us; others among us chose others . . . And at least some persons can humbly claim that they have done their bit, keeping the <u>Talisman</u> in view. And when I said that the intent of the liberalisation programme in 1991 was entirely in line with the <u>Talisman</u>, there was no need whatever of any eye-brows going up. It was a case of clear conceptualisation and equally clear projection.

***

While taking a good look at our economy over the decades, let us briefly examine what position it reflects today at first sight. Here we need to keep aside both our propensity for self-condemnation, as also for excessive self-adulation. Our population has trebled since independence. The increase was not because of any sudden explosion of procreation in free India. The birth rate was already high in the past, but the mortality and morbidity rates were also high. Our health schemes in the last 50 years did bring a marked improvement in infant survival, mother survival, relief from several communicative and non-communicative diseases-- thus increasing net population and life expectancy. This is a happy example where success brings its own problems; we do not grudge them, evidently.

With this burgeoning population we became self-sufficient in food and clothing. And the Indian farmer has proved that even without much formal education, he is quick to adopt every single scientific method brought to him, the moment he is convinced that it is for his benefit. This augurs well for the future.

However, where India has *not* done well enough is on the quantitative, mass side. Already poor when freedom came, she clearly lagged in meeting the ever-increasing current needs at mass level, plus the large backlog of unmet needs inherited at the time of freedom. Primary and secondary education, primary health, housing for the poor, primary levels of nutrition etc., everything at the primary and mass level. I said 'well enough' because even in these areas, what was done was nothing short of massive (such as the phenomenal expansion of educational facilities all over the country etc.) but the needs have galloped faster, leading to overall shortfall. Besides, quantitative expansion was not accompanied or followed by qualitative improvement, such as in education. The main (though not the sole) reason for these inadequacies was paucity of resources (meaning continuing poverty) and not any inherent complication in solving the problems, by and large. If the government could build, say ten million rural houses (admittedly) it could as well have built twenty. And so on. No matter which Party rules, these are basic, irrefutable facts.

It is clear therefore that more incomes to the people *at all levels* would be the main solution to these ills, if the country does not have to lose its independence and become a mendicant or a dependent. In any event India is too big to find an adequate alms-giver or a big enough prop to lean on for all time, without crushing the prop itself. The Indian elephant *must* stand on its own legs.

Next, the rationale of the mixed economy pattern adopted in the early fifties under Jawaharlal Nehru needs to be understood in perspective today, when newer generations sometimes seem to be critical of it. What were the options in this respect before India in 1949, for instance? The realisation of the bitter truth of India having been exploited and virtually robbed under foreign rule was strong at the time. A system in which the big fish devours the small fish could not have been considered good for the country, which was still echoing the powerful patriotic songs that had aroused millions of people-- *daridranarayans* in Gandhiji's words-- and created a pervading spirit of nationalism and Swadeshi. In a word, to accept *the lassez faire* system with no holds barred would have been unthinkable. On the other side the Soviet Union was emerging as a power to reckon with and the Marxist ideology was catching the imagination of intellectuals and political leaders alike all over the world. Nehru was following these developments very closely since the twenties and developed his opinions on these matters studiously and with clarity. He developed an absolute abhorrence of dictatorship, having personally witnessed some scenes in other countries. And equally naturally, he did not approve totalitarian methods wherever they were practised. The corollary of all this was that he did not approve for India the Soviet economic system either. He took what was relevant for a poor country, and also what was relevant for giving primacy to the will of the people. The combination was an amalgam of socialism and democracy. On the economic side it became the mixed economy, with private ownership retained in many areas such as agriculture and some categories of industry, and also giving an important role to the state in huge infrastructural ventures like irrigation and power projects and several other areas where private enterprise was just not possible then.

There has been a lot of misunderstanding and deliberate disinformation about the Public Sector. An impression is sought to be created that it was totally unnecessary and that the private sector could have done wonders with industrialisation. As a person who lived through those stages and possesses some personal knowledge about those policies, I wish to reiterate that the emergence of the Public Sector was the one good thing that happened to the country at that juncture.

The Public Sector, then -- being in charge of the 'commanding heights' of the economy-- was to take care of the establishment of the infrastructure from public funds and its expansion, to the maximum extent possible from out of its own earnings. But for various reasons, this did not happen; instead, the Public Sector itself soaked more and more Government funds, decade after decade. The basic infrastructure set up by the Public Sector was magnificent by any standards and has stood the country in good stead. It is valued at rupees two lakh crores today. However, Government could not adequately fund its much-needed expansion and timely modernisation. The result has been stagnation, compounded by obsolescence. Therefore, somewhere on the way the inefficacy of the public sector alone to meet the country's needs in full, could be clearly seen. The fault did not lie with the public sector alone; it was compounded by Government's mounting financial stringency also. It had entered a kind of vicious circle.

Here I would like to add an interesting and crucial piece of information which, I am sure, would surprise many. I learnt from the Prime Minister of Singapore recently that their policy too had all along been to keep huge infrastructure projects-- in other words commanding heights-- under State control, run them efficiently and to allow a free play of private enterprise in other medium or minor industries, in their thousands. It is only now, he said, that they are doing corporatisation. Curiously enough, this shows that Jawaharlal Nehru and Lee Kwan Yew followed the same route from two totally different ideological standpoints. The difference seemed to lie not between sectors, but between efficiencies in the same sector. It proves that inefficiency is not the monopoly of a particular sector . . . I had occasion to emphasize this point in Parliament with particular reference to the Singapore Airlines as early as 1991.

It is to be noted that the Public Sector, as conceived by Nehru, was not detrimental to the private sector's vital interests. It was a parallel sector, but not a predatory one. Despite grumbling against the public sector, captains of the private sector were also fully aware of the huge benefits that accrued to them from the public sector. In a public expression of these benefits, Naval Tata had said:

'I am one of those who always believed that on our country attaining political independence, had our Government not shouldered most of the infrastructural industries like coal, steel, rail and air transport, power, fertilizer, and a number of other basic industries, the industrialists like Tatas, Birlas, Goenkas, Kirloskars and dozens of others would have found it extremely difficult to attain the extent of industrial development they have been able to achieve... To that extent, the private sector owes a debt of gratitude to the Government for accelerating the tempo for industrialisation, which alone made possible our claim to be amongst the first dozen of the most industrialised countries of the world.'

The Public Sector has seen many ups and downs over the decades. During the eighties, particularly during Rajiv Gandhi's regime, efforts were made to minimize its inefficiencies through management tools like the MsOU. In the Reform package of 1991, the tool was 'competition'- provided by the Private Sector. However, there was no intention of transferring 'ownership' as a remedy to solve the problems either of the Public Sector or of the economy. Indeed it *does not* solve the problems. All the relevant aspects of the new policy, including the Public Sector, were thoroughly examined and certain parameters were clearly formulated and unequivocally announced at home and abroad, including Davos, the Mecca of the world-wide capitalist industrial fraternity. Throughout the first two years of that regime as far as I could recall, Government took great pains to explain that it had not abandoned-- nor intended to abandon-- the mixed economy concept formulated by Jawaharlal Nehru. Even after the Lok Sabha election of 1996 when the Congress went out of power at the Centre, no one is aware of any reversal of that policy having been decided upon by any government. It is obvious therefore that any decision to sell off the PSUs flies in the face of the accepted and fully extant policies of the Nation, to date.

So, any decision of sale, or one amounting to sale, of our Public Sector Undertakings is a serious one. This news must have come as a rude shock to those with a background knowledge of India's economic policies since independence . . . Mixed economy was part of a package that epitomised an ideal combination of 'middle path' policies. It was a wholesome balance between the world's contradictory economic-ideologies of the time-- and above all,

3

the only viable guarantee, such as was feasible, for strengthening sovereignty and independence in decision-making in the conduct of our economy. Thousands of patriots and political activists everywhere understood this very special dimension of the mixed economy, almost instinctively. Indeed it was appreciated in terms of the Nation's essential self-reliance and not in terms of profit and loss. And the nation's resolve of self-reliance cannot be computed in terms of money. Therefore, the primacy of that sovereignty and independence in decision-making needs to be kept intact, *in fact*.

Obviously, any decision to sell off is completely irrevocable. No future government will be in a position to reverse it. For instance, we were able to bring back the Nation's mortgaged gold in 1991. However, had it been outright sale instead of a mortgage, we could not have done anything about it. Some decisions of this nature would have to be dealt with in a manner different from the ones adopted under a rigid party system. These have to be very carefully scrutinised and decided only by a clear consensus bordering on unanimity. The question whether to go in for the Public Sector in 1950-51 was vastly and qualitatively different from what we have today as the question of what to do with the huge edifice that is the Public Sector already. It cannot be answered in a yes or no format for a variety of reasons. What I wish to emphasize is that this decision is not confined to the government or the political parties. This is essentially concerned with the ownership of the entire people of India-- the *de facto* and *de jure* ownership, which no government for the time being can deprive them of, for all time. No one has a right to do so, least of all a Government with a clearly unclear popular support. In this form it is unacceptable. Further, it is not a question of the terms on which the sales are to be made. In a large number of cases, it is the very idea of permanent alienation of the Nation's own joint property-- the structures along with the land they stand on-- that cannot be countenanced. The clear difference between permanent right of the people in the property on the one hand, and the function of the government in holding that property for the time being on behalf of the people, on the other, is a very real one and needs to be realised-- whatever may be the scope of legal quibbling. People's property is *not*, strictly speaking, goverment property; if at all, government can deal with the property only as a trustee, and without tampering with the people's *basic* ownership. Even a piece of land assigned by government to a landless person, is not permanent alienation; it is liable to be revoked under certain circumstances. And let the government not take recourse to the specious plea that 99 years' lease is only temporary alienation! . . . So you cannot sell off the people's property worth two lakh crores without batting an eye. Even a lease of our airports for a longish period could put our interests, especially security interests, at serious risk. I would like to remind countrymen how India could retain the Kashmir Valley in 1947 against the raiders by the one single feat of taking control of the Srinagar Airport just in time. After personal observation and experience over the decades, I am compelled to say that India's geo-political situation will never never allow any act that loses, or parts with, the control of our airports at any time. It is difficult to imagine the position of a person who lives in his house but allows someone else to control its ingress and egress points. Anyone with his eyes and ears open and his sense of history intact, can feel in his bones, what security implications India is destined (or condemned) to live with every moment of her existence as a Nation. Either one feels it, or one doesn't; there is no need to elaborate.

The proposal of dis-investment in the PSUs, which was thought of in the 1991-96 period, has to be distinguished from the present decision of outright sale. Whatever the shrinking global village may bring, I for one do not see the complete withering away of the nation state in the foreseeable future. I do not see the end of exploitation of the weaker states by the stronger ones. The methods, of course, will be almost unrecognisably different-- and

4

more alluring. While dis-investment was essentially a pragmatic idea without impinging on ownership or on the basic policy, sale clearly amounts to giving up the accepted policy of mixed economy. Surely, the people of India have never approved of this *volte face, whichever way one interprets their chaoticmandate* ... It causes some consternation, therefore, to see no effective public reaction at the impending destruction of the entire edifice of the Nation's fifty-year old policy, without so much as a serious scrutiny or a nationwide debate.

Coming to the practical aspects of this decision, the anticipated complications are truly mind-boggling. In the first place, nothing is known about the urgency for the decision or the alternative use to which the sale proceeds are intended to be appropriated. If, as seems reasonable to surmise, the proceeds are to form part of the admittedly uncomfortable budgetary assets, the decision would be tantamount to selling one's dwelling house to pay the grocer's bills. The illogic is patent.

The total assets of the PSUs are approximately being estimated at around Rupees 200,000 crores. And yet they are just able to fulfill the country's needs only to the extent of 30 to 35%, which would naturally be a decreasing figure in the context of increasing needs. After the purchase of these huge undertakings it is only reasonable to think that the buyer would remain engrossed in sorting out the multifarious problems thrown up by the purchases for the next several years. While it is possible that the units will be run somewhat more efficiently and may even receive marginal expansion, it would be impossible for them, in the short run, to be able to make any appreciable dent on the 65% of the unmet needs of the country. If this is the prospect for several years, one wonders what net gain can be expected today from these unadmitted distress sales. It is also not at all difficult to imagine the cut-throat competition among MNCs etc. in grabbing our PSUs and the utter improbability of those who are neck-deep in the competition (or those who fail in the competition) rushing in to make fresh infra-structural investments in India.

One is thus left totally unconvinced of either the correctness of this decision, or about its urgent necessity. It is doubtful whether the common people will appreciate it, when they eventually come to know of it in all its stark details. As things stand, there seem to be few other issues of such crucial nature, which the thinking people in the country are duty- bound to take up with all the vehemence at their command and take it to its logical end. It is too early to tamper with the Public Sector, as such. In the evolution of the liberalisation process, a time will come when more colear-cut decisions would possibly be taken regarding the emerging pattern of the economy, including the Public Sector. While no pattern will be valid for all time, a change for change's sake also would be meaningless. So this Sector as a whole should not be made a victim of ad hocism meanwhile.

It is most unfortunate that the Government should be thinking of selling off Air India/ Indian Airlines. I simply cannot think of India selling off her national carrier, which carries the national flag.

Now to return to liberalisation. The utility of foreign investment, when it was first tried in a big way in 1991 was to relieve the Government of its massive commitments on large infrastructure projects (such as power, fertiliser, highways etc.) Given these inescapable priorities, we could not spare enough for human resource development-- viz, something that converts a human being into a human *resource*. Government had spread its resources too wide, too thin, on too many things, for too long. If only foreign investment could take over a major part of these giant infrastructure schemes, this substitution would have enabled Government to utilize more of its own resources on education, health and social assistance. In addition, industrialisation would bring jobs to the educated sector. This sector was growing fast despite inadequate overall educational facilities. It tended to become an almost frightening problem-- particularly in urban areas wherein its striking visibility attracts instantaneous attention anyway. The young men and women had to be looked after, to the extent possible, on a priority basis.

So in the eyes of the layman, the practical advantage of foreign investment (which was understood as investment from outside the Government, whether foreign or Indian in origin) was the huge extra investment expected to come in for his benefit. This formed part of the package called economic reforms, which have enjoyed consensus ever since, by and large. Thus the new thinking of 1991 did not fly in the face of our mixed economy. Government simply altered the mix, as required by circumstances. It is now clear that this policy outline is definitely about to be destroyed. The present Government's message seems to be one of 'Clearance Sale.'

The new package of 1991 did work out as intended, in the beginning. A massive allocation of Rs.30,000 crores for rural development in the 8th Plan (actually rising to Rs.33,000 crores) from around Rs.10,000 crores in the 7th Plan; a courageous public commitment that India would step up its expenditure on education to 6 per cent of the GNP by the end of the IX Plan; launching several 'yojanas' targeting almost every group among the poor; well-conceived schemes of social assistance nation-wide-- these measures are enough to show how our liberalisation began with great promise and enhanced our self-confidence. The fund flows for rural development to the DRDAs continued steadily; indeed in some instances, the money going from Delhi accounted for the *whole* of the development activity in the State, though labelled differently while reaching the beneficiaries... It must be emphasised, besides, that India's liberalisation was well tailored to the country's specific needs and priorities. No 'exit policy' was accepted, as such, since the consequent risk of large numbers of workers losing their jobs simply could not be overlooked. Again, liberalisation in India, unlike in some other countries, did not *ipso facto* mean conversion of the Public Sector into private enterprise, although it did mean a vast enlargement of private enterprise, to co-exist with the existing Public Sector; the difference is worth noting. Government clearly told prospective investors not to be eyeing our existing Public Sector for take-over, but to concentrate on starting new industries to fulfil the large requirement not covered by the Public Sector. As anyone can see, these parameters were entirely different from what is now being done in the name of reforms. ***To put it bluntly, sale is certainly not the next generation of dis-investment. Let us not delude ourselves. Sale is a totally different species, not any generation of dis-investment.*** What makes me feel unhappy is the disinformation being spread that it originated in 1991-96.

However, the sum-total of foreign investment was not massive enough to make a real dent on the situation, even though the direction was right. A hundred-fold increase in investment would still go unnoticed in this vast investment-parched country. What was worse, the emphasis on infrastructure became a halting starter and the results have been poor. If infrastructure is left out, it is difficult to see how large-scale foreign investment would be of any specific public benefit here. The power sector, for instance, has belied all our high hopes so far; it deserves top priority. Some reasons of these shortfalls are said to be-- the investor's perception of our political stability and practical difficulties in restructuring procedures, some of which are said to continue as irritants. Much has been done, admittedly, but this is a continuous process and could be hastened only up to a point and no further, at any given time, for obvious reasons. Even so, investment on infrastructure is of the essence in the Reforms package. Only this investment can release Govt.'s funds for human development. *It is precisely in this area that the government's political and diplomatic sagacity and perspicacity are generally tested. Success in this field does not consist merely*

6

in high-profile visits, nor even high-sounding communiques; they are all hopelessly outdated todqy. An over-whelming part of diplomacy is therefore economic diplomacy now.

*   *   *

Meanwhile, time flew. The Millennium changed. A new Century arrived. A New decade was ushered in... Yet nothing really changed. Being one of the lucky individuals who can claim to have straddled two millennia, I was trying, in the all-pervasive euphoria of the transition, to be enlightened about what the enthusiastic entrants to the new millennium think is in store for them. At that moment, I had a chance to read a booklet named 'December 1999 Compilation from World Bank, UNDP and other Reports.' To anyone witnessing the scenario painted in the compilation for the first time, it would make a really depressing reading. The Report graphically describes the situation in some countries that had made remarkable progress in the last two decades. A short report on India is also included in the compilation. The net effect that was seen in these countries are as follows:-

1.   Economic insecurity;
2.   Education and Health budgets coming under strain;
3.   Longer time needed for human recovery than economic recovery;
4.   Job and income insecurity;
5.   Cultural insecurity;
6.   Personal insecurity;
7.   Illicit trade-- drugs, women, weapons, laundered money;
8.   Political and community insecurity.

The Reports came in 1999. However, may I point out that some of these were anticipated for a long time in the past in India and particularly in the context of our liberalisation policy in 1991? May I respectfully submit that these are quite well-known in the experience of developing countries, including India, and were being raised time and again with the World Bank and the IMF etc, only to be summarily ignored? Today the World Bank, in very plain language, seems to have retracted its earlier assertions, as is evident from some passages I shall presently quote, since they fully reflect the woes of the world's down-trodden people today.

I would also like to remind those who chose to forget or ignore, for whatever reason, the fact that apart from the trebling of the allocation for rural development in the VIII Plan as mentioned above, special nationwide 'Yojanas' were introduced from time to time during 1991-1996 (in addition to continuing the programmes initiated in Rajiv Gandhi's regime). *This was not meant to be confined to one Plan. It was the precursor of a new strategy to be repeated on an increasing scale in subsquent Plans. It was a timely and deliberate intensification in the objectives of the planning process, so as to shore up a poor country's flanks from some of the anticipated negative effects of liberalisation.*

A brief overall view of the Yojanas of 91-96 is given below:

*Prime Minister's Rozgar Yojana;
*Mahila Smridhhi Yojana;
*Employment assurance Scheme (EAS);
*Revamped Public Distribution System of essential eommodities;

Midday meal Scheme for school children funded by the centre for the first time;
Commitment and decision to spend 6% of the GNP on education by the end of the IX plan.
Large-scale national Social Assistance Programme from the Centre for the first time.
Introduction of an improved and modern tools scheme for village artisans all over the country;
Safai Karmacharis' Welfare and Development Commission for the first time from the Centre with funding provision of around Rs.500 crores;
Statutory status to SC & ST, BC Commissions;
Conversion of metre and other smaller gauge railway lines into broad gauge for the first time after independence to a distance of around 6,000 kms amounting to one-half of the entire small gauge length in the whole country, so as to complete it by end of IX Plan. This was taken up on priority for its intensive employment potential also.
Fillip to Rural Housing raising the number of houses built to one million a year by 1995 and planning to continue the annual increase so as to complete the construction of houses for all the houseless poor people in the whole country in 7 or 8 years.
Continuous and unprecedented increase in rice and wheat procurement prices by at least Rs. 40 to Rs. 50 per quintal per year over the entire five-year period; in order to improve the terms of trade of the agricultural sector and bring it closer to the industrial sector;
Enormous increase of export opportunities to farmers;
Enouragement to growing palm oil crop in India along with other commercial crops, in a bid to make the country self-sufficient in edible oil at the earliest and to save a huge foreign exchange outgo;
Concrete steps initiated to introduce a new scheme for crop insurance.

A quick analysis of these programmes would reveal that they were conceived with every section of the population in mind. They were formulated for actual and quantified benefit, not merely as expressions of support and sympathy on paper.

This was a deliberate combining of the new policy with suitable independent programmes to siphon development benefits and employment opportunities to the grass roots levels as a direct by-pass. This was the largely unnoticed other side of the much-noticed 'opening up' part of the liberalisation programme. The huge outlays on these programmes were to be made possible by a large portion of massive infra-structure projects being entrusted to the private sector.

Everyone agrees that these massive programmes need to be taken up. There has never been any difference on this. In fact, there was a public commitment that from Rs. 30,000 crores in the VIII Plan, the outlay would be raised to close to Rs. 80,000 crores in the IX plan. This was the commitment by an elected Central Government. No one can say that this would be in excess of the country's need. Even if it was not written on stamped paper and registered, it was no less an official commitment. And we have an authentic Report that Rs. 33,000 crores in the VIII Plan has made only a limited impact. There is no need either to gloat, or to beat one's breast, over this proven inadequacy. The most obvious conclusion is that a much higher outlay on rural development is absolutely necessary in several successive plans. We have to find the funds required. One way we adopted for getting the funds in 1991-96 was the substitution I have mentioned above. There is no need to stick to this route alone; there is nothing sacrosanct about it. If the government finds equally massive sources in any other way, it would only redound to its credit and the people would certainly be grateful. If neither of these two alternatives comes forth, it will only mean that we don't mean what we say in regard to the Indian village. There can be no other interpretation or inference.

Another significant fact that has come to notice in the UNDP report is that in the reforms era Government planners and others concentrated on the capital market with emphasis on making the market safe for foreign and NRI investors... This, it is said, has resulted in investment in the financial assets yielding higher returns (such as stocks and shares) than investment in physical assets. After pointing out this fact, it is asserted that we need more investment on growth- inducing, employment-generating and wage-goods-producing projects.

In my understanding, what the UNDP sources say is the same as has been said above, that infrastructure projects need to be brought into the country in a big way.

*   *   *

It may be of interest to the Indian people to know what the World Bank has said now. After over 50 years, the World Bank has admitted that many of its past policies were misguided. The Bank's annual World Development Report painted a bleak picture of the developing world which has fallen even further behind rich nations. It also said that in many ways the Bank had failed in its mission to improve conditions of poverty, disease and poor education in the developing world and admitted that it cannot carry the burden alone if its ideas are to work. It also said "trickle-down economics"-- the practice of cutting taxes for the rich hoping it would benefit the poorer in society-- does not work. (We in India have said it time and time again, based on our own experience of our own stratified society.) But whatever policies were used over the past 50 years, one thing is certain: Poverty continues to rise.

About India, another report reveals some astounding data. Although relative differentials exist, absolute deprivation is high in most parts of rural India. For example, about half the population of rural India is illiterate and suffers from 'capability poverty'; about 40 per cent have extremely low incomes.

The Report exhorts that a determined, concerted and sustained effort to eliminate poverty and social disability is necessary in India. The belief that a relative cost recovery is needed to sustain many social service investments is a reality. However, over 50 per cent of India's population is still vulnerable and cannot afford the cost of education and health care. Public action, therefore, is needed to restructure and eliminate the current anomalies in the dispensation of social services so as to target them to the most needy and at the same time recover costs from the better- off by allowing the private sector to cater to the needs of the latter. Whatever may be said about recovery, our age-old tradition of the free school and free medicine-- such as the country could afford-- has now been more than vindicated. The materialist trend that was scoffing at the 'free' idea now seems debunked, when applied to the poor people in India, as per these high-brow reports. While on this subject it may be useful to recall that the Public Sector was not essentially meant to grab profits, in the fifties when it was started. it was an extension of compassionate social values, as adumbrated by our saints and leaders over many centuries past. The idea of making profits for its own consolidation emerged, as of necessity, gradually towards the end of the fifties, if my recollection is correct.

The Report suggests synergistic efforts to invest in the rural and agricultural sectors so as to enhance rural incomes and also to generate broad based employment opportunities along with guaranteed real wages. It concludes, saying that the challenge for India in the next century is to improve the levels of living and concurrently reduce relative deprivation within

9

a limited time.

I wish to remind the authors of these Reports that India's development philosophy and plans were predicated precisely on these ideas-- right from the word go. We seem to be getting our own ideas back as original advice now. So be it. We do not claim the first authorship; but it is a good thing to know that we have at last been found right (without saying so) by those whose opinion counts.

The brighter scenario, however, is also evident. Our own undeniable experience is that the middle class in India-- that is, the class which can be expected to fend for itself, by and large-- is constantly growing. There is optimism in the air. Liberalisation is like another new-found freedom. It is a wonderful tool. It has opened many doors and the Indian innovator has now got numerous openings. He has suddenly grown wings and is flying high. His self-confidence is a sight to see. A few things that have not yet begun happening need to happen now. They are: Applied research to meet our own problems based on our own assets; and a distinction between satisfaction of legitimate needs on the one hand and mindless consumerism on the other. So let there be no meaningless conclusion that liberalisation itself is bad, simply because many more good things are still to happen. *However, let us also clearly understand that liberalisation is at the crossroads, from where it needs to be steered carefully and with imagination so as to yield the bountiful results it is capable of.*

The contours and purposes of liberalisation started in 1991 stand fully vindicated. 'Caution' is the watchword. On his visit to India some time back, the Singapore P.M. also said something very definite about the vagaries of indiscriminate capital movement all over the world. Very wisely, he declared that he wants Singapore to be a global hub of knowledge-based industries. Now, India can also derive the maximum advantage, from her proven prowess. in this field. But can India, with her vast size and unending problems of poverty, afford to remain confined to knowledge-based industries alone? Can our knowledge of how many steel plants we need bring us even one scrap of steel? Quantifying poverty seems rather superfluous where poverty in its massive dimensions is there for anyone to see, except for those who don't want to see. India is the land of the Vedas and Upanishads, she never lacked knowledge and insight-- whether memorised or computerised. Thousands of saints, savants, leaders, preachers, poets and experts have declared what needs to be done. The process is continuing unceasingly. But the mechanics of implementation is what seems to be faltering. A slogan has to be converted into an idea, the idea into a thesis, the thesis into a programme, the programme into implementational components, the components have to be related to human beings in a system called the administration. While this is the long journey, with all its hazards and uncertainties, not to speak of human frailties, we still seem to be teetering on the fringe of slogans. When the Singapore Prime minister hinted at erratic capital movement, he was also politely warning us not to fall in the debt trap by short-term borrowings for unproductive purposes. Centuries ago, we had the Charvakas who merrily said, *rinam krithva ghritam pibet.* (Meaning: Make debts and enjoy yourself!)The reason they cited was: *bhasmeebhutasya dehasya punaraagamanam kuthah?* (Meaning: Once your body is consigned to the funeral pyre, where is it going to come back from?) The Indian society definitely rejected this philosophy even in case of the individual. And when it comes to a State or the nation, this reckless outlook is still more disastrous, since the State and the Nation will last for ever, unlike the individual. So between the Charvakas and the Indian elephant, caution is the only sensible bridge.

I can only hope that eyes will open in time.

(P.V.Narasimha Rao.)

Annexure 10:

Interview of Dr K.N. Raj to *Frontline* in mid-July 1991 that greatly
bolstered the confidence of the prime minister and finance minister

THE ECONOMY

'Drastic measures needed'
Interview with Dr. K. N. Raj

Dr. K. N. Raj, an internationally reputed economist who has distinguished himself in a number of areas including theoretical work, feels that though the outlook is not bad, India has to be extremely careful about external borrowing.

The joint author of the famous Raj-Sen model, Dr. Raj has made wide-ranging contributions in development economics over the years. As Director of the Delhi School of Economics, he contributed to shaping it as a centre of excellence.

Dr. Raj spoke to **C. Gouridasan Nair**. Excerpts:

▶ *What is your assessment of the present economic situation?*

Essentially, what we are faced with now is a balance of payments (BoP) problem. Underlying this are the other issues of which the most important, I think, is the enormous deficit in the Government budget. It is as part of the efforts to deal with the deficits that the Government has to consider enormous cuts in expenditure and a major candidate there is Government subsidies. It could also be many other things like a sizable cut in defence expenditure. *Otherwise, basically, the economy is in a very strong position.* The rate of economic growth in the last ten years has been remarkable. The economy has been able to grow quite rapidly. *I basically agree with Dr. Manmohan Singh's assessment that the outlook is not all that bad and, in fact, it is quite reassuring.* It will not be possible to bring about changes in the economy overnight.

▶ *What is at the root of the present BoP crisis?*

For years, we have been depending on what you might call soft aid — which meant either grants for which no interest is payable or loans at very low rates of interest. This period gave way to a period of loans available only at very high rates of interest. This is the period during which we developed large deficits. *The import liberalisation of the period also resulted in deficits which had to be financed with these*

high interest loans. It is these high-interest loans which have really grown in the very short period. *It really shows the dangers of external dependence in a sense.* Once the rates of interest are high, in no time you lose control. It is this that has happened. We have to get ourselves out of this mess. *In future, we have to be extremely careful about external borrowing. We have to depend very much more on our own resources.* We must have an enormous export promotion drive so that we earn the foreign exchange we need, both for development purposes and for all our repayment needs. China is also doing exactly the same. The Chinese are entering the market of the Far East as well as the U.S. in a big way.

▶ *Manmohan Singh says there is no alternative to a large IMF loan involving conditionalities if India is to tide over the present crisis. How do you view this?*

There are two propositions here. One, that there are certain conditions attached by the IMF to the extension of the loan. Second, that we have no

Phil Roy

alternative. *I do not myself know what are all the conditions that have been imposed. But I have sufficient confidence in Manmohan Singh because he has very wide experience.* He is not another economist; he is a person who has worked in a very wide range of organisations so that he is familiar with the entire background. He has also been in the IMF, the World Bank and so on. So I have no reason to question his assessment.

▶ *Manmohan Singh has also stated that we have been fed on soft options till now and that if we do not wake up now, we shall lose our economic independence.*

Quite right.

▶ *But there is also a contrary viewpoint. That we would stand to lose our economic independence and more if we go in for the loan, accepting the IMF conditionalities. The Left parties, for instance...*

I am not terribly bothered about the leftist position because they have a high-minded, doctrinaire approach when they are out of power. If the leftists were in power today, I know exactly what they would have done. They would have accepted these. So that does not affect my judgment. People will, of course, make noises when there are substantial reductions in subsidies and when there is an increase in prices. That is quite true. But as Manmohan Singh has said, we have certainly taken easy options earlier. *If we had not increased our expenditure on the scale that we did from the early 1980s, we would not have been in this situation.* The Economic Advisory Council to the Prime Minister, of which I have been a member right through this period, had drawn the attention of the Government to these problems. The Council's reports had focussed on the current economic situation, highlighted structural imbalances that underlay the problems, and tried to indicate priority areas for action for removing the imbalances. What I am trying to say is that it is not as if these have come to us all of a sudden. They were there and were well understood. *But I don't think — though it is an unfortunate thing to say now — that Rajiv Gandhi quite understood the magnitude of the problem.*

▶ *Now that we are left with limited options, should the country have a financial emergency?*

I do not understand the precise implication of the term 'emergency' here. Is it that we should have a period in which all rights of citizens are terminated? *I am one who believes that open expression of points of view is an excellent thing and we should be able to explain to our people why this has become necessary.*

▶ *What about the measures? Some drastic measures would be required...*

Yes, of course. I think that is at the back of the mind of whoever is suggesting a 'financial emergency.' It will be fairly drastic, I imagine.

▶ *Who should tighten the belt then?*

You see, this involves questions like which subsidy to remove. Take, for instance, two forms of subsidy — one, the subsidy on foodgrains, and the second, that on fertilizers. The subsidy on foodgrains benefits a large number of very poor people. *It would be absurd to talk of an adjustment that removes the support that the poorest people in the country get.* But let us at the same time remember that in India as a whole *the foodgrain subsidy* is not one addressed primarily to the poorest people. It *is a subsidy for people living in the cities and towns. Nothing in the rural areas!* It is only in Kerala that we have a foodgrain subsidy which cuts across rural and urban areas and, by and large, reaches the poor also. If one goes by the equity consideration, only the subsidy as it applies to the higher income groups should be removed and that is administratively difficult. *So, on the whole, it is better not to touch the subsidy on foodgrains.*

But on the other hand, a cut in the subsidy on fertilizers could be thought of. Fertilizers are used by all classes of farmers, but access to the fertilizer subsidy and the intensity of fertilizer use is greater among larger farmers with resources.

▶ *Would you say that the IMF conditionalities are a bitter pill which we will have to swallow in the interest of the future health of our economy?*

As I said earlier, I do not know what the conditionalities are. Therefore, I do not know how much of it is bitterness which could have been avoided or how much of it is merely a listing of measures which sound to you as harsh, but in reality we cannot avoid. Depending on one's ideology and so on, some measures mentioned in these can be seen as a bitter pill. But I would rather look at them differently. *Are these the things we would do for ourselves in any case? If so, what does it matter to me if they put them in their list?* One should not have any complexes in these kind of things. The major effort should be to make the people understand that we are in a crisis in which we have very few options and that radicalism being used to create very strong political resistance will be completely counterproductive. ■

Index

Chief Controller of Imports and
　Exports (CCI&E), 64–65
Chowdhury, Renuka, 54
Committee on Tax Reforms, 126
Communist Party of India (CPI), 41
Communist Party of India (Marxist)
　(CPM), 122
Confederation of Engineering
　Industry (CEI), 128
Confederation of Indian Industry
　(CII), 128
Congress (I), 14, 29
Congress' 1991 Lok Sabha election
　manifesto, 28–30, 65, 97–98,
　136, 139
Congress Parliamentary Party (CPP)
　meetings, 7–8, 73, 83, 108–109,
　111
Congress' plenary session in
　Bangalore, 2001, 132
Congress Working Committee
　(CWC), 4, 14–15, 25, 30,
　96–97, 126

Damodaran, Ramu, 9
Dandavate, Madhu, 33
Dasgupta, Dr Asim, 62
Dasgupta, Gurudas, 41–42
Datta, Bhabatosh, 58
debt obligations of India, 1991,
　49–50
debt rescheduling, issue of, 49–51
Deora, Murli, 109
Desai, Ashok, 105
Desai, Padma, 18
Deshmukh, C.D., 25
devaluation episode under Indira
　Gandhi, 35–43
Dhar, P.N. (PND), 52–53, 56, 58

Dhawan, R.K., 109
Directorate General of Foreign
　Trade (DGFT), 65
Drabu, Haseeb, 131
Dubey, Muchkund, 105
Dubey, Suman, 4
Dunkel Draft, 131

Economic Administration Reforms
　Commission, 2
economic development of Jammu
　and Kashmir, 131
Eighth Five-year Plan, 129
Enron power project, 133
exchange rate adjustment, 68–69
exim (for export-import) scrips, 65

Faleiro, Eduardo, 119, 121
Farmers' Parliamentary Forum, 109
Federation of Indian Chambers
　of Commerce and Industry
　(FICCI), 103, 128
Fernandes, George, 33, 132
fertilizer pricing system, 107,
　110–112
　subsidy issue, 110
fiscal deficit and balance of
　payments deficit, 18
foreign exchange reserves, decrease
　of, 11–12
Foreign Investment Promotion
　Board (FIPB), 123
Fotedar, M.L., 91, 96

Gandhi, Indira, 2, 4, 22, 26, 78, 107,
　127, 137, 145–146
Gandhi, Rajiv, 2–13, 16, 23–26, 48,
　94, 137, 140, 143
　death of, 4